CREATOR

SUSTAINER

GOD

PROTECTOR

COME TO
THE SECRET GARDEN

SUFI TALES of WISDOM

by

His Holiness M.R. Bawa Muhaiyaddeen

THE FELLOWSHIP PRESS
Philadelphia, PA

Library of Congress Cataloging in Publication Data

Muhaiyaddeen, M. R. Bawa
   Come to the secret garden.

   1. Sufi meditations.   I. Title.
BP189.62.M624   1985   297'.43   83-49210
ISBN 0-914390-27-9

Printed in the United States of America
by THE FELLOWSHIP PRESS
Bawa Muhaiyaddeen Fellowship
First Printing

His Holiness M. R. Bawa Muhaiyaddeen

About the Author

Muhammad Rahīm Bawa Muhaiyaddeen is a revered sage and holy man who was first discovered in the jungles of Sri Lanka in 1914. Little is known of his history prior to this time, except that he traveled extensively throughout the Middle East and India.

His Holiness has spent his entire life as an observer of the subtle secrets of God's creation, and for the past seventy years he has been sharing his observations with thousands of people from all over the world and from all walks of life. A life-long student of the world's religions, he is respected by scholars and leaders of many different philosophies and spiritual traditions. His Holiness has the unique ability to distill the essential truth from all religions and to renew faith within the hearts of men.

In response to the invitation of several individuals, His Holiness first came to the United States in 1971. During his subsequent visits to this country he has appeared on many television and radio programs and has spoken on university campuses throughout the United States and Canada. He is the author of over twenty books. *Come to the Secret Garden* is his second collection of short stories, many of which have been dramatized on national public radio. His Holiness has also been the subject of numerous newspaper and magazine articles in publications such as *Time, Psychology Today,* and *The Harvard Divinity Bulletin.*

The Cover

ismillāhir-Rahmānir-Rahīm. In the name of God, Most Merciful, Most Compassionate. The painting on the cover of this book illustrates the secret of everything in all of God's creation. Within this wondrous secret is the secret heart, within the secret heart is the secret life, and within the secret life is the secret soul, the soul of light. This secret heart is a beautiful flower garden filled with the blossoming flowers of truth, wisdom, unity, compassion, God's duty, His three thousand gracious qualities, and His ninety-nine actions.

Just as the stories in this book have many meanings, this painting has many meanings. The tree depicted here is the tree of life. It represents the body, which is the house for this life, and contains four hundred trillion, ten thousand spiritual thoughts. These thoughts come from illusion, mind, and desire, and they spread throughout this spiritual tree of life, happily enjoying the tastes of the fruits of illusion.

The hawk above the tree is the mind which flies around in search of food. Desire is the eagle that sits waiting for the food that the mind brings to it. The peacock represents the five elements of the body. It accepts and absorbs everything that comes, both the joys and sorrows of life. The peahen is illusion, or maya. When the peacock of the five elements dances, all the four hundred trillion, ten thousand spiritual energies fall from its feathers. Then the peahen of illusion picks them up and eats them with pleasure, but it never finds peace. All created beings are like this peahen.

The red cardinal represents the cravings of the mind and the arrogance of the I. It has taken the form of blood ties and thinks, "I am the boss of everything." It is filled with arrogance, karma, illusion, and the qualities of the three sons of illusion known as *tārahan, singhan,* and *sūran.* It has the six evils of lust, anger, miserliness, attachment, fanaticism, envy, and the five sins of intoxicants, cravings, theft, murder, and falsehood. The cardinal proclaims with pride, "I am the guardian of all these things."

The candle burning inside the tree is the light of life, wisdom, and truth, the light of man's soul. It too is a secret. We must know this light within our hearts and understand it in order to look at all our thoughts with clarity. When we see with this clarity, we will be like the dove who lives in unity with its mate. After the female lays an egg, they take turns sitting on the nest. First the male protects the egg while the female searches for food, and then the female guards the egg while the male goes in search of food. Doves demonstrate this kind of unity. Together they work to protect the egg until it hatches, and then they continue working in unity to protect the young chicks.

If all creations lived in love and unity like the doves, then we all would see other lives as equal to our own. If all creations in the world knew this truth, we all would understand how we must lead our lives. We would consider all mankind as one race, one family, with one God and one truth.

At the bottom of the painting is a silver ribbon with a gold heart at each end. The heart on the left is the mind. It looks at all the scenes of the outside world, then takes them into itself and enjoys them. This is a waste of time. The heart on the right is the inner heart, in which God, truth, and the kingdom of heaven can be known.

In the center of the silver ribbon is a sharp point. This represents man's appearance on this earth. On either side of the point are two curves, one is birth and the other is death. In life this body appears and then disappears. We have to think about this.

Above are two rose-colored ribbons with three loops on either side. These are the six levels of wisdom. The three on the left represent feeling, awareness, and intellect, which are innate within all creations. But beyond these, man has judgment, subtle wisdom, and divine analytic wisdom. These are the loops on the right side. The seventh level, the divine luminous wisdom of life, is depicted in the resplendent light of the candle at the center of the tree.

This painting is only a small example of all that is spoken about in this book, *Come to the Secret Garden*. We must understand everything in this tree of life—the secret heart, the secret truth, the secret of wisdom, love, and compassion, and the secret life, the light of the soul.

My love you, my children, my brothers and sisters, my sons and daughters. May truth show you the path. *Āmīn*.

Acknowledgements

The stories compiled in this book were first heard in 1982 by a small group of people visiting with His Holiness in Colombo, Sri Lanka. From July to October, in the early hours of dawn, His Holiness would begin every day with a new and original tale of wisdom. Presented in the oral tradition of Sufi lore and in the ancient language of Tamil, these stories were simultaneously translated into English by Mrs. Rajes Ganesan, Mrs. Crisi Beutler, and Mrs. Lauren Toomey.

The work of transforming these words into a printed publication then became a family project of the Bawa Muhaiyaddeen Fellowship in Philadelphia. Hundreds of people gave freely of their time, energy, and talents to make this book possible. From the transcribing to the typesetting, from editing to proofreading to illustrating, from printing to collating to binding, *Come to the Secret Garden* was compiled with love.

May God bless all those who took part in this venture and all those who read this treasury of wisdom. *Āmīn.*

NOTE TO THE READER:

The following traditional supplications written in Arabic calligraphy will be found periodically throughout the text.

⊕ following Prophet Muhammad or Rasūlullāh stands for *Sallallāhu 'alaihi wa sallam*—Blessings and peace be upon him!

⊕ following the name of a prophet or angel stands for *'alaihis-salām*—Peace be upon him! After two or more names it stands for *'alaihimus-salām*—Peace be upon all of them!

⊕ following the name of a companion of Prophet Muhammad, a saint, or *khalīf* stands for *radiyallāhu 'anhu/'anhā*—May Allah be pleased with him/her!

Contents

Introduction

All praise and glory belong to Allah alone. *Āmīn.* May all our duties be to Allah alone, the Unfathomable Ruler of grace, the One who is incomparable love. His thoughts and His focus are perfect. Nothing He does is wrong; everything He does is right. May we pray only to that One who has no comparison and no equal. May we believe solely in the Everlasting One and focus on Him alone. May we dedicate all the days of our lives to Him, seeking only His help. *Āmīn.*

May we learn good qualities and true justice from Him. May we make the effort to learn how to rule our lives from the Infinite One who rules all the universes. May we search for the peace in which He abides. May we merge with His state, so that we can live in unity with all lives, offering them the peace, equality, and tranquility that He gives. *Āmīn.*

My grandchildren, God has created everything in pairs of opposites as examples, so that we can understand the difference between good and evil. There is heaven and hell, this world and the next, truth and falsehood, right and wrong. God has provided us with these contrasts so that we can study them, act according to what is good, and avoid what is evil.

All human beings experience happiness and sadness. God knows both yet exists eternally in bliss, discarding sadness. All human beings experience hunger, illness, and old age. May we live without hunger, may we live without disease, and may we become youthful. May we exist in a state of peace as God does. We must experience both life and death, but He discards death and lives forever. May we follow His example. May we discover the source of this eternal life and ask for His help to attain it. *Āmīn.*

My love you, my grandchildren, my brothers and sisters, my sons and daughters. May we obtain the wealth of God's actions, His qualities, and the treasures of wisdom, grace, and love. May we obtain the wealth of the world of the soul, of this world, and of the next world, then, now, and forever.

At this very moment and at all times, without fail, God is performing countless duties in an unattached and just way. We too must perform our duties in this way. We have to do our duty to the soul, duty to this world, and duty to Allah who is the Father of our souls. We must understand His actions and do as He does. May we learn His gracious qualities and all the actions He performs while creating and protecting all lives. Knowing how He acts, may we act in this way, progress in our lives, and serve Him alone.

Children, we describe God by the ninety-nine names of the *Asmā'ul-Husnā.* He has revealed these ninety-nine actions, or *wilāyats,* to us so that we can know Him. To teach us, He sent us His prophets, lights, *qutbs,* saints, men of wisdom, and so many who possess the divine knowledge known as *'ilm.* He sent all these representatives to tell us of His state, so that we can understand and know peace, unity, tranquility, and serenity. He sent them so we can know that all men are the children of Adam ☼ and all mankind is one family, one community. He sent them to teach us of the one God to whom all worship belongs.

My brothers and sisters, you who have been born with me, let us think about these teachings that God has sent. Let us search for the explanation of their meaning. Let us see both the wisdom and the qualities within their meaning. Let us understand the love, the justice, and the completeness of the Resplendence, the *Nūr,* contained within their meaning. Let us understand all this with the clarity of the seven levels of wisdom. Let us understand it with the wealth of *īmān,* the wealth of absolute faith, certitude, and determination. Let us understand it with inner patience, contentment, and surrender, giving all praise to God who rules all creation.

We need to obtain peace, justice, and love. With these qualities, we must perform our duty to the world, to our souls, and to Allah. This is why we have come to the world. This is why we are living. Wisdom and tranquility are essential in our search for Him. Understand this, my grandchildren, my brothers and sisters, my sons and daughters. You must think about this.

Within this secret garden you will hear the speech of birds, trees, bushes, flowers, rocks, water, and mountains. They speak to you of wisdom, grace, and tranquility.

My grandchildren, everything we need to know is clearly shown to us through the examples of God's creations. In this collection of children's stories, these outer examples are shown and their inner meanings revealed. Within this book, *Come to the Secret Garden,* you will find many explanations of this world and the next, of heaven and hell, man and creation, wisdom and ignorance, light and darkness, good and evil, patience and impatience. You will find explanations about the subtlety of wisdom and the suffering man undergoes when he lacks that subtlety, about intelligence and actions performed without intelligence, and about the qualities of animals and the qualities of human beings.

Within this secret garden you will hear the speech of birds, trees, bushes, flowers, rocks, water, and mountains. They speak to you of wisdom, grace, and tranquility. They speak from the power of the soul that God has given to every creation, to the lands and the oceans, to the earth and the sky, to the sun and the moon.

This book teaches us of separation and war, of unity and peace. It tells us what results from believing in races, religions, castes, scriptures, and other divisions, as opposed to what results from practicing the qualities of Allah which are devoid of such separations. It shows what we gain from seeing mankind as one family, in contrast to seeing the divisions of many families. It describes torpor, darkness, and unreality, while revealing the resplendence of wisdom. How very deep that wisdom is, yet how easy to attain. It shows the world to be a tiny dot, and the heart of man to be a vast universe. It explains to us about mental and physical visions and the forms that arise from the thoughts of man. It shows us how true love must act. It explains what justice and conscience are. It speaks of the things that we see with our eyes, in contrast to the realities we see with wisdom and the goodness we see with love. It shows us how wisdom and peace can rule our lives. It reveals what arises from the peace, the grace, the qualities, and the clarity of Allah, the Infinite One.

This unique collection of stories tells us about the celestial beings, the saints, the lights of God, the angels Gabriel, Michael, Israfil, and Israel (may the peace of Allah be upon them all), and about the prophets Adam, Noah, Abraham, Ishmael, Idris, Isaac, Job, Salihu, Joseph, Solomon, Moses, David, and Jesus (may the peace of Allah be upon them all), and finally about Muhammad (may the peace and blessings of Allah be upon him). It explains why Allah created and sent the prophets, the truth they revealed, the words they brought to us from Allah, and the effect of those words upon us.

This book speaks about the One Treasure which is everlasting and infinite, as well as the treasures which are subject to death. It explains the meaning of truth and falsehood, life and death, heaven and hell, this world and the next. It tells us who rules this world and the hereafter, who is the moving force, who rules hell, and who has created it to be ruled. It tells us about both the physical body and the soul within. It reveals to us the nature of destruction and the nature of the indestructible, the impure spirits and the pure soul.

Come to the Secret Garden explains how perception, awareness, and intellect exist and function in all creations. It shows the way in which judgment, subtle wisdom, analytic wisdom, and divine luminous wisdom have been given to man. And it shows how man, through these higher levels of wisdom, can understand God's creation, the earth and the sky, the sun and the moon, himself, his soul, and the One who created all things.

This book can reveal the truth to those with evil qualities and turn them toward the good path. The benefit we can obtain from these stories is to learn what is right and what is wrong, and then to follow what is right. It can show us how to understand and avoid evil. That understanding can bring us to a state of peace. It can cause love, serenity, and compassion to grow within us. It can strengthen our wisdom and determination, giving us more faith and trust in God.

Come to the Secret Garden is for children just learning to talk, for children approaching old age and death, and even for children who have gone beyond that state. Everyone needs this book—all children, young and old, immature and mature, the infant and the aged, those who have wisdom and those who do not have wisdom. Anyone who understands this book will attain peace in his life. These words will not hurt any life. They will bring only goodness to our own lives and to the lives of others. The more we understand from this book, the more good it will do, the more peace and tranquility it will create. It will bring love to everyone: the love of divine knowledge, the love of wisdom, the love of God's qualities, and the love of His words. Such love will bring great benefits to all.

My precious children, my brothers and sisters, it is not enough to read this book once. Countless deep meanings are within every word. Even if you read these stories fifty or a hundred times, there will always be new and deeper meanings to be found. With each reading, as your wisdom grows, you will gain further understanding. These explanations are crucial to man.

How did these meanings come? They came from God. If a man surrenders to God and becomes His slave, then God will be the One acting within him, and God's sounds will emerge from that man. God is the cause and man is the effect. If the house of man's heart is made into God's house, then God will speak. However, if man keeps the house of the heart for himself, God will never speak through him. Just as a microphone transmits the sound of one's speech, a man whose heart belongs to God will automatically give voice to His sound. And when that sound emerges, we will know it as truth. It is such a sound that has come to this book and to hundreds of thousands of other discourses as well. However, in these stories the words have emerged in the form of simple examples. If you read it thoroughly, you will know that this book truly belongs to everyone.

These are not our words, they are the words of God. This book was written to explain God to us. Once we attain clarity, we will understand His words for the rest of our lives. We will understand the *Allāhu* who lives in all lives. This book is a way to understand His qualities, His life, His truth and purity, and the soul. Then we will know how to obtain peace and wisdom in the world of the soul, in this world, and in the hereafter. We will understand our duty to God and to all lives.

There is so much clarity and goodness contained within these pages. For our wisdom, our faith, and our determination, this book provides a way of understanding. The book itself is not the way, but within its inner meanings the path can be found. It is not enough to understand the letters and the words; we must understand the meanings within them. Then we can understand the many forms of goodness that exist in our lives and dispel all the separations and divisiveness within us.

We must read this book with patience, inner patience,

contentment, and trust in God. May God give us this awareness. May He give us understanding. Even if we cannot understand everything in this book, we will still benefit greatly if we at least understand a few points and subtleties. Even if we can understand only one atom of it, it will bring peace to our lives.

There are so many explanations within this secret garden. We have just mentioned a few. Each child, you and I, all of us should read this book, try to understand the wisdom in it, and obtain its good benefits. We all need this.

O children of Adam ⊛ , my brothers and sisters, the community of mankind is one family. There is one God. It is our birthright to pray to Him and to have His qualities and actions. We must live in a state of love, compassion, and patience. May we establish this wisdom and tranquility in our hearts. May we try to obtain His qualities and act with His wisdom so that we can know Him.

Allah, the Unfathomable Ruler of grace, the One who is incomparable love, is the Lord who creates, nourishes, and protects this creation. We need His help alone. We need His knowledge alone.

Only if we obtain His qualities can we do the correct work on the farm of our lives. May we search for His qualities and His wisdom with determination. May we have absolute faith in Him. *Āmīn. Āmīn.* May He give us His grace. May we search only for His help. *Āmīn.*

My love you, my grandchildren, my sisters and brothers, my daughters and sons. Come close and sit down. Each one of you should look at me and listen carefully to what I am about to say. You must learn how to conduct yourself properly. Your life is very subtle, and so you must conduct it with subtle wisdom.

"God created me and covered my head with fruits that give others peace."

The Orange Tree Believes in God

y love you, my grandchildren, my sons and daughters, my brothers and sisters. Tell me, my grandchildren, what do you think about God?

"Father, what do you mean? God is truth. How can we have any opinions about God? We know that we need Him, and so we are searching for Him. But many people say, 'There is no God!' and that troubles us. Why do they say such a thing?"

My grandchildren, the world says many things. It is true that there is only one God, one prayer, and one community of mankind. But many people in the world have separated into different groups that say different things. So, my grandchildren, rather than saying what we think, let us ask another kind of being what it thinks. Let's ask that beautiful orange tree over there.

"O orange tree, do you believe that God exists? Or do you believe that there is no God? What do you think? Is there a God or not?"

"O great one of wisdom, I will tell you what I think. God has given me branches full of fruits that are useful and pleasing to others. When I wonder who could possibly have given me so many fruits and put so much good taste in them, I have to believe in God. These fruits are proof enough for me. If there were no God, how could I have so many fruits with such delicious taste?

"God created me and covered my head with fruits that could give others peace. If I were to say that there is no God, then it would be like saying, 'I have no fruit, I have nothing.' How can I say I have nothing when I have so much? I could only say such a thing if I were completely ignorant. If I possessed even an atom's worth of wisdom, I would have to say that there is a God. Yes indeed, I do believe in God.

"O great one, there are many trees that look just like me. Their leaves and bark have the same colors and hues. They too are called

1

orange trees, yet their tastes and qualities are different from mine. Some taste sweet, some taste sour, some are bitter, and some are stringy. Their tastes and textures differ because of the various qualities that have been working within them. It is ignorance that makes some fruits sour, just as it is ignorance that causes differences of opinion among men. Such opinions come from their qualities.

"Men are like us. They are all created by the one God as the children of Adam ☺, and they all belong to the family of mankind. There is but one prayer and one taste for everyone. This is the way it is. Yet some men say that there is no God. That is like my saying I have no fruit. These opinions come from ignorance. If they had an atom's worth of wisdom, they would have to believe that there is a God. This is what I think.

"O great one, God created us all. It is He who gives you food, and gives your tongue the ability to taste the good and the bad. It is He who puts light in your eyes, makes your nose able to smell, and your ears able to hear. And so that you can understand what you hear, He endows your heart with the grace of His wisdom. He gives you hands and legs so you can give and take and do whatever needs to be done. He gave you the face and the beautiful form of a human being. Day and night, whenever you are hungry, He feeds you. According to your state at each particular time, He gives you water, fruit, or other kinds of nourishment, sometimes more and sometimes less. He knows your needs.

"Allah is the One who gives us all nourishment. Without Him, not an atom would move, not a blade of grass would bend. We must believe this with absolute certitude. A man who does not accept this, who does not believe that there is a God, is like a fully-laden tree that cries, 'I have no fruit.'

"God lives with man. He created him, He protects him, and He helps him with all his needs. When man has been given so much, it is only his own foolishness that says there is no God.

"If you have wisdom, you will realize that man will not believe in God until his ignorance, selfishness, desire, jealousy, and egoism begin to leave him. When he starts to conduct his life properly, leaving the left side and approaching the right, wisdom will come into him. Then he will believe in God. But as long as he remains ignorant, wisdom cannot enter him. O wise one, what is your opinion?"

"I accept what you say, O orange tree."

It is truly like this, my grandchildren. Do you understand now? If a tree can discover that there is a God, then surely man can do as much. You must understand. *Āmīn.*

The birds along the Nile are so lovely. Aren't they a treat for our eyes?

Birds Along the Nile

y love you, my grandchildren, my daughters and sons, my brothers and sisters. Today let us go to the Nile River in Africa. This river is close to six thousand miles long. It runs the length of Egypt and then empties out into the sea.

Thousands upon thousands of different kinds of birds live along the banks and in the trees near this river. Come and look at the beautiful white storks, the pink flamingos, and all the different kinds of cranes standing along the riverbanks. There are also eagles and vultures. All these birds have gathered here for different reasons. Some came to catch fish, some to eat water bugs, and some to feed on certain kinds of crabs. Others just come here to sit. Look at them all! There are small and large birds, tall and short birds, birds with very long beaks, and birds with bright red beaks. Look at the variety of colors in their feathers: gray, pink, white, black, red, and sometimes the colors of the earth and trees. Even the birds' legs are colored, some red and some black. Aren't they all beautiful? Do you see the bird with the lovely rose-colored feathers? People use the colorful feathers from all these birds to make hats and headdresses.

My grandchildren, the birds along the Nile are so lovely. Aren't they a treat for our eyes? They are even more beautiful than the river. But all their beauty is in their feathers. Without these feathers, the birds aren't useful to anyone except the dogs, foxes, hyenas, and people who like to eat them. If you pluck all their feathers, what will happen? The brilliant colors and subtle hues will be gone.

My grandchildren, man is like these birds. His form, his color, and his titles are all just feathers, covering him like clothing. This clothing with its many colors is the outer beauty of man, and this is what people look at in others. They are struck by outer appearances and distinctions, and they belittle or praise people accordingly. "Oh, that man has such a high rank, such honorable titles. This man is rich, that one is a king, and that one is a president." That is the way people talk. They gossip about clothing, money, titles, and family names.

So what is the difference between men and birds? A bird has two wings, and man has two arms. They both have two legs, two eyes, and two ears, even though the bird's ears are only little holes. The bird has a beak and man has a nose. There is really no difference at all. As soon as you take away his signs, symbols, clothing, and make-up, man is just like a plucked crane. Once he is stripped of all his outer distinctions, he has lost his value, and the foxes, jackals, lions, tigers, worms, insects, and beetles will be waiting to devour him.

The crane's feathers are beautiful, but this beauty is of no use. Man is in the same state. Like a bird without feathers, he is of no use when all his outer trappings are taken away. Yet he holds on tightly to these things so people will be impressed by him. He is praised or blamed for the way he looks. But this kind of beauty is useless, for eventually, he is left naked in the grave.

However, my grandchildren, there is a wonder and a beauty within man. There is a man within man, and within that inner man is a truth. Within that truth is a light, within that light is a brilliance, and within that brilliant light is the resplendence of wisdom and divine knowledge, or 'ilm. Within that 'ilm is another 'ilm, and within that inner 'ilm is the Rabb, the Lord God. And ultimately within God is a plenitude which is His justice.

That is the great wonder within man. God's three thousand gracious qualities and His ninety-nine duties and actions, His wilāyats, all exist in that man within man. This is the greatest, most amazing beauty in the whole world. It is the greatest wonder in the kingdom of the soul, the kingdom of the world, and the kingdom of the hereafter. It is the greatest wonder in the eighteen thousand universes. Except for the wonder of Allah, which is within this wonder, there is no other beauty, taste, or joy. For man's life, for his wisdom, for his qualities and actions, for his patience, inner patience, contentment, and surrender, for his love, his prayer, his worship, and his devotion—this is the most amazing and most beautiful treasure.

If man can understand this, then he will be truly beautiful. Then his body, his form, his vision, his speech, and his thoughts will have that original beauty. There is no wonder or beauty greater than this.

My grandchildren, wherever you look in the world, the beauty you see is not lasting. If you look at these birds, at man, or at the trees, what do you see? When the leaves fall, the beauty of the tree is gone. When the feathers are plucked, the bird's beauty is gone. When you take away a man's clothing and titles, all that remains is skin and bone.

There is no wonder or beauty in these outer things. The secret of the man within man is the real wonder. It is a beautiful, exalted wonder which you and I must try to know and understand and follow.

My grandchildren, my daughters and sons, my brothers and sisters, you must search for God's beautiful qualities and His divine knowledge, or *'ilm*. You must know this wonder of your life with absolute certitude. My love you. May God help you.

He doesn't even lift a paw to help her.

The Lion Family, the Tiger Family, and the Human Family

My love you, my grandchildren, my brothers and sisters, my daughters and sons. Come with me, and we will visit the jungle.

Many wicked and dangerous animals live here, so be careful. Do you see that lioness over there with her two cubs? Look how the baby lions are struggling to get milk from their mother. They tug on her and pull her this way and that, causing her great discomfort and making it very difficult for her to move about.

The male lion is lying off to the side by himself, watching his wife give milk to the cubs. Suddenly he roars, "I am hungry! Stop wasting your time with them. Bring me some food!" Look how big and fat he is. He has a full mane and looks so strong, but he roars for the lioness to serve him.

The mother looks at her small cubs. "They need their milk," she thinks. "It's a shame to stop feeding them now." But the male lion roars again and again and again. Finally, the lioness pulls herself away from her children to go hunting for her husband's dinner.

Look, she has found a herd of zebras! Watch how she stalks them. First she runs, then slows to a walk, and then stealthily creeps closer and closer. But the zebras are alert and sense her presence. Suddenly they begin to stampede. The zebras are running for their lives, and the lioness is running to catch food for her husband. Finally, after a long chase, she catches one of the zebras by the neck and drinks its blood.

Now look, my grandchildren. She is dragging that heavy zebra to her husband. He just lies there watching her, waiting for her to put the food right in front of him. He doesn't lift a paw to help her. Seeing their mother, the cubs run to her side, but the lion roars at them. And the mother once again has to push them aside so they will not disturb their father as he tears away at the body of the zebra.

9

Only after the male lion has eaten his fill does he let the mother feed her children whatever is left. He licks his chops and once again stretches out to rest. But still the work of the lioness is not finished. First she must take care of the needs of her children, and only after that can she eat.

Finally, all that remains of the zebra is the skeleton and a few shreds of meat scattered here and there. The vultures will eat those, and then the jackals and hyenas will come to take anything that is left.

My grandchildren, did you notice how much stronger and healthier the male lion was than the lioness? But even so, he did not think, "My wife is working so hard taking care of the children. I must go and find some food for all of us." Instead, he roared at her, "Stop what you're doing! Bring me my food!" He did not even move aside for the children until his own belly was full.

Although human beings are born with divine analytic wisdom, the same thing often happens in human families. Sometimes all the responsibility falls on the woman's head. In addition to caring for the children, she may have to go out and earn a living while the man just sits around like a lion, not doing anything. Even though he is not working, he still won't look after the children. And he always eats first, with no thought for their hunger.

A man who behaves like this is worse than an animal, and he will have many difficulties in his life. Because of such men, families split up, and that creates even more problems. But those men do not realize this.

ᑐ ᑌ

Look, there is a family of tigers, a father, a mother, and three cubs. Come along, my grandchildren, and let's watch how a tiger family behaves. Listen to the hungry children complaining to their parents. The moment the father hears their cries, he jumps up and goes off to hunt, while the mother stays behind to protect the cubs.

Soon the father spots a deer drinking at a water hole. Watch how he stalks his prey. Like the lioness, he stealthily creeps closer and closer and suddenly he pounces! In one leap the deer is caught. He drags his catch home, and the whole family eats together happily, sharing the food.

My grandchildren, some human families behave like the lions we saw earlier, while others are like these tigers. If both the man and the woman realize the difficulties in caring for a family and share the work, they will have some peace in their lives. It is very important to remember this and have the same kind of unity and love in your own families. You must also realize that we all belong to one family, the family of Adam ☺. Just as the tiger realized his children's hunger and went out to find them food, each of you must think of the whole human race as your family and help those who are in need. When you notice that someone is suffering, you must do your best to ease his pain. When you see someone who is troubled, try to comfort him. When you are aware of another person's mental suffering or hunger or disease or old age, try to understand and help.

If you can make others peaceful, it will bring goodness to the life of your soul, and it will bring about unity in the human family. Then if there is water and food in one house, there will be water and food in all houses. And if there is joy in one house, all houses everywhere will be filled with joy. If everyone were determined to live in this way, then it would be heaven wherever the human race existed. Such unity and love are the heaven of God's kingdom and the essence of a joyful life. On the other hand, no hell is more hellish than the life of a man who lives without unity and love. The fire of the thoughts raging in the heart of such a man is worse than any fire in hell. With this fire, he burns the hearts and lives of all his brothers and sisters.

My love you, my grandchildren. Each of you must think about what I have said and understand what it means for your own life. Show at least as much understanding as the father tiger did. If man would use even that small amount of wisdom, he could do so much good. You can do that much, can't you?

Do your very best to live a life of unity, love, peace, and patience in your own families and in the world family. All people must live in unity with themselves and with God and truth.

Do not lie around like the lion, waiting for someone else to feed the hunger of your life or the hunger of your soul. You cannot look to others for heaven or expect benefits from their prayers. You cannot gain the wealth of the soul, the wealth of grace, or the wealth of wisdom through the efforts of others. When it comes to prayer and

11

the soul, each of you will have to work for your own gain. No matter how many problems you have, you will benefit and become good through your own searching and striving. Then your karma will end, the hunger of your soul will be appeased, and you will find peace.

My love you, my grandchildren, my daughters and sons, my brothers and sisters. You really must think about this. Each of you must make great efforts to bring about peace in your daily life and in the life of your soul as well. Very humbly and with great love I am asking you to develop the qualities and the wisdom that will help you to lead such a life. May God help you. Āmīn.

The Patient Fisherman Catches the Fish

y love you, my grandsons and granddaughters. Somewhere nearby there is a good clear pond filled with beautiful lotus flowers. Let's walk a bit and see if we can find it. Ah, there it is, just beyond the main intersection.

All kinds of people come to this pond for all kinds of reasons. Look, some people are fishing. Shall we watch them? Do you see that fisherman over there casting his line into the clear water? He has already caught two or three fish and is trying to catch some more. The man next to him has snagged his line on a lotus plant. See how he yanks and yanks at the line, trying to free it. Finally he tugs so hard that it breaks. "What the devil!" he shouts. "This lotus plant broke my hook and line!" And he stomps off in anger. He came to catch some fish, but all he caught was a lotus plant.

Look, that man over there is casting his line again and again but isn't catching anything. He too is getting angrier and angrier. The fish are swimming by in every direction but they just aren't biting. "Oh, you satanic fish!" he yells. "Why won't you take the bait? Why can't I catch you? I can't wait here forever!" He's making so much noise that he's scaring the fish. They are swimming off in all directions, and that makes him even angrier. Once again, he casts his line but still the fish won't come near it. Finally he breaks the rod and throws it in the water, shouting, "You satan! I've been wasting my time with you!" And he stomps off in anger, just like the first man.

But look, three other people are still here, trying their luck. Listen to them complaining. "This pond is no good! There aren't enough fish here and they're not the right kind. Maybe we should go to the river." So they also leave, blaming the pond.

Now here comes a traveler to fetch some water. But instead of filling his clay pot, he stands on the bank and watches what all the others are doing. "This is terrible!" he complains. "Look at these

All kinds of people come to this pond for all kinds of reasons.

people! Some are washing their backsides in the pond and others are washing their feet. This water is no good now!" So he stands on the bank, urinates, and leaves with his water pot empty.

But look, a man in a carriage has stopped him on the road and asked for some water. "Don't drink the water in that pond!" the traveler warns, "It's filthy!"

"That may be so," the man in the carriage argues, "but this is the only water available for the next fifteen miles. People may do all sorts of things that dirty this pond, but somewhere a clear stream must feed into it. Please fetch me some of that water or I will die of thirst."

"No, no!" protests the traveler. "You must not drink that dirty water!"

But the man keeps insisting, "Don't pay any attention to what the others do. Just find some clear water and bring it here, or I will die."

Oh no! They've started fighting. Look, the water pot has been shattered, and they're practically killing each other! Finally, beaten and half dead, they both stumble off.

Now everyone has gone, except for the first fisherman we saw. He has been sitting there very patiently all this time, casting his line and catching a fish now and then. It looks as if he has caught about twenty fish. Everyone else left empty-handed and angry.

My grandchildren, every day many people come to this pond for different purposes. One comes to pick flowers. Another comes to clean his backside. A few come to fetch water. A cow comes and urinates. But do you see how the pond always remains the same, no matter what the people do? The beautiful lotus flowers continue to lie on the clear water, while the fish and other creatures swim about below the surface. Even though each person comes here and acts out the disturbances of his mind, nothing affects the pond.

People come to the pond to fulfill some desire, and when they fail, they blame anyone or anything but themselves. The fisherman whose hook caught on the lotus plant blamed the plant, but it might not have happened if he had been more careful. The traveler who criticized what everyone else was doing, found fault with the pond and left without any water. The man who couldn't catch anything became furious and blamed the fish. But the one who sat there patiently caught so many fish.

Did you watch everything carefully? Was the pond at fault? Were the fish or the lotus plant to blame? No, it was not their fault. Those who were unsuccessful placed the blame elsewhere, but it was really their own carelessness or anger or impatience that kept them from getting what they wanted.

Each person sees his own faults in others. His own ignorant thoughts cause him to attack others. Whatever state or quality he himself possesses, he sees that same state or quality in others and then blames them. This is the way of the world.

But God is not like that, my grandchildren. Just as the pond remains the same no matter what people do, God is unchanging and eternal. For Him there are no separations of color, race, or religion. He is beyond all philosophies and dogmas. He treats all lives alike. His power is perfectly pure. His state is perfectly pure. His qualities, grace, and wisdom, His unity, peace, justice, and equality are all perfectly pure. He is the All-Perfect Purity. He is plenitude and completeness. That is God. Such is His state.

If people with religious differences were to come into God's presence, one would say, "Oh, this is a Hindu god," and leave. Another would say, "This is a Zoroastrian god," while another would say, "This is the Christian God," and still another would say, "This is the God of Islam." They would all complain, "This person's devotion is not right, that person's god is false, and that person is not one of us."

Thus, when each one comes before God, he brings his own qualities and then finds fault with that One Truth. He murders the qualities of love and finds fault with the compassion, unity, peace, justice, and power of God. And even though it is his own actions that are at fault, he scolds God and finds fault with His kingdom. Such people are like the fishermen who blamed the pond.

The difference between God's kingdom and the kingdom of the world can be seen in the qualities and actions of man. Man cannot understand the kingdom of God unless he acquires the qualities, actions, and unity of God. But instead, man exhibits his own qualities and his own differences in this world.

God is not in that state. Even though He dwells within all lives, you will only see Him reflected in one who has purity and good conduct, one who has God's qualities and compassion and patience. God shines in the heart of such a person. The image of God can be seen in him, even though he remains in the form of man. This is how God does His work and conducts His kingdom.

My grandchildren, did you understand everything that happened at the pond? There were eight or ten people who spent their time finding fault and criticizing. Only one man had patience and did his work with care and one-pointedness. Because of these qualities, he was able to catch many fish. The world will always find fault, but the patient man will catch the fish.

My grandchildren, my daughters and sons, my brothers and sisters, it is like this in the world. The one who has patience and contentment will receive whatever he needs in life. The one who surrenders to God and gives praise to God, who acquires wisdom and a loving way, and who has the virtuous qualities of shyness, modesty, reserve, and fear of wrongdoing; the one who has absolute faith, certitude, determination, and trust in God—such a one will receive the wealth of God's grace, His love, His qualities, and His awakened wisdom, His *gnānam*. He will receive all the wealth of God and live peacefully in both this world and the next. But those who are always impatient and find fault will lose everything. You must think about this.

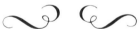

My grandchildren, do you remember the two men who were fighting? Remember the man in the carriage and the traveler who refused water because he found fault with the pond? Let's see what has happened to them. Look, their bodies are lying by the side of the road. It looks like they both died of thirst.

A third man is lying next to them. He seems to be dying too. His lack of wisdom is destroying him, his arrogance is making him suffer, and his ignorance is killing him. He is crying out for water. Children, the pond cannot come to him, so you must run and get him some water in this piece of broken pot. Ah, look, after drinking just this little bit of water, he is beginning to gather strength.

"Who brought this water? Where did you get it? If you brought it from that pond, then it is no good!" he shouts, throwing away both the broken pot and the water.

People without wisdom act just like this. As soon as they gain a little strength, their arrogance and ignorance come to life again. Whatever help we give such people will be like poison to them. So we must be very careful. If someone threw a pot at us we could be hurt.

You must understand this and only teach God's qualities to those who have God's qualities. Only talk about wisdom to those who can understand it. Remember, my children, all man's faults are due to his own ignorant actions, to his lack of wisdom. Nothing is God's fault. Think about this.

God is within man and man is within God. He is our Father, the only One worthy of worship. Whoever understands this and performs God's duty with His qualities and grace will rule in God's kingdom. May God help you. *Āmīn.*

Children, Be Good

y love you, my grandchildren, my sisters and brothers, my daughters and sons. Come close and sit down. Each one of you should look at me and listen carefully to what I am about to say. You must learn how to conduct yourself properly. Your life is very subtle, and so you must conduct it with subtle wisdom.

First you must think about what is good and what is bad, then you must throw away all that is bad and do only what is good. See how those good things taste. And if someone does something good for you, you should do good in return. But if someone does something bad to you, just forget about it. Never do anything bad in return.

Also, my grandchildren, you must always respect your mother and father. Not only must you respect them, you must also obey them. If someone is slightly older than you, then he should be treated like your older brother. If someone is older than that, you should respect him like a father. If someone is younger than you, you should show him love and compassion and take him under your wing like a younger brother or son. You must respect him, too. Even to the cows, goats, and other animals, you must show love and compassion. Throughout your life you must show God's three thousand gracious qualities to all people. You must do your duty and respect those who are lowly as well as those who are great. You must do this without any discrimination and regardless of their station in life.

Whatever duty you do for others, you should perform that duty with love, compassion, truth, and with an open heart. Do not do it with selfishness or attachment, and do not expect a reward. Whether you help a young child or an adult, do not expect any help in return. Show them love, and when your work is done, go happily on your way.

You must never have the thought, ''I did this for you, so now what

My children, whatever you do, perform that duty
with love, compassion, truth, and an open heart.

will you do for me?'' Never harbor such thoughts. If you help someone and expect something in return, then you are a selfish person performing a self-business, and any help, love, or truth you give will come back to harm you. It will gather karma for you. If you give help in that way, it is evil, not good. You should never be in that state. Your reward comes from the help you give, not from the one you help. It is his responsibility, not yours, to remember the help he receives. You should simply be of assistance and then go on your way. It is wrong to expect something in return.

However, if you serve any life with your heart full of love, such love is even greater than the ocean. It will become a limitless treasure in the heart of each person. If you perform your duty in the right way, finish it, and then move on, this will give peace to the hearts of others. Such duty will be a treasure of God's grace.

My grandchildren, you should never be angry. Anger is the guru of sin. It will lead you on the path of sin and take you straight to hell. Hastiness will consume your good, true wisdom. Impatience is an enemy to your wisdom. All that glitters is not gold. Do not think that whatever you see is truth. A golden pot needs no decoration, nor does a heart of truth. Truth does not have to be adorned.

If you have true wisdom, you do not have to put on any acts. Every word you speak will be beautiful, loving, and compassionate. There will be sweetness and dignity in those words. If your wisdom has come from truth, that in itself will be beautiful. It will need no make-up. So do not speak words you pick up here and there or read in books. Your words should come in an automatic way from within your heart and reveal the truth. Simply speak that truth. There is no need to embellish it and make it eloquent.

My grandchildren, do not steal. Do not lie to your parents because you are afraid of them. Tell them the truth with love. Say, "I made a mistake. Please forgive me for what I have done." First ask God to forgive you, then ask your parents to forgive you. Next ask forgiveness from anyone else you have wronged. If you realize your mistake and repent, your sin will be erased. But if you do not realize your mistake, if you do not ask for forgiveness, that sin will stay with you.

Never say anything to hurt anyone; always speak with love. Show others a look of love and compassion; do not stare at them like tigers do. Do not pick fights with others; try to live with them with love, affection, trust, and peace.

You must not keep hostility in your heart toward others. Discard that hostility and all the evil qualities within you. Do not hold onto doubt, it is a huge cancerous disease. Get rid of it. Get rid of whatever suspicions you have toward others. They are your brothers and sisters. Live without any doubt. That will make you happy. It will be heaven for you.

Do not hurt, torment, or cause suffering to any being. Even the bull that pulls carts should be used in a loving way. Do not overload it with more weight than it can bear. After all, when you are given a load too heavy for you, can you carry it? Isn't it difficult for you? Then think of the suffering you cause a bull when you give it more weight than it can carry. My grandchildren, you must know the capacity of each one's body and know each one's state. Only then can you give him the correct work, treat him with respect, and protect him.

My love you, my grandchildren. Whenever you give someone food, know the capacity of his stomach and give him the correct amount needed to fill it. If you give too much, he will not be able to eat it; if you give too little, he will suffer because he will still be hungry.

Know the qualities in each one's heart and then serve him. But first, try to know your own heart. Only then can you understand the hearts of others. If you have that understanding, then whatever words you speak and whatever duty you perform will be true duty, God's everlasting duty. If you are in that state, the love you give to each one will be God's complete love. In every situation, perform your duty with this understanding.

Precious jeweled lights of my eyes, my grandchildren, my brothers and sisters, my sons and daughters, when you go to school, pay attention to what you are learning. Do not pay attention to what others are doing. Do not spend time looking around at other things. Concentrate on whatever you are doing at the moment. That is the only thing you should be thinking about until it is finished. If you go to prayers, concentrate on prayer. If you read a book, concentrate on that book. If you have some other work, focus on that. Concentrate deeply with your wisdom. Intend to do each thing in this way, and do everything in the name of God.

My grandchildren, do not listen to what other people are saying. Do not listen to find out if they are talking about you or me. In the world there is so much talk and so much ignorance. Do not give your ears to the sound of the world, to words of ignorance. Give your ears to the sound of God. Have love for the duty you must perform and give your ears to that duty.

Precious jeweled lights of my eyes, perform each of your duties in a good way, without paying any attention to the world within you. In this way, perform all the countless actions that you do every day. Ignorance, illusion, and satan are always playing there within. Dispel the playing that is going on inside, and forget about playing in the outside world.

My love you, my grandchildren. Each of you should think about this. Always discard what is bad, keep what is good, and act according to the good. Acquire God's qualities, actions, and behavior and discard all other qualities.

My grandchildren, if you grow up in this state of goodness, you will be the children of God. You will live as good children in this world, and you will be needed in both this world and the next. God will accept you as children of faith and truth. You will receive His goodness, and from that goodness you will attain everlasting benefits.

Live as good children to all and as good children to God. Be good to your own heart and good to your wisdom.

My love you, my grandchildren. Think about this and conduct your lives in this subtle way. *Āmīn.* May God help you.

"O hunter, most men would feel sorry if they killed a deer who had a fawn. But you don't seem to have any compassion."

The Hunter Learns Compassion
from the Fawn

y love you, my grandchildren, my sons and daughters, my brothers and sisters. Have you ever seen a baby deer? Let me tell you a story about a fawn and its mother. Please listen carefully. This story will show you the difference between the awareness of man and the awareness of animals.

Once there was a man who liked to go hunting. He would go into the forest carrying a gun or a bow and arrow, and he would shoot deer, elk, and other animals. Like most hunters he enjoyed eating all the animals he killed, but he found deer meat especially tasty.

Now, this man had been hunting, killing, and eating like this for most of his life. Then one day he came upon a deer giving milk to her fawn. This made him happy because he was tired, and he knew that the deer could not run away while her baby was nursing. So he shot her. But before dying, the deer cried, "O man, you have shot me, so go ahead and eat me, but do not harm my child! Let it live and go free!"

"I understand what you are asking," the hunter replied, "but I plan to take your child home, raise it, and make it nice and fat. Then one day it too will become meat for me to eat."

The little fawn heard this and said, "O man, are such thoughts acceptable to God?"

The hunter laughed. "God created animals for men to kill and eat."

"O man, you are right. God did create some beings so that others could eat them. But what about you? If there is a law like that for us, then perhaps there is also such a law for you. Think about it. There is only one person ready to eat me, but there are so many eagerly waiting to eat you. Don't you know that? Someday in the very presence of God Himself, grubs, worms, the tiny insects of hell, and even the earth itself will be quite happy to devour you. You who are a human being must think about this. When we deer are killed, we are eaten right away, but when you die you will be consumed in hell ever so slowly, over a long period of time. You will be subjected to hell in so many rebirths.

"O man, God created me and He created you. You are a man. God created you from earth, fire, water, air, and ether. I am an animal, but God created me from these same elements. You walk on two legs, I walk on four. Even though our skin and color are different, our flesh is the same. Think about the many ways in which we are alike.

"If someone had killed your mother while you were nursing, how would you feel? Most men would feel sorry if they killed a deer with her fawn. They would cry, 'Oh, I didn't know!' But you don't seem to have any compassion. You are a murderer. You have killed so many lives, but you never stop to think how sad you would be if someone killed your mother. Instead you are happy to kill not only my mother, but you also want to kill me and eat me. Since you are a human being, you should think about this. Even the cruelest and most demonic of beasts would stop to think about what I have said.

"Can't you understand the sadness of a child whose mother has just been killed? What you said to my mother and to me is terrible and has caused me great pain. O man, you have neither God's compassion nor human compassion. You do not even have a human conscience. All your life you have been drinking the blood and eating the flesh of animals without realizing what you have been doing. You love flesh and enjoy murder. If you had a conscience or any sense of justice, if you were born as a true human being, you would think about this. God is looking at me and at you. Tomorrow His justice and His truth will inquire into this. You must realize this.

"Even though you are a man, your thoughts are much worse than those of four-legged animals. Do not think you are a human being. We certainly don't think so. You have the face of a man, but to us you are worse than a demon or the most dangerous beast in the jungle. When we look at you, we are afraid. But when we see a true human being, we have no fear. We might even walk right up to him, because we are like small children who embrace everyone as readily as they embrace their own mother.

26

"O man, I am only a baby. If I lie down by mistake on a poisonous snake, it will not hurt me. Or if I accidentally step on a snake, it still won't hurt me, because it realizes that I am young. Even insects know I am small and will not sting me.

"So how can you do this, O man? You who have been born as a human being must consider your actions. It is terrible to keep me as a pet only to eat me later. Every day when you fed me, I would be thinking, 'I might be eaten tomorrow.' This would torture me constantly. Day by day, my weight, my happiness, and my life would decrease. In the end all that would be left of me would be skin and bones. I would be grief-stricken and emaciated. I would be no good to you at all. I would be too sad to live, so just kill me and eat me right now.

"It is better to eat me at the same time you eat my mother. If you kill me now, before I experience that sorrow, at least you can enjoy the innocent, happy flesh that has drunk its mother's milk. Later I will have no flesh. Do not make me suffer any longer. Kill me now, so that I will suffer for only one day. I am too sad to talk about it any more."

"Little fawn, everything you have said is true," the hunter admitted. Then he gently picked up the body of the mother and led the baby deer home.

That night he told the other hunters what the baby deer had taught him.

All who heard the story cried. "So often we have eaten deer meat, but now that you have told us this, we see the karma that has come to us through the food we enjoyed. Our bodies are in a state of turmoil. We realize now that we had no compassion or wisdom." And they all decided to stop eating such food.

"Let the baby deer go," one man said.

"No, give me the deer," said another. "I will raise it until it grows up and then I will set it free."

But the hunter decided to raise the fawn by himself. And over the years that deer showed him more love than his own children did. "This gentle being is capable of more love and gratitude than a human being," the man thought. "It kisses and licks me and makes contented sounds when I feed it. And it even sleeps at my feet."

So the years passed until the deer was fully grown. Then one day the man took it into the forest and set it free.

My children, each of us must be aware of everything we do. All young animals have love and compassion. And if we remember that every creation was young once, we will never kill another life. We will not harm or attack any living creature.

My children and grandchildren, think about this. If we think and act with wisdom, it will be very good for our lives. My love you.

Don't Fight Like Chickens

y love you, my grandchildren, my brothers and sisters, my sons and daughters. Come along with me, and we will visit a chicken farm.

If you look through the wire fence, you can see how well these chickens are cared for. They have everything they need, food and water and a cozy place to sleep and lay their eggs. They have trees to give them shade, branches to roost upon, and plenty of room to run about and play. But they cannot leave and wander wherever they wish.

My grandchildren, why do you think the farmer has shut them in? Because if the chickens were free to wander, then dogs, foxes, and thieves might catch them and eat them. The farmer put a fence around the yard to protect the chickens. Do you understand?

Now, my grandchildren, there are certain things you can learn by watching chickens. Look, two hens are coming out of the coop with their husbands. Do you see them? The moment the two roosters see each other, they start to fight. They stick their heads under each other's wings and peck. Each one thinks the other has come to steal his wife. Watch them. Whenever the hens approach, the roosters fight even harder. Look over there, my grandchildren. One hen is running after another's husband, but he is chasing still another hen. Now all the hens and roosters are fighting.

"You took my husband!"

"Why did you steal my wife?"

The fighting is endless. One hen is missing an eye and another is missing half her gullet. One rooster has lost the crest from his head and another is bleeding. And look, do you see the chicken with cuts all over the chest and the one over there with a broken leg?

All of them are wounded, but still they keep on pecking each other on the neck or head or under the wing. None of them will ever admit

People are like chickens, always pecking at each other and starting fights.

that they lost, but they never really win, either. When they become too tired to fight, they just circle around and around each other. And if one becomes even more tired, it will hide its head under its wing. But pretty soon another chicken will come along and start the ruckus all over again. This is how chickens fight.

My grandchildren, people are like chickens. Even though they have plenty of money and property and possessions, they will peck at each other and start fights. Even if they are family men with children, grandparents, and in-laws, they will bare their teeth and punch each other. Even if they are so old that they have great-grandchildren, they will still end up locked in each other's armpits, battling to the death.

Man is not satisfied with one woman, so he goes out looking for others. Even if a man has an extremely beautiful wife, his eyes, ears, and nose will turn in the direction of any female who passes him on the street. He will stare and grin and show his teeth, or hang out his tongue and drool like a tiger or lion. Man is not satisfied with one of anything. He wants variety. Craving land, women, and gold, he creates his own misery and destruction. These three terrible desires ruin him.

Women are like this, too. They smile at each other's husbands and soon they are all fighting like hens. Women fight women and men fight men. My grandchildren, do you understand this? You must think about it.

There are other things chickens do that you should also think about. Look how they scratch at the dirt near the fence and try to escape from the very place that provides for their needs, gives them comfort, and protects them from dogs, foxes, and thieves. They also scratch and peck at the earth to dig up worms and insects, even though there is plenty of food lying right on the surface. Why do chickens do that? That is their nature. That's what chickens do.

Man also does not appreciate the wealth that God has bestowed upon him. His mind is like a chicken, scratching at hell, digging up worms and insects. God has given him a place to live, a house, light, food, water, and a body for his soul. God provides nourishment, saying, "Eat the food that I have given you," yet man does not respond in the proper way. He does not accept what God has given. Instead, the monkey mind and the dog of desire crave the things of hell and drive man into danger. Man's thoughts wander everywhere, thinking that there is more here than there, or more there than here. Failing to eat the loving food or drink the loving water, he digs for what God has discarded.

Man does not appreciate the protection God has given him. He scratches at the protective fence of *imān*, trying to tear holes in the wire mesh of faith. He knocks down the fence posts of wisdom, thinking, "If I break through the fence, I can be free." But when man leaves God's protection, when he refuses God's beautiful food and water, he is captured by illusion. While he is digging in hell for worms, he is slaughtered by satans, demons, devils, ghosts, dogs, and foxes.

But man does not think about what is going to happen to him. He has not established the state of patience, contentment, trusting only in God and giving all praise to God, the state of *sabūr, shukūr, tawakkul,* and *al-hamdu lillāh.* Although he could live in health and happiness, he has broken through the protection of his faith in God.

You must think about this, my grandchildren. A man who is wise will stay within God's protection. He will be satisfied with the water and food that God has provided. His heart will be very happy and he will be in a state of love, compassion, wisdom, justice, and peace.

My grandchildren, God has given you the beautiful house of the innermost heart, placing His food and loving compassion within that innermost heart, the *qalb.* God's protection surrounds it and keeps it safe. Do not let go of that protection, do not forget it, and do not tear it apart. Try to learn God's qualities and wisdom and build a peaceful life. Then you will not meet with accidents.

Remember how those chickens fought? They caused their own suffering. Remember how they were trying to break through the fence? They were seeking their own destruction. You and I must dispel the qualities and actions of the chicken from within ourselves. We must search within our Father's qualities for peace, tranquility, and serenity. *Āmīn. Āmīn. As-salāmu 'alaikum wa rahmatullāhi wa barakātuhu kulluhu.* May the peace and blessings of Allah be upon all of you.

The King Who Wanted to Make Gold

y love you, my grandchildren, my sons and daughters, my brothers and sisters. Come with me and we will visit what was once a great kingdom. A century ago it was ruled by a mighty king.

Look over there. That is where the king's palace once stood. And here on this spot where we stand today, he built an ashram for wandering gnanis, swamis, gurus, yogis, and men of wisdom to rest and refresh themselves. See how crumbling and desolate the ashram is now. The foundation still stands, but the walls have fallen to ruin. My grandchildren, I will tell you a story about this king and why he built a special resting place for wandering wise men. This is a story you should know.

Once upon a time before he ruled this kingdom, the king was just a common man, living in the mountains to the east. How do you suppose he became king? In olden days, rogues would band together, choose a leader, and plunder the countryside in all directions. If the leader was clever, his power would grow. That is how this man came to be king. He was appointed the leader of a band which grew in size and power, capturing more and more land, until he had acquired a whole kingdom. And as he and his men conquered the adjoining kingdoms one by one, he became mighty in wealth and power.

One day the king thought, "This is how things happen in the world. If someone more clever than I comes along, he will capture my kingdom just as I captured the kingdoms of so many others. Even if I escaped with my life, where would I go? If someone seized my wealth, how would I earn a livelihood? What would I do?"

Then one day, the king read in the Puranas about the wise alchemists who knew how to make gold. "If I could learn how to make gold from metals such as copper and iron, I'd be safe," he thought. "Even if someone seized my kingdom and all my wealth, it wouldn't matter. I wouldn't need a kingdom. I could make gold anywhere. I must find such an alchemist.''

And so the king built an ashram for wandering wise men. The roof and pillars were made of copper. There were two doors, one in front and one in back. Over the entrance was a sign which read:

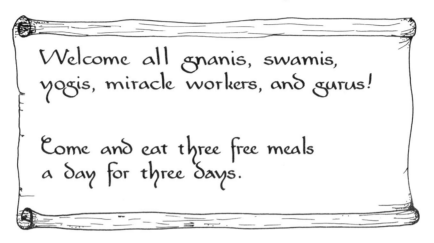

Welcome all gnanis, swamis, yogis, miracle workers, and gurus!

Come and eat three free meals a day for three days.

And over the exit there was a sign which read:

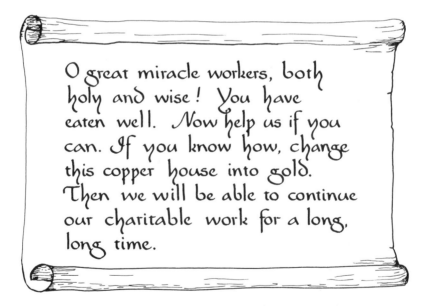

O great miracle workers, both holy and wise! You have eaten well. Now help us if you can. If you know how, change this copper house into gold. Then we will be able to continue our charitable work for a long, long time.

The king posted guards all around the ashram, instructing them, "If anyone turns this ashram to gold, stop him and bring him to me. Don't let him leave!"

Millions of people stopped to eat and went on their way, but not one knew how to turn copper into gold. Then one day, at long last, a guru arrived with ten or eleven disciples. The guru read the first sign. He knew his disciples were hungry, so he led them inside. Although the guru took only a little, his disciples ate well.

As they were leaving, the guru saw the second sign. Telling his disciples to wait, he went outside and returned with a special herb. He stood in the middle of the room, between the entrance and the exit, crushed the herb between his hands, and blew on it. The bits of crushed herb scattered through the air, and the whole ashram turned to gold.

As the guru walked toward the exit, the guards immediately surrounded him. "Swami, please do not leave. The king wants to see you. You have given us so much wealth. Please, you must come to the palace."

And so the guru was carried on a palanquin to the palace. The king had no sooner paid his respects, than he began to plead, "You are my god. I built the ashram and invited people of wisdom to come so that I could learn how to make gold. I have waited so long for someone as wise as you. You must teach me this secret art."

"Is that so, O King?" the guru asked. "Very well, you can learn to make gold, but do you really want something that changes and disappears? Gold will not remain with you. Neither wealth nor poverty are permanent. Both will leave you, just as you too will have to leave this world one day. So what is the use of learning to make gold? O King, do you understand?"

"But Swami, learning to make gold is my life's desire! Please teach me how. Please!" he begged.

"Well, if this is what you want, you must come and stay with me for twelve years. Then I will teach you. But first you must make yourself look like my other disciples. You must leave behind your jewels, your luxurious clothing, and even your sandals. You can bring only two sets of clothes, one to wear and one for a change."

The king's desire to learn how to make gold was so strong that he agreed to sacrifice all his comforts and go with the guru. After handing over the entire kingdom to the care of his ministers, he walked out of the palace, leaving behind all of his wealth and finery. Barefooted, he presented himself to the guru and began his journey.

They walked and walked. How the king suffered! He hobbled along painfully, his tender feet burning from the hot sand and stones. Finally, the group stopped to rest in a small cave deep in the jungle. Every day, the guru sent the king and another disciple deep into the jungle to pick fruit, dig for wild yams, and fetch water. Thorns stabbed the king's feet and tore at his face and body. Because he was accustomed to great comfort and cleanliness, the king found it extremely difficult to live in the jungle. Within a few weeks his whole body was covered with sores, and he became feverish.

"O God!" he thought to himself. "Why do I have to suffer? I don't need gold. How comfortable I would be if I had stayed in my palace! Even without knowing how to make gold, I could have enjoyed my daily food. As it is, I haven't learned any wisdom, and I haven't learned the art of alchemy. I am just suffering."

Day by day, year after year, his suffering increased. From head to toe he was covered with oozing, bloody sores that would not heal, and he itched all over. He could barely walk, yet he and another disciple were sent out to do every chore that needed to be done. The other disciples took turns, but the king had to go out every day for eleven years. Often he cried, and there were many nights when he could not sleep. Many times he wanted to give up and run away. But then he would think, "No, I have come here to learn, and I must see it through."

Finally, one day the guru said, "Bring the king here."

When the king came before him, the guru asked, "Are you a king or a disciple?"

"I am a disciple," he replied. "I am no longer a king. Soon I will die."

"You have not yet learned what you came here to learn."

"More than eleven years have passed, Swami."

"Come with me," the guru said, and he led the king to the foot of a mountain of rocks. "Pick that herb," commanded the guru. "Crush it between your hands, blow on it, then rub it on those rocks. You will see them change. Then make a pile of all the ones that changed."

The king did as the guru instructed, and the rocks changed into chunks of iron. That was on the first day. On the next day, the guru told him to take a different herb, crush it, and blow on it. This time the rocks he rubbed turned to lead, and the king piled them up on one side. On the following day, the guru instructed him to use another herb, and this time the rocks changed into copper. The king made another pile. The next day the guru said, "Take these two herbs, crush them together, blow on them, and spread them over the rocks." These rocks turned to silver, and the king made yet another pile. On the next day, the guru told the king to pluck and crush still another combination of herbs. This time the rocks changed into a gold alloy. On the following day, the king was told to gather yet another combination. He crushed the herbs, blew on them, and the rocks were transformed into ingots of pure gold. The king piled them up. He now had six huge piles.

Then on the final day, the guru instructed the king to pick nine different kinds of herbs. The guru said, "After crushing these, blow them onto nine different sections of the remaining rock." When the king had finished, the rest of the mountain had been transformed into nine huge mounds of sparkling gems. There were emeralds, diamonds, rubies, lapis lazuli, cinnamon stones, pearls, sapphires, coral, and topaz.

"King, you may leave now, if you wish. But first look carefully at the wealth before you, and then tell me what your final decision is."

The king stared at the mounds upon mounds of gems and gold. He picked up handfuls of gems, tossed them into the air, and let them shower down upon himself. Then he rolled around in the glittering riches. But after a while he thought, "What am I doing? This is not what I need." And he returned to his guru.

"You have finished the work that you came for," the guru told the king. "All this is yours. You can take it with you."

"O Swami," the king answered, "I have been with you for twelve years, and I have finally come to realize that what you told me is true. I see now that I do not need this wealth. Wealth is something that comes and goes. You have the ability to make a mountain of rock into a mountain of gold, yet you have chosen to give up this worldly wealth

The king stared at the mounds of gems and gold. But after a while he thought, "What am I doing? This is not what I need."

and live in a simple cave. The wealth you have is different. You have chosen the wealth of God's kingdom, the wealth of God's grace, which will never change or diminish. Nothing can be compared to the wealth of wisdom, love, justice, equality, peace, and compassion. It has no equal.

"I have seen everything my mind wanted to see, everything my desire searched for. Gold is not true wealth, it is only earth. Once I desired and enjoyed the things of the earth, but not anymore. Although I was a king, I did not have the peace that you have." Looking at the gold and precious gems heaped up around him, he said, "I will not benefit from all this. Someone might try to kill me for it. It is a disease that could destroy me and also destroy the wealth of grace.

"Swami, please accept me as your disciple. I need the wealth that is undiminishing and indestructible. Please give me that. I want to learn how to gain the wealth of God's grace from you."

"Now you are indeed my disciple," replied the guru. "You are God's child, and you are a child of my love. Come."

And so the man who had been king was cured of all his sores, and his body was transformed into a beautiful form. The guru taught him about God's wisdom and grace, and he became a light to the kingdom of God. Having received the undiminishing wealth of grace, he lived as a child in the kingdom of God, able to serve all lives and see them as his own. He served the soul, he served God and his guru, and he served the world and all of mankind. He never returned to reclaim his kingdom, for he no longer wanted it.

My grandchildren, little did the king know that shortly after he had followed his guru into the jungle, enemies invaded his kingdom and killed all his ministers. Kings from far and near came to fight over the gold roof and pillars of the ashram. They grabbed whatever they could and carried it back to their kingdoms.

This broken-down building you see in front of you, my grandchildren, is the ashram the king built for the wandering wise men. Now it has crumbled and mingled with the earth, along with those who died fighting for the gold and gems of the world. And look over there at the king's palace. It is also in ruins, nothing but dust and ashes, a haven for birds and bats.

Think about this, my grandchildren, my brothers and sisters, my daughters and sons. Like the king who wanted to make gold, people think they need to search for worldly wealth. It would be better if they would search for the wealth of grace and divine knowledge, for the wealth of God's qualities and love. Those who understand God's love and show it to others, considering every person's life as their own, will know real freedom. Those who serve others with God's love will become peaceful and serene. They will receive God's everlasting wealth in the world of the soul, in this world, and in the hereafter. But the lives of those who do not search for the permanent wealth of God will crumble into ruin, just as this palace crumbled.

Think about this and make the effort to search for God's wealth. The effort you put into gathering worldly wealth is wasted. The things of the world will not turn into gold. They are billboards for hell. Surrender to God and prepare your heart to accept whatever He gives with patience and praise, both in this world and in the next. Have the contentment to believe that whatever Allah gives you is enough. To attain this contentment, you need wisdom, the divine knowledge of 'ilm, and the faith, certitude, and determination known as īmān.

You do not have to suffer, my grandchildren. Your Creator will give you the necessary food at the correct time, but you must do your part. Look at the animals. See how chickens find their food in the earth, and the birds find their food in the trees and grass. Allah has provided for them all, but they must make the effort to find what He has given them. And through your own efforts, you too must find the permissible food that God has created for you.

My children, as you search for Allah, try to become peaceful and attain a state where you can share your peace with others. Always be as thoughtful of others as you are of yourself and share what you receive with your neighbors and those who are hungry. Prepare your heart to do this work. Make your love for Allah clear, and when wisdom and His qualities come within you, you can transform yourself as the king did. If you strengthen your īmān, you can receive Allah's wealth of grace and rule in the three worlds. That is certain.

Good qualities, actions, conduct, and love rule Allah's kingdom.

God has one hundred powerful qualities which are His duties. Of these He has kept for Himself the one duty of creating, protecting, and sustaining His creations. But the other ninety-nine are there for you to share. Therefore, perform your duties and try to find wisdom.

You can never find lasting peace by collecting gold and gems. They are not permanent. Instead, fill your heart with God's qualities and with peace and tranquility. They are the greatest wealth, the wealth of grace, wisdom, and justice.

My love you, my grandchildren. May you think about this. God is all we need for our lives. Strengthen your faith, your *īmān*. Be patient and be content. Surrender to Allah and praise Him. Pray to God, bow to Him, and pay your respects to Him. Make this firm and definite in your lives. That will be very good. When you reach this state, it is certain that you will receive the beauty of youth and the light of His *rahmat,* which is the wealth of His benevolent grace.

My love you, my grandchildren. May you have the faith to make your lives complete and to receive the wealth of peace that never changes and never ends. May Allah bring the perfect fulfillment of His qualities, His beauty, and His light to shine in your hearts and in your faces. *Āmīn.* May He give you the divine knowledge called *'ilm.* *Āmīn. Āmīn. Yā Rabbal-'ālamīn. As-salāmu 'alaikum wa rahmatullāhi wa barakātuhu.* So be it. So be it. O Ruler of the universes. May the peace of God and His beneficence be upon all of you.

41

Everyone likes to hold a baby. It melts their hearts.

Everyone Loves a Baby

y love you, my grandchildren. Do you see the first little buds on that tree? How beautiful they are! Soon they will change into tiny pale green leaves. Later they will turn a deeper green, and then the tree will flower and bear fruit. Still later the leaves will turn yellow, and finally they will become brown, the color of earth. This is a sign that they will soon die and mingle with the earth.

We are like those little buds, my grandchildren. We are so beautiful when we first emerge from inside our mothers. Right away they embrace us and we hold on tightly. At that age, we also cling tightly to God. We do not see any differences or create separations between races and religions. Because we do not yet have the world within us, we are still very beautiful. We exist in the pure state of God.

Everyone likes to carry us in their arms. It melts their hearts. Mothers are not the only ones who feel this way. Everyone thinks a baby is beautiful. Have you noticed this? Even his sounds and his shape are beautiful. Everything about a newborn baby is so beautiful. Everybody praises him, saying, "Such a lovely baby! Such a good baby!" And the baby speaks to all who embrace him. As soon as one baby sees another, they speak to each other in their common language, "Aiioooeee" and "Ooooannneee." Babies love each other so much.

My grandchildren, God is like a baby, a compassionate baby of love. God is the most beautiful of all. Everyone loves Him. He dwells within us, and whenever He comes forth from anyone's heart in the form of words, intentions, thoughts, meanings, or love, He is embraced by every heart. It is very beautiful.

My love you, my precious grandchildren. If you can be in that state, you too will be beautiful. You will understand God's language and He will speak to you as a baby. God will grow within you as faith, certitude, determination, good qualities, actions, and love. And when He emerges from your heart, His compassion, love, and beauty will be seen in all your words and actions.

Everyone will embrace you and their hearts will melt. Truth is like this. All those who focus on God and follow His path will embrace the words and qualities that come forth from your heart. Your mother and father will embrace you. Your relations and blood ties and neighbors will embrace you just as they do a baby. Those who love God will be happy when they see His love, His wisdom and truth, His actions and qualities. When they embrace you, they will be embracing Him. My love you. Think about this, my grandchildren.

Then, now, and forever, God is embraced by the hearts of all who need His beauty. If your love is in this state, everyone will trust you. If your actions and qualities are in this state, everyone will accept them. These are your original qualities, the qualities of the baby when it first emerges from the womb. If you achieve this state, you will be the children of God, the sons and daughters of God. If you do not, you will be the children of illusion, satan, and hell.

My grandchildren, have you noticed how young branches laden with new leaves bow down like the branches of a weeping willow tree? The small branches are so soft and gentle, but as they grow, they become less and less supple. In the same way, as children grow older, their beauty, their qualities and their actions change. They are still green like the emerging leaves of the young branches, and this green is cooling to the eyes, but it no longer melts the heart. Nor does it bow to compassion, wisdom, or justice. Older children become like the older branches, more rigid and leathery, not bending for their mother or father or anyone. Even their words will not bend. The mother and the father in turn refuse to bow to the new rigid qualities in their children. Thus separations arise between children and their parents.

Once a branch becomes stiff, the leaves can be blown off by any storm or gust of wind. Those that remain clinging to the tree eventually change, turning from yellow to brown, until finally, one by one, they too drift to the ground. Soon they are either consumed by fire, or they turn to dust and mingle with the earth.

My grandchildren, if our qualities change like the leaves, eventually we too will fall and die and mingle with the earth. But if we keep that beauty and those qualities we had as babies, then we will not fall. God will embrace us, and we will be indestructibly intermingled with Him. As He embraces us, His qualities will come into us, and we will feel no separations. Think about this. Think about God and how He embraces those who love Him.

The state of God is like the state of a baby, and the state of a baby is like the state of God. God is love, and His speech is like the loving speech of a little baby. If His qualities and His plenitude come into you, then you will be a baby too. And when you see that Baby, you will know His language, and you will be able to speak to Him and understand the meaning of His words. If your speech and your breath are like His, then your Father and everyone else will play with you, and you will have a connection to God.

Always remember the words of your Father, the actions and unity of your Father, the compassion and justice and conscience of your Father, the embrace and love of your Father. Always reflect upon His three thousand beautiful qualities and His ninety-nine *wilāyats*. If your own actions are filled with these qualities, you will be the son of God, and you will represent Him. You will have no enmity within you. Your words, your actions, and your love will be embraced by all hearts. You will be the child of Allah.

But if a man does not come to that state, if he does not embrace the loving qualities of a baby, then God will not speak. It is only if a man acquires God's qualities that he can understand that loving baby language, and then both can speak to each other.

My grandchildren, even though we cannot see God, He has formed man in His image. Thus, we can see God in the heart of a man who acts with God's qualities and His truth. Think about this. Discover this state, realize and know it. Do you understand? My love you.

May Almighty God help us. He is the Unfathomable Ruler of grace and the One who is incomparable love. There is no end to His grace and no limit to His love. May God who is our Father protect us, without ever forsaking us. May He give us His grace. *Āmīn.*

"My name is lime. I can cure all of the 4,448 illnesses of man!"

The Pride of the Lime

y love you, my grandchildren. Shall we walk this way? Look at the beautiful green limes hanging from that branch. Come, sit closer, and I will tell you a story about something that happened to the lime fruit long ago.

There was once a doctor who gathered herbs to use as medicine for his patients. One day as he was searching in some fields, he heard a small voice coming from the lime tree. "O man, O physician," it called, "what are you looking for?" He looked around in every direction, but saw no one. Again and again the lime called out to him. Finally the physician shouted, "Who are you? Who is calling me?"

"My name is lime." And with that, the lime shook itself. "I am over here on this branch. Look at me. Why are you wasting your time searching for herbs to cure diseases? I, the lime, am the one who can cure all of the 4,448 illnesses of man. I can cure the burning eye disease, the diseases of the ninety-six kinds of bile, and the diseases from fat deposits that choke the heart. I can even delay the Angel of Death for five minutes.

"First you must pick me, then squeeze me, and then add certain things to the juice that you extract. This mixture will cure the sick. I can dissolve all that is harmful inside the body and heal all the diseases for which you usually use herbs. I can bring forth the good things that develop strength. I am so powerful! I am the most important fruit of the entire plant kingdom!" the lime boasted.

"Ohh, that is wonderful!" the doctor said, truly impressed. And he began to pick some limes.

Suddenly, the words of God resounded. "O lime fruit! Do you have so much pride and arrogance that you have forgotten who created you? Do you think it is you who possesses all this power? It is I who made you with such beauty and simplicity, but in your boasting you have forgotten Me. So, because of your pride, your essence will be divided. Your one seed and single segment will be changed into many segments with many seeds. You will become the mother of a whole family of fruit, and your power will be shared among them.''

At once the lime was divided into many segments filled with many seeds, and from that lime came the entire citrus family. Each kind of fruit was given a portion of the lime's qualities. One portion went into the lemon, one into the orange, one into the grapefruit, and one portion into the tangerine. The lime itself was left with the green color and sour qualities.

Like the lime, man becomes ripe for his own downfall, when he forgets God and allows the I to arise within him. No matter how educated a man may be or how much he knows, no matter whether he is a king or a beggar, if he forgets his Creator and becomes arrogant, God breaks down that man's power into many different sections. And as his ability and talent are divided into many portions, his goodness also diminishes. He loses his wisdom and sinks to the state of the lime. Eventually he becomes prey to hell, to the earth, and to worms and insects.

But the one who remembers the treasure of Allah will increase in wisdom, and his state will be elevated. He who considers the Creator as the source of all his actions will flourish. His search, his wisdom, and his qualities will all flourish.

My precious grandchildren, when wisdom comes to you, all the bushes, the trees, and even the weeds will speak to you. But if you become proud, goodness and truth will not speak to you from within any of God's creations. Instead, hell will speak to you. Illusion, demons, and ghosts will speak to you. Fatal illnesses will speak to you and make you suffer. Ignorance will speak to you. Religious and racial prejudices will speak to you. But wisdom will not speak to you. Neither will your inherent potentialities, nor God's qualities, truth, or love. Your desires, or *nafs,* demons, ghosts, and four hundred trillion, ten thousand spiritual things will all prick you and pinch you from inside. When that happens, you will feel tired and disturbed, full of torpor and doubt. In that low state you will not be able to cure anyone's illness or give peace to anyone.

If you attempt to give peace to others while you are in such an arrogant state, your help will be worse than the poison of a snake. Your arrogance and your karma will kill the other man, and you will even expect a reward for the poison you have given. If you have differences, pride, arrogance, jealousy, envy, deceit, intoxication, religious fanaticism, and prejudices, your life will be filled with destruction and obsessed with doubt. That poisonous state will destroy your goodness and the goodness of others. It will eat away at the qualities of God and hinder His justice. That poison will destroy everything.

My love you, my grandchildren. You must cut away all these evils. You must listen with the ear that can hear the speech of the entire creation, see with the eye that can see everything, smell with the nose that can smell everything, and speak with the tongue that can reply to everything. You must take it all in and understand with the heart that knows. When this happens, wisdom will come to you and all creations will speak to you. You will understand the power of God and praise Him.

When you surrender yourself to Him and dedicate yourself to Him, when you give your wisdom and love to Him in your breath and in your speech, then all creations will speak to you, and you will be able to understand them. You will know the essence and movement of each and every life. When you reach that state, then you will truly become the son of God.

My love you, my grandchildren. Do not be like the lime. Destroy this pride of the I. Destroy your differences. Become a man. Become a true believer, a *mu'min*. Become a messenger of God and a slave to God. Become His son, become His child. Serve God, perform your duty in His kingdom, and help all lives.

Every child should know this and understand it with wisdom. My love you. May God help you to realize this state. *Āmīn.*

We must get rid of this karma, this stench. It cuts away at our entire life and severs our connection to God.

It Hurts to Be Washed

y love you, my grandchildren, my brothers and sisters, my sons and daughters. Look at your clothes. See how dirty they are? They have changed so much since you first bought them! The colors have faded, and the cloth is full of sweat. Smell them, they stink!

Now smell your body. The odor of everything you eat is present in your sweat. If you eat beef you can smell the cow, if you eat goat meat you can smell the goat, if you eat fish you can smell fish, and if you eat chicken then you will stink like a chicken. Even if you take medicine, you will smell it when you burp. Where do all these odors come from? From inside your body. They come from the things you have eaten and put into your body. That is why you smell and why your shirt smells, from the sweat of all that you have accumulated inside.

The stench and dirt that collects on your clothes can be washed, but what can be done for the smell inside the body? My love you, my grandchildren, try to think about this.

You wash your clothes, don't you? You think, "I must look good. I have to look important," and so you keep your clothes nice and clean. In olden days, people had to beat their clothes on stones by the riverside to clean them, but now science has given us the washing machine and all we have to do is add a little soap. But the clothes really suffer in the machine. Someday, watch how a washing machine works and you will see how the clothes suffer. They are tossed about, tangled, rubbed, and scrubbed. Even if you wash them by hand you have to soap them, scrub them, and rinse them. That's the only way dirt can be removed. Clothes go through so much, just for you to dress up and look attractive, like a new bride or a bridegroom.

My children, in the same way, you have to wash away the smell coming from each pore of your skin. This smelly, karmic illness, this illusion, pride, jealousy, doubt, arrogance, hatred, lust, anger, miser-

51

liness, greed, fanaticism, envy, the base desires of the *nafs,* the differences of I and you, mine and yours, my possessions and your possessions, my religion and your religion, my language and your language, my child and your child—how they all stink! They reek every second, from every pore of your body.

It is very difficult to wash away this stench which comes from the things you have searched for and accumulated within yourself. And because it is so difficult, it might hurt a little when you try to remove this stench. If you have an infected sore and the doctor cuts it open with his scalpel, you might cry from the pain. If you step on a thorn and the doctor removes it, it may hurt so much that you might try to hit him or even bite him. It is hard enough for the doctor to do his job without your resenting him and calling him a terrible man.

You may react the same way when you come to a man of wisdom and good qualities and he tries to help you rid yourself of your karmic illnesses. It will certainly be difficult. You will suffer when someone who knows reveals your illnesses to you. Your mind and desire, your hunger, disease, old age, and death will suffer. The four hundred trillion, ten thousand illnesses you harbor within yourself will experience sorrow. If someone tells you to discard the things you have nourished so carefully, it will make you unhappy. You will yell at him and be full of doubts, resentment, and envy, and you will run away.

It would definitely be easier to go to someone who has the same qualities as you, someone who would just say, "Oh, nothing's wrong. There's no problem. You smell fine, just apply a little deodorant. I love you. Eat whatever you want and recite whatever mantra you choose. Then you'll be happy." You will like him. You will say that he is a fine doctor, a good guru, and a good sheikh.

But think about it. Since he smells just like you, he will not mind your karmic smell. His stench and your stench go together very nicely, but even animals will run away from it, the stink is so foul. Consider the skunk. Everyone thinks a skunk smells dreadful, except another skunk. So, when two skunks get together, they are happy. But human beings will do everything possible to get rid of that terrible odor.

My grandchildren, just as one skunk does not know that another skunk is smelly, karma does not know the smell of karma. But a man of wisdom will know. He will try to get rid of the stench. A false guru will only enjoy the smell of karma. He will not try to help you get rid of yours, and so it will continue to grow in you. He will ask for money and say, "Do this, do that. Give me two hundred dollars, and everything will turn out well." A false guru asks for money, but a true wise man says, "I want nothing. It is enough if you become well."

A true healer who tries to cure your illness might cause you pain. It is hard to wash away that condition, because the sickness is part of your flesh, your blood, and your mind. It sticks to you like paint. Trying to peel or scrape it off is very difficult. It must be done with *sabūr* and *shukūr*, with inner patience and absolute contentment. My grandchildren, you need that *īmān* of faith, determination, and certitude. You need all the qualities of Allah. Then the paint can be scraped off with wisdom and love, and you can be clean.

My love you. It is difficult to get rid of the karma of this birth. It is difficult to wash and scrape away arrogance, karma, and illusion, and *tārahan, singhan* and *sūran,* the three sons of illusion. It is difficult to get rid of lust, hatred, miserliness, greed, fanaticism, and envy. It is difficult to eliminate intoxicants, theft, murder, falsehood, anger, haste, impatience, selfishness, pride, doubt, suspicion, and the separations the mind creates between religions and colors. Only if you have patience, contentment, faith, determination, and all the qualities of God, will the wise man be able to make you as beautiful and clean as he possibly can. He keeps trying to do his duty always. He does not seek anything from you.

My love you, my grandchildren. Think about this and strengthen your faith. We must get rid of this karma, this stench. It destroys the life and freedom of the soul. It cuts away at our entire life and our connection to God. The skunk's smell is in its skin, but man's smell is in his mind. It is easy enough to skin a skunk, but to get rid of the mind's smell is very difficult. Reflect upon this deeply. Get rid of your pride, your resentment, and your anger. Acquire humility, peace, and serenity. You must have these qualities. That would be good.

My love you, my grandchildren. May this karma be gone and that fragrance be ours. May we believe in our Father, and may we have absolute faith, determination, and certitude. Cherish those qualities. Be patient. Then that good doctor can use his wisdom on your behalf. May God help you. *Āmīn.*

This fish has a subtle light which allows it to see,
as it swims about happily searching for food.

The Fish with a Light on Its Forehead

y love you, my grandchildren. Today we are going into the depths of the ocean. Come and look through this special lens, and you will see the countless creatures that live there. You can even examine the minute details of fish eggs, single-celled creatures, viruses, and many other forms of life. Do you see them all?

My love you, my grandchildren. Look at that light over there. What wonder is this so deep in the ocean? That light comes from an unusual fish. Focus the lens carefully and you will see that the light is located directly above the two brows of this fish. It resembles the reflectors found on road signs, and it glows in the dark like fluorescent paint. This luminous paint is one of man's many recent scientific discoveries, but God invented something just like it a long, long time ago when He created this fish.

Though there are many varieties of fish in the ocean, only this particular fish has a subtle light which allows it to see, as it swims about happily searching for food. This light enables it to avoid accidents and difficulties. If it sees a dangerous fish above, it can dive down, and if it sees one below, it can swim higher up and escape. But because the other fish cannot see in the darkness of the ocean, they are often caught and eaten.

This fish is not as beautiful or as big as some of the other fish, nor does it have magnificent coloring, but when you look at its face, the subtle glowing light gives it a unique kind of beauty. As you watch a school of these fish swimming by, you can see a bright blue path of color shimmering in front of each one. These lights look like sparkling gems in the water. Out of all His creations, God gave this light to only one kind of fish.

Man, who is so exalted, also has a natural light to help him. This light, which is in his heart, enables him to look at the whole world and choose what is right.

When man was created, he was given the luminous paint of truth. God placed wisdom at the center of man's eye, in the pupil, and He surrounded it with this shining truth. There is a tiny point within that pupil of wisdom through which light emerges. That point within wisdom is God. Through that point comes the light which enables man to see everything and allows his heart to understand everything. By showing him what is coming and what is going, it gives him the power to escape from any accident or danger. This light gives man the vision to understand.

Just as the fish has a light to help him search through the dark ocean to find the food that is right for him, man has a light to help him travel through the dark ocean of illusion to find his proper food. With this light he can see good and bad, right and wrong, permissible and impermissible, heaven and hell, truth and falsehood, and he can evaluate all that exists. Then he can discard what is wrong, or *harām*, and take only what is right, or *halāl*, and enjoy its taste. This light was given to help him choose what belongs to God and discard what belongs to hell. This luminous truth joins with faith, certitude, and determination and shows him the good path.

My grandchildren, you must open this beautiful eye of wisdom and look at your life. With it you can see everything. God placed His power within it and gave it to you. It will protect you and enable you to have a long life without accidents.

The natural power of this light comes from God's kingdom, from His throne. With this light in your heart, you can avoid what is wrong and take what is right. If you avoid bad foods, you will not be subject to disease. If you look with God's gaze and His qualities, you will not be subject to destruction and death. Then you can lead a peaceful and serene life, with God's beautiful form and God's kingdom of heaven in your heart. Wouldn't this be good?

My precious children, this is something that is natural to you. Even before you came to the world and entered the house of this body, that light was made ready for you. While you were still in the kingdom of the pure soul, that sharp and subtle wisdom was given to you. With it you must understand all that you see with your eyes. Look at and understand the kingdom of the soul, the kingdom of this illusory world, and then the kingdom of our Father. Avoid what must be avoided, take what must be taken, and conduct yourselves correctly.

My love you, my grandchildren. This light within your heart is the true light of the soul. If you use it to see your way and guide your life, what sadness, what difficulties, what karma, what sin or suffering can you possibly have? What evil can ever approach you? Neither darkness, satan, nor illusion will be able to come near you.

My love you, my grandchildren. Think about this. Like the fish, see with the help of this light. Look with your truth and wisdom so that you can follow the good path in this ocean of life. My love you, my grandchildren, my brothers and sisters, my sons and daughters. Think about this. My love you. *Āmīn*. May Allah help us.

*Despite their differences, the trees stand united. Even
the animals live here together happily and peacefully.*

The United Forest

My love you, my grandchildren, my brothers and sisters, my daughters and sons. Shall we go to the forest? Come along with me.

Look how beautiful it is here! The forest is filled with many subtle kinds of beauty. The trees reach upward, tall and straight, like pillars of light. Each stands alone, erect and strong. Not one is bent.

How did these trees grow so well? By standing close to one another, allowing nothing to grow between them. This unity protects them against destructive forces. Even though there are many varieties of trees, with leaves, buds, flowers, and fruits of all different colors and types, they stand united despite their differences. Together they can weather winds, storms, and hurricanes. And if poisonous chemicals should fall upon one tree, the others will help to absorb the poison, because they are so near. Even the animals live together happily and peacefully here. If an enemy attacks, they can find refuge by jumping from tree to tree.

How lovely the trees are, how elegant! Each one grows alone, yet they stand together, making the forest beautiful and cooling to the eyes. Here the rain that falls is shared equally as it splatters on every leaf. This is a united forest.

My love you, my grandchildren. This is unity. We must think about the beauty, happiness, and contentment we have seen today in the forest. If all of mankind could live in unity like these trees, without differences of race or color, how happy and peaceful we would be! If man could grow to be strong and stand erect by himself, and yet be united with others, how happy and free his soul would be!

Just as this forest is almost heavenly in its beauty, man could also be so beautiful if he lived in unity and justice. Then one man would not kill another. In the face of a forceful wind, one man would protect another, just as the trees in the forest protect each other against the forces of the elements. If troubles came to a man in such a united world, he would be able to escape, just as the animals in this united forest escape from danger by jumping from tree to tree.

If man would grow tall and strong and free of hatred, this world would be heaven on earth. It would become the indestructible kingdom of God, a united world with all people living as one family and one life, without divisions. With such unity, mankind could never be destroyed by the discord that arises from differences of races, religions, or colors.

But if man does not live with the qualities that can turn this world into heaven, his life will be hell. He will destroy himself and others through the storms and volcanoes of differences. His life will be a life of vengeance in the kingdom of destruction. If only man would reflect on the beauty of the united forest and create that kind of unity in his life, destruction would not come to this world. There would be no separations, no divisions, no differences.

My love you, my grandchildren. You must think about this. Love and unity can never be diminished or destroyed. They constitute the justice of God's kingdom and are the duties by which He protects all lives. Everyone, our brothers, sisters, fathers, mothers, and all our relations should make an effort to live in unity. This is the way God is, and man must strive to live in the same way. To reach this state is to reach heaven and a peaceful life in God's kingdom.

Please reflect upon this, my grandchildren. Like the trees in the forest, try to live together with God's loving qualities, performing God's duties. If we can live in unity, the terrible forces of the world will not attack us. We will be saved from destruction and accidents. Please make an effort to grow in peace and to attain complete wisdom on this path. My love you. *Āmīn.*

Tiny Red Ants Can Cause Destruction

y love you, my grandchildren. Come, will you journey a little way with me? Wait a minute! Something is happening over there. Look, an army of tiny red ants is marching swiftly toward us. They are *cuttay* ants, the most terrible kind of ant. Their poisonous bite is as bad as that of a scorpion. Do you see how their heads and back portions are much bigger than their necks and middles?

Even though these ants are so small, they strike terror in the hearts of larger creatures. If a single red ant bites the inside of an elephant's trunk, it will cause so much pain that the elephant will think he is going to die. He will trumpet and slam his trunk against a tree, but still that ant inside will not let go. It will bite him over and over again. A tiny red ant can make a huge elephant suffer so much.

When these *cuttay* ants gather into an army, they are even more terrifying. They destroy everything in their path. They attack quickly and completely devour their victim. First they attack the eyes, blinding their prey, then they crawl into its ears, and finally they tear its whole body apart. They can reduce any creature to bones in a very short time. These ants will not leave anything alive. They destroy leaves, trees, and all the creations subject to their power. Look! All the animals and insects and even people are fleeing in fear of this army. Come children, run quickly and escape from them!

My love you, my grandchildren. There are four hundred trillion, ten thousand thoughts in your mind which are so tiny they cannot be seen. Without your even knowing it, they have crept into you like an army of ants, bent on destroying you and the whole world.

What are some of these tiny thoughts? A doubt is only a small thing. A desire in the mind is also a small thing. Illusion is just a

*Even though these ants are so small, they
strike terror in the hearts of larger creatures.*

small point in our lives. Selfishness and falsehood are very small. But if a man has any one of these, his entire life will be consumed and destroyed, no matter how large or clever he might be. His wisdom, his purity, his good thoughts and qualities, the life of his soul, his life in this world, and his life in the kingdom of God will all be devoured by these ants, these evil qualities. They do not know what truth is, nor do they understand what is wise and good. They will attack and consume everything.

My love you, my grandchildren. You must be careful not to let even an atom of evil come into you. One atom can destroy your whole life. It will devour your body like those *cuttay* ants. Its poisonous bite will cause both your soul and your life to tremble. The qualities of God, your love, and your wisdom will shiver from its bite.

As soon as you see this army coming, you must be very, very careful. These tiny ants won't let anyone escape. What will they go after first? They will attack your eye of wisdom and then eat away at your love. Once they have conquered your wisdom and intellect, and you lie there stunned, they will swiftly devour your faith, certitude, determination, your *īmān,* and your good qualities. Then you will become blind and open to attack from all the karma of the world, all the desires, sins, the egoism of I and you, mine and yours, all the connections and intoxicants, theft, lust, murder, and falsehood. All the four hundred trillion, ten thousand thoughts will join together in a huge force and gobble you up piece by piece until there is nothing left. Your whole life will be devoured.

My grandchildren, flee from this army! Do not think that your doubts and suspicions or your thoughts and desires are only small things. They will destroy your life, your soul, and your treasures in the three worlds. Just as you should not think, "Oh, these ants are nothing, we can crush them," do not think, "This is only a small fault, just a tiny evil." Do not be deceived into thinking you can easily get rid of them at any time. If you waste time and ignore them, you will end up with a huge problem. You must stop them before they even come near you. This matter is much greater than you think. You have to use a large amount of wisdom and grace to get rid of these ants.

My precious grandchildren, you came to this world as a pure soul.

God created you in such a beautiful way. When you arrived you were beautiful, resplendent, and pure. But by the time you were three, so many evil connections began to come to you. And now this army of ants has captured you and is bent on destroying you. These four hundred trillion, ten thousand thoughts are destroying the freedom of your soul. They are destroying wisdom, God's qualities, God's actions, His equality, peace, unity, love, justice, integrity, and tranquility. Your thoughts are eating you up like ants devouring an animal. These ants are out of control, running in every direction, destroying everything in sight. Do you understand this?

My grandchildren, ants are afraid of only one thing—fire. Even though they may try to attack the fire, still they are afraid of it. They do not fear anything else. They can float on water and drift with the wind, but they cannot withstand fire. So if you want to stop these ants, you must build within you a huge fire of wisdom. That is the only thing that can stop them. Use your faith, certitude, and determination to light that blaze. Then when these thoughts approach you, they will be scorched and burned. Good will be protected and evil will be destroyed.

Therefore, my children, with the logs of faith, certitude, and determination, build a blazing fire of wisdom. Build a huge fire of divine analytic wisdom until it reaches up as high as divine luminous wisdom. Then the four hundred trillion, ten thousand energies and thoughts can be stopped.

My children, you must be very careful. And you must be strong, or these terrible thoughts will eat you up. They are dangerous, wicked things. They can destroy the whole world. Do not let them devour you.

Think about this. Be ever watchful. May God help you. *Āmīn.*

The Perfect Balance of the Crane

y love you, my grandchildren. Come, let us go to the shallow lagoon where the fish come in from the ocean. We can sit by the shore in the shade of this tree and watch the birds. Look at that flock of cranes. There are small ones, large ones, and very tall ones. Some are soft gray, some are pure white, others are a brass-colored red, and still others are a deep saffron color. The very tall ones tower above the small ones. They are all so beautiful, standing there motionless on one leg.

Do you see how long they can remain still? Their bodies are quite large, and yet they can balance on one very thin leg. Look, some are standing on the shore, sleeping with their heads tucked under their wings. A few others are standing in the lagoon with heads bent down, their eyes focused on the water. Why do they stand that way hour after hour? To catch fish. They are waiting for their food to swim by. Even those on land stand patiently, perfectly balanced and still. This is natural for cranes. How beautiful they are!

My grandchildren, my daughters and sons, my brothers and sisters, just as the cranes need balance to stand motionless in order to catch a fish, we must have the balance of wisdom to catch what we need. With subtle wisdom, analytic wisdom, and divine luminous wisdom we must stand ready, every minute of every hour of our lives. To catch the grace of God, the *rahmat* of Allah, we need to have that single-pointedness of wisdom. We need that faith, determination, and certitude. All our thoughts and intentions must be focused on Allah's love, His grace, and His qualities. We have to balance on this one point and then catch hold of God.

To catch that subtle meaning, our wisdom must be ever so subtle and sharp. We must catch wisdom with wisdom and find subtlety

*Hour after hour, the crane stands motionless on
one leg, waiting for a fish to swim by.*

with subtlety. We must stand motionless, balanced on the point of truth. Awake or asleep, even while walking, we must maintain that point of wisdom, that thought, that intention, and that faith. Neither our shadows nor our minds should move. Our desires must be still. Everything must be perfectly motionless. Day and night we must stand in this way, balancing on that subtlety. All of our attachments and relationships, our selfishness, hunger, illness, and old age must be perfectly controlled. Our happiness and sadness must be controlled with analytic wisdom. We have to stand in that subtle state to catch Him. We have to catch the point of truth, which is Allah.

My grandchildren, if we can be like this, we will taste the love and the flavor of that one meaning. We must imbibe His food and taste its bliss. Then we can satisfy the hunger of our souls, the hunger of the karma of this existence, and the hunger that we have as slaves. We can end the suffering in our lives and attain peace, tranquility, and love.

Just as the body of the crane is heavy, this body of ours is also heavy. Mind and desire are heavy. The world is heavy. Desire for earth, women, and gold is heavy. But no matter how heavy they are, if we control them and stand balanced, we will not fall.

My grandchildren, think about this. We must remain perfectly balanced. Otherwise, we cannot catch God or obtain His meaning. In the way that the crane controls itself, we must use wisdom to control everything within ourselves and then catch hold of God. This will bring us a great blessing. My love you. May Allah give us that balance and control. *Āmīn.*

My grandchildren, these tricks are natural for animals, but not for you.

The Circus

y love you, my grandchildren. Come, let's go home. The sun is going down and it is getting dark. So many people are out tonight. Everywhere there are posters with colorful pictures of bears, lions, tigers, dogs, and many other kinds of animals. Let's go see what the posters say. Oh, it's a circus! Look, here comes the parade! Let's watch the animals and acrobats. Look at them dancing about and jumping up and down.

Now the men have put up the tents. Shall we go inside and watch the show? What a wonder! Five or six people are climbing on top of each other and doing somersaults. Others are flying from one trapeze to the next, twisting in the air, and grabbing onto each other's hands and feet. These people can perform so many different tricks.

My love you, my grandchildren. Can you see that monkey over there? He is swinging and jumping just like the acrobats and trapeze artists. These tricks come naturally to a monkey, but people have to learn how to do them. Perhaps they learned by watching the monkey. Swinging on a trapeze is regarded as a great art, but I have seen better performances in the jungle, where monkeys cling to the vines with their hands and feet, hang upside-down, and leap from one vine to the next. Still, man's tricks are fun to watch. He can fly through the air, holding on to the trapeze with his feet, then flip around and do many amazing things. Wearing only a small loincloth, man plays gleefully high up in the air, but he cannot stay up there. Eventually he has to come down to the earth.

Man can perform so many different tricks in all the realms, on the ground and in the air. Sometimes he even seems to be suspended by nothing. However, if we look at this with wisdom, we will see that he is only mimicking the behavior of monkeys. So who is man's guru? The monkey?

Have you been watching all that is happening at this circus? Oh, look over there. Two monkeys are fighting and punching each other very hard. They look like they're boxing. The kangaroos are also boxing, using their hands and feet and even their snouts and heads.

My love you, my grandchildren. Why does man mimic such things? So that he can become famous. People praise his tricks and call his accomplishments miraculous. He enjoys boxing like a kangaroo and swinging through the air like a monkey. But who is the best when it comes to boxing? Kangaroos. And who is best at swinging? Monkeys. Why? Because this behavior is natural for them.

My grandchildren, although people have learned to copy the acts of monkeys, they haven't discovered what the work of a true man is. There is another side to man's life that he has not learned anything about. He hasn't learned the qualities and actions of God. He hasn't learned to love God or to believe in Him. He hasn't realized the unity and wisdom of God, His light and integrity, His peace and serenity, His conscience and justice. Man has not learned the qualities of the One who is incomparable love and the Unfathomable Ruler of grace. He was born as a rare and exalted creation, but he has forgotten this.

Instead, man is learning from the animals, who do not even possess analytic wisdom. They defecate where they eat, and sleep where they defecate. That is what man is learning. Just as fish swim in the water, man has learned to swim underwater. Horses and other animals can run swiftly across the land, and man has also learned to run very fast. Beetles fly in the air, and man has learned to put on wings and fly. Certain birds dive into the water to catch fish, and man has learned to dive beneath the water just like them. Man imitates the acts of kangaroos, monkeys, goats, cows, dragons that blow fire out of their mouths, donkeys, snakes, peacocks, crows, cats, rats, dogs, foxes, and many other animals. He learns their tricks and adopts their qualities.

My grandchildren, if you look back at your own experiences, you can see how man mimics the animals. He has learned to imitate countless things in God's creation, but he has forgotten everything that belongs to the section of God. His wisdom, his qualities, and his actions have degenerated so much, even though his outside appearance has not changed. He still has the same face, hands, and eyes he always did. But he prefers to play, enjoying these animal qualities and the dancing, swimming, and jumping.

Thus man has come to his present state. He has not changed one bit for the good. He has not understood the power of God—that strong, endless, limitless love and grace. If he would only turn to that power, if he would only acquire wisdom and God's qualities, how much he could learn! God created him as a human being and gave him a rare and exalted life, filled with love, compassion, and wisdom. He was born beautiful, but he has not turned to the ways of the One who created him. Is that not a wonder?

My grandchildren, you must understand that when God created the animals, He gave them certain qualities and actions. These are natural for the animals, but not for you. So do not try to imitate their ways in order to win prizes in this world. Understand that God created a different section for man. And that section is so very exalted!

This is what you should try to understand and then act accordingly. Do not harm or kill any life. Protect all lives as you protect your own. Then you will know compassion, unity, harmony, and peace. You will learn to be always in a state of love. My grandchildren, think about this. May God give you His great wisdom. My love you.

Don't try to find fault with the storm.
That will only lead to your own destruction.

Finding Fault

y love you, my children, my grandchildren. Come closer, and I will tell you something to help you in your life.

Children, do you ever criticize others and find fault with them, complaining, "Why are they doing that?" Or do you ever look at the sorrows of the world and ask, "Why is God doing this?" A man of wisdom will never have such thoughts. He will study each situation and try to understand the cause and the effect. Finally, he will say, "Ahh, so that is why this happened." He will never find fault with God or question the way in which God does things.

If you stand in the middle of a gale and criticize it, saying, "Why is this wind blowing so hard?" then you too will be caught up in the storm. Don't try to find fault with the storm. That will only lead to your own destruction. Instead, understand the nature of the storm and look for a way to escape.

My children, God has created pairs of opposites to teach us about our lives. He created right and wrong, good and evil, sweet aromas and bad odors. If life did not provide us with these opposites, how could we understand anything? We can only understand goodness when we have known evil. We can only know light when we have seen darkness. We can only understand heaven if we have experienced hell. We can only know if there is a truth when we have witnessed falsehood. Only if we have experienced base desires and the harm that comes from them can we understand the heavenly messengers. Only if we have experienced selfishness and attachment can we find our way to non-attachment and unselfishness.

Thus there is no point in finding fault and criticizing God or anyone. Instead, we should try to understand each situation and find clarity within it. Each thing within creation is there to teach us something, and it is our duty to discover the lesson within it. We can understand the truth through examples. That is what maturity is. A man of maturity understands the cause and the result of everything.

Without this understanding, man is only an animal. He will perform an evil act and then say it was his duty. His actions will bring harm to himself and to others. But a man who understands before he acts will receive many benefits and will be able to give peace to others. He will complete the work of the All-Pervasive Treasure. If this state is established in a man, he will be called man-God, *manu īsan,* and *insān kāmil,* a perfected, God-realized being. He will understand.

We must discover the point of everything in our lives. We must use our wisdom to clearly understand each and every thing. Then truth will arise from within us, and within that truth we will see the radiance of God. That is the beauty and grace of the soul.

Jeweled lights of my eyes, you must think about this deeply. This is life. Criticizing and finding fault will only bring harm. You have to realize where the faults lie and then dispel them. Are the faults in God? Are they in others? Or are they in ourselves? Where do the faults lie? We have to understand this and avoid them.

My love you.

The Secret Room

y love you, my grandchildren. Today we are going to a place where there are many subtle wonders. There you will find certain things that you must bring back and keep very carefully in your room. They cannot be kept in any other place. What are these things? Let's go and find out.

Come along with me, children. Look up at the sun. It is so bright that it dazzles our eyes. See how this brilliant sunlight chases away all the darkness. What must you take from the sun? Take the point within it. And what is that point? The essence of its light.

Now come along, we have still more things to gather. What do you see over there in the sky? Ah, the moon! Look how pale it is in the daylight. At night the moon is very bright, but when the darkness ends it loses its power and brilliance, leaving only a pale image. Take this image of the moon with you, my grandchildren, and come along further.

Oh look! Can you see that object swaying back and forth high up in the sky? It's a kite! It has stopped moving now and remains balanced in one spot. Watch it carefully, my children, and take that point of balance from the kite.

Come, let us walk about in this lovely flower garden. Can you smell the sweet fragrance in the air? You must extract the fragrance from the flowers and bring it with you.

Now we have come to an orchard, filled with various fruits. From here you must take the good taste of the ripened fruits. That is all you need. Now, my grandchildren, what else must you gather? Do you see that man planting seeds? Bring some of those seeds with you.

All right, that is all we can do today. It is growing late. The day is over and we must go.

Did you do what I told you to do? Have you brought everything with you and put it all safely away in your room?

"No. We didn't bring anything home with us. Some of them were so far away that we couldn't reach them. We didn't know how to bring those things."

Is that so? That is because you have locked up your heart, which is the room of love and truth, and you do not have the key of wisdom to open it. The effort and faith needed to open the door to the house of your soul has not developed within you. If you cannot open that door, what is the use of learning any of this?

You need wisdom so that you can grasp the treasures of truth that you saw and then keep them in your room of love and truth where you can take good care of them. If you had wisdom, you could have brought all those things with you.

ᴄ·ᴜ ᴄ·ᴐ

My grandchildren, what was the first thing I showed you? The light of the sun. I told you to take only the essence, the point within that complete light, the subtle resplendence of its rays. That sun is within you, and that light is wisdom, the light of your life. That incomparable resplendence is God, and you are the light-filled child of God. Your life should be filled with goodness and plenitude. I told you to take that completeness into you. But, my grandchildren, you did not do what I said. You did not extract that light with the subtlety and sharpness of wisdom.

Next I showed you the light of the moon. Because it was daytime, the moon appeared faint and pale. My grandchildren, the light of your worldly life is the same. It can only be seen in the darkness of illusion. Your whole life goes by in that darkness, and what remains in the end? Only the soul. The body ages, loses its energy, and perishes in the darkness of this illusion. In the end only the soul remains.

Why did I ask you to bring this image of the moon with you? It can teach you about the limit of your life. I wanted you to understand what will happen; your body will go, but your soul will remain. My grandchildren, you have to understand that point and make yourself complete and ageless. That was the point to be taken from the moon.

Next we looked at a kite. It swayed to and fro high up in the sky and then found a point of balance. You too have to balance your life in this world. When things in your life begin to sway, you must maintain a state of balance with your qualities, never wavering from the center. First one side will pull you down, then the other side will tug at you. You must be able to adjust and balance between the two. Do not be pulled to either side. Use your wisdom and good qualities to maintain your balance. That was the point to be taken from the kite.

After that we looked at the flowers and smelled their fragrance. I told you to know their beauty and take only their good scent with you. Next I told you to find out how each fruit in the orchard tastes but to take only the sweet taste. In the same way, you have to understand life and extract the good essence from it.

Then, do you remember the man who was planting the seeds? Just as he planted the seeds in the soil, you must plant in your heart the seeds of *īmān,* of faith, certitude, and determination; the seeds of truth, wisdom, love, compassion, equality, and tranquility; the seeds of inner patience, contentment, trust in God, and praise of God, known as *sabūr, shukūr, tawakkul-Allāh, al-hamdu lillāh;* and the seeds of God's qualities and *wilāyats,* His actions and duties. A point of truth grows from each of those seeds. Take the point from each one and plant them all within your inner heart. Cultivate them and they will bloom within you as completeness. These are the seeds I asked you to take.

My love you, my grandchildren. Think about these points I told you to gather. From the sun, understand the resplendence of grace-awakened wisdom, the resplendence of *gnānam.* From the moon, know that the soul exists even when the body is gone. From the kite, learn to use your wisdom and good qualities to maintain your balance in life. From the fragrance of the flower and the taste of the fruit, learn to extract the essence of life. From the seeds, learn to plant and cultivate the points of truth in God's kingdom of the heart. Do this farming with wisdom, and when all these seeds develop and reach completeness within your heart, then you will become the plenitude.

My grandchildren, I took you on this journey and showed you all these examples so that you would understand the points within them. I told you to take these points and place them in your secret room, but instead you thought you were supposed to carry the things themselves. If you try to carry even one of these things, you will perish on the spot. If you try to carry the form, it will destroy you. However, if

*To find peace in your life, you must keep the essence of each
thing in the right place. That place is your secret room, the
room of your heart where your real life is lived.*

you take the point, the essence, it will make you grow. That is all you need for your development.

My love you. You must think about this. Open your heart so that you can place within it the point of everything you observe. Then keep those treasures in that perfectly pure place, the secret room of your heart. Only in that way can you protect them from destruction.

You must keep each thing where it belongs or you will lose your balance. You must keep an electric current within an insulated wire or it will give you a shock and throw you down. Take truth and keep it in the place of truth. Take wisdom and keep it within wisdom. Take the light and keep it within the light. Take justice and keep it within justice. Take conscience and keep it within the conscience, the witness. Take goodness and keep it within goodness. Take your life and keep it within God's life. Keep God within God.

To find peace in your life, you must keep the essence of each thing in the right place. That place is your secret room, the room of your heart where your real life is lived. This room is the kingdom of heaven, the kingdom of *gnānam,* the kingdom of the soul, the perfectly pure kingdom of bliss. You must take only what is right and keep it within this pure place. Then you will find that completeness, and your life will flourish. But if you put the wrong things there, the room of your life will be destroyed.

My grandchildren, you must know where each treasure should be kept and how to protect it. Walk on the right side. That is heaven. The left side is hell, the wrong side. Gather what you need and keep all that is good and fragrant within your heart on the right side, in the kingdom of heaven. Throw your hellish thoughts and visions and whatever is evil off to the left, to the kingdom of hell. Plant the seeds in the right way, conduct the journey of your life in the right way, and maintain the correct balance. If you lose your balance, you will fall into hell, into illusion, torpor, desire, lust, fanaticism, backbiting, the divisions of race and religion, and the hypocrisy of saying one thing while thinking something else. The qualities of poisonous beings, ghosts, and demons will come into you.

My love you, my grandchildren. Evil qualities are all poisonous. If you keep such poisons within you, they will end up killing you. The snake has poisonous sacs within its mouth so that it can attack others.

But when it thunders, the poisonous sacs burst, and the snake dies of its own venom. Like this, my grandchildren, whatever evil you keep within yourself will kill you the instant the thunder of God's compassion and *rahmat* strikes. If you keep these poisonous qualities within you, they will destroy the truth, the kingdom of the soul, the kingdom of grace-awakened wisdom, and the kingdom of that perfect purity and resplendence. Your life will be destroyed.

My love you, my children. Your every thought must be a good thought. Make use of the good. Discard the bad qualities and actions that come to you.

Every one of you must think about this. We see so much in our lives, and we listen to so many beings. But remember, from whatever you see or hear, extract only the point of truth and keep it in your heart. You only need that one point of truth which is found within everything. God's *qudrat,* His power, is within that point. Let the rest go, and then your load will not be heavy. Do not try to keep within you those poisons that are filled with so many bad odors. The body, other creations, and illusion are all connected to earth. They all smell. There is only one point that does not have this stench. That is the soul of truth, the one point of fragrance. Take only that and leave the rest behind. Then your life will be peaceful and your journey easy.

Every child must think about this. Walk with your father of wisdom and joyfully look within each thing he points out to you. Extract the point, understand it, and keep it within you in the secret room of your heart. Your father of wisdom will show you the way. This is why you travel with him.

My love you, my grandchildren. God, your Father, must protect you. Truth, the Father of your soul, must help you. *Āmīn.*

Do Not Follow the Chameleon of the Mind

y love you, my grandchildren, my sons and daughters. Have you ever watched a chameleon? Some people believe that if you follow a chameleon, it will lead you to a buried treasure of precious gems.

Look, see that man trying to catch one? But as soon as he approaches, the chameleon quickly runs up a tree, stops, and turns around, so that its head points toward the ground. Then it nods its head up and down and looks very wise. The man thinks the chameleon likes him, because of the way it rolls its eyes. But when he tries to move closer, the chameleon runs even further into the darkness of the jungle. Still the man follows it, thinking it is calling to him.

Finally the chameleon climbs up still another tree deep in the jungle and stays there. When it becomes dark, the man finds himself in the middle of the jungle, surrounded on all sides by tigers, foxes, snakes, and bears. What a predicament he is in now! Lost and alone in the jungle, he will be swallowed by the poisonous beings of darkness.

My children, people do not realize that chameleons always nod their heads, as if saying, "Come. Come here." The chameleon of the mind is also like that. It keeps on nodding its head, leading man on. He follows his mind and desire, thinking he is going to see a great wonder. But the mind always remains out of reach in front of him, nodding its head, calling, "Come, come." And man continues to follow. The mind finally leads him to that dark place where the Angel of Death awaits. Then it climbs into a tree leaving man to become firewood for hell. Oh, how he suffers!

My children, know with wisdom that the mind will lead you on and then abandon you in the darkness. It will lure you into believing what

The chameleon of the mind lures you into believing what the world and the intellect say. But in the end you will be prey to foxes, dogs, snakes, scorpions, ghosts, devils, and demons.

the world says and what the intellect says. But in the end you will be prey to foxes, dogs, snakes, scorpions, ghosts, devils, and demons. You will tremble with fear during the night and finally become food for hell.

If you believe what your mind tells you, if you trust it and follow it, this is what will happen to you. Think about this. You must understand the nature of the mind and what will happen if you follow it blindly.

You must follow only the truth and God. Do this with _imān,_ with faith, determination, and certitude. Then you will not run into danger. Acquire God's qualities and you will find peace in life. May God help you. _Āmīn._

*No matter where rain falls, the water will flow downhill
and collect in natural hollows, forming ponds.*

Strengthen the Walls of Your Pond

y love you, my grandchildren, my brothers and sisters, my sons and daughters. Let us look at a pond. No matter where the rain falls, the water will flow downhill and collect in the natural hollows of the earth, forming ponds.

In the same way, the grace of God fills the pond of the heart. A natural hollow is formed within us at the time we are conceived. It is formed from our parents' or grandparents' continued faith and belief in God and from their connection to His qualities and actions. The fresh water of God's grace, His *rahmat,* collects in this natural hollow and can then be of benefit to all lives.

However, my grandchildren, even if you have this natural hollow, it is still necessary to be under the guidance of someone with wisdom, a true sheikh, a father who can teach you how to continue receiving this supply of fresh water. And if for some reason you lack that hollow, then he will show you how to make one. He will point out where the terrain is suitable for forming such a pond. He will select a spot where there is already a slight incline on both sides and the beginnings of a hollow in the center. Then the father will teach you how to build supporting walls around that area for the water to collect.

What must the walls of the pond be built with? With the faith, certitude, and determination known as *īmān,* with effort, perfect vigilance, concentration, and the qualities of God. These materials will make the walls strong. You must build the pond with the point of God. You must prepare this pond in the heart so that the waters of grace can collect there when the *rahmat* of God's justice, the *rahmat* of His qualities and actions and duties, the *rahmat* of the divine knowledge of *'ilm,* the river of honey, and the river of milk come rushing in. The pond has to be strong in order to hold the water.

"My children," the sheikh will caution you, "if you do not build these walls and strengthen your pond, then gales, storms, floods, or earthquakes will break them down.'' And when these forces do come to attack you, the sheikh will focus his gaze upon you and say, ''You must have determination! You must stand firm! Add more of God's love and compassion to strengthen the walls of the pond. All responsibility must be given to the One who is responsible. Strengthen your good qualities. The storms are approaching, make the pond stronger!''

The walls of the pond might shake when the gales of the five elements, the waves of illusion, the turbulence of the base desires, and the agitation of your mind come to attack you. The safety of the pond will be threatened by selfishness, jealousy, vengeance, treachery, evil actions, murder, revenge, doubt, envy, hypocrisy, intoxicants, lust, falsehood, theft, and so many other evils. Every one of satan's qualities will come to attack you, your soul, the truth, your devotion to God and His grace, and the milk of awakened wisdom, or *gnānam*. The sheikh will beat away these evils to save the good things from being destroyed. He will be firm with you in these times of danger, because he knows that the things which can break you down are approaching rapidly. He will rebuke the attachments of your mind and desire, your blood ties, your connections to your religion, race, and family. At such times it may seem that your father of wisdom is hurting you. He may look hard at you, he may chastise you with wisdom, but he is not trying to hurt you. He is breaking down the forces that are trying to destroy you.

Initially the sheikh's actions might cause pain, but if you stand firm you will see that it was for the best.

If you remain patient, then later when you look back, you will see the things that came to murder you lying dead all around you. You will see the corpses of the dogs, cats, lions, and bears that came to kill you. You will see the demons, ghosts, and all the dangerous beasts that came to destroy your exalted birth.

If you stray toward any of those things, they will destroy you. This is why you must have faith, certitude, and determination in your sheikh and in God. This is why you must give the responsibility to your sheikh. He is making you build that pond to protect your life, your soul, your duties, and your actions, to prevent them from being broken down and scattered. Wisdom must hammer down the rock and earth and make it compact. And while wisdom is beating you, every part of you must be firm in patience, contentment, trust in God, and praise of God, in *sabūr, shukūr, tawakkul,* and *al-hamdu lillāh.* As soon as you feel any pain, you must turn to faith, certitude, and determination. Only then will you have the strength to accept the beating.

If, instead, you cry, "It hurts!" and run away from the wealth of the pond, from the wealth of helping others, then the sheikh will tell you, "If you have wisdom, you will return. But if ignorance prevails, you will leave and never come back."

This is what a sheikh will tell you. If you stand firm, you will be within the sheikh, he will be within you, and God will be within both of you. Your pond will be filled with the honey of grace and the milk of *gnānam* which can feed all lives, quench their thirst, and satisfy the hunger of their souls, their lives, their stomachs, their karma, and their illusions. You will know how to dispel all that is bad and take only what is good. You will become God's child, existing in His kingdom with His qualities. In the world of the soul, in this world, and in the kingdom of God, you will be His child, living with His treasures. It is for this reason, my precious children, that the sheikh will fashion the pond of grace-awakened wisdom, of *gnānam,* within your heart.

All the things which attack and try to shatter your heart will be destroyed by the sharp arrow of the sheikh's wisdom. That arrow must enter your heart in order to destroy the things that have come to attack you. The arrow may appear to be piercing your heart, but it is those evil qualities that are being killed. The arrow will not kill you. It might brush you as it flies by, but it will only kill your enemy and God's enemy.

Never think there is enmity between you and your father. Your father is only attacking the evil which separates you from God. He is trying to save that unity. My grandchildren, you must think about this and build a pond of wisdom so that everyone may drink its grace, quench their thirst, and wash away their dirt. All who do this will attain the treasures of God which bring peace to the soul.

My love you, my grandchildren. May God help you to strengthen the walls of your pond. *Āmīn.*

"O man, you planted only one potato, yet you were given a thousand in return. But did you ever give as much as we did?"

The Potato Speaks to a Greedy Farmer

My love you, my grandchildren, my sons and daughters, my brothers and sisters. There was once a farmer who planted many crops which grew tall and strong. His harvest was ten times greater than the effort he put forth, but he never gave any of it to the poor and hungry or to the people who worked in the fields. In fact, because his crops were better than average, he charged very high prices. If they had grown poorly, he would have been forced to charge less.

One day the earth scolded him. "You do just a little work, and look how much I do for you! But do you ever share your good fortune? No, you don't pay your workers enough, and you charge your customers too much."

And so the happiness of the earth decreased, and in the next growing season, where a hundred seedlings once would have appeared, the earth produced only fifty. But still the farmer kept raising his prices, and the earth's happiness decreased some more. Then, in the next season, where fifty fruits or vegetables would have grown, the earth yielded only twenty-five. The more the man increased his prices, the less the earth produced. Finally, out of all the trees in his orchard, only two bloomed.

"It's not fair!" the man complained. "I put forth so much effort! I worked so hard! Perhaps the soil isn't any good. Perhaps these aren't the right crops." He was exhausted. "Hardly anything has grown this time. What a terrible loss!" he complained to everyone.

Then a potato called out to him, "O man, we have to laugh when we look at you. You planted only one potato, yet you were given a thousand in return. But did you ever give as much as we did? You were so happy, but did you ever give anything to the poor or hungry? Did you feel compassion for the people who worked on your farm? Did you ever reduce your prices for anyone? No, you sold your crops to both rich and poor for ten times what they were worth.

"We have never heard anyone say anything good about you. Not a single person ever said that you gave them anything or increased their wages. We only heard about how much you profited. But despite all your profits, you were never generous.

"Did you ever say, 'O God, You gave me so much. You gave me such a great harvest'? Did you ever attribute that to God, O man? No, you never did.

"Then when your harvest and your profits decreased, you began to cry, 'It's not fair! My farm is not yielding anything. Nothing is growing. Everything is going wrong. My harvest is so small, and I have suffered such a great loss.' You told everyone your sad story.

"This is your ignorance, O man. What did you ever do to deserve anything? Your workers did all the work and your neighbors helped by giving advice, while you just stood around. Nevertheless, we happily gave you ten to a hundredfold in return. But did you ever lower your prices for the poor? No. And when the poor came to ask for alms, you never even gave them a mouthful of food. That hurt them, it hurt us, and it also hurt the earth. As our happiness decreased, your harvest decreased. And it will go on decreasing because you are not farming with a clear heart. In the end you will have nothing left but the barren earth. This is what happens when you do not share and give charity. This is what happens when you gather everything for yourself.

"O man, this is your karma. You are happy when things go well, but as soon as your share decreases, you scold and curse the earth. You do not seem to have been born as a human being. You take everything for yourself. Even an elephant takes only its share and then moves on, leaving enough for others. It eats one leaf and spares the next. It eats one fruit and leaves the rest for the birds. But you do not leave anything for anyone, and that is why your mind is forever dissatisfied. While other beings are content, your mind is always desiring something. You never have enough. It is because you do not make others happy that your mind feels dissatisfied.

"O man," the potato continued, "your harvest will decrease to the extent that your charity decreases. As soon as your charity increases, your harvest will increase. If your heart is open and you have compassion toward other lives, you will reap one hundred vegetables instead of ten. And as your harvest increases more and more, you should charge less and less.

"The earth is a mother. It gives you so much. Look how much the earth made us multiply from one seed! God gave you this harvest so that you could share it equally with others, but instead you gathered it all for yourself. Think about it. Look what happened when you kept everything for yourself. If you change your ways, then the earth will again increase your harvest, and all lives will open their hearts to you.

"Do not complain like this, O man. Do not say you worked so hard and your crops are not growing. Understand what has happened and ask for forgiveness. If you can satisfy the needs of others, then your needs will be satisfied." This is what the potato told the greedy farmer.

My precious grandchildren, God gives us so much. When He gives us one handful of anything, we should give at least a half or a quarter of that to others. If He gives us two handfuls, we should give one away. If He gives us four handfuls, we should give two away. If we share in that way, our lives will be exalted, our goodness will be exalted, and we will experience tranquility. We will know peace in our souls and peace in the world.

If man realizes this in every aspect of his life, if he cares about others in the same way that he cares about himself and then does his duty, the earth will be happy, the trees will be happy, the animals will be happy, and all hearts will be soothed and cooled. Then he will attain the treasures which come from that peace and tranquility. But if the hearts of others are hurt, his heart will also be hurt, and in the end he will be sad. Try to think about this. Try to understand what the potato told the farmer. My love you.

Only if we stand in the shade of God's truth and
act with His qualities and wisdom will we be sheltered.

Stand in the Shade of God's Truth

y love you, my grandchildren, jeweled lights of my eyes. Come, let us rest in the shade of this tree and find some relief from the heat. If we sit beneath its branches, we will be protected from both the sun and the rain. But if we remain at a distance, we will never find comfort. Instead we will complain, "Oh, the sun is scorching!" or "The rain is beating on me! I cannot bear it! This useless tree is not giving me any protection!" Why blame the tree when it is our own fault for not standing in its comforting shade?

Man also blames God like this. He has not sought shelter in the place where God is. He has not sought shelter in God's actions, His qualities, or His beauty. Instead, man stands exposed to the sorrows, the heat and the cold, and to the storms and fevers of the world. He stands in the darkness of illusion and blames God and the truth for not protecting him. "What is God?" he asks. "Where is He now, when I am faced with so many dangers and suffering from so many difficulties? The storms and the scorching heat are tormenting me," he cries. "Why doesn't God help me?"

My grandchildren, it is ignorance to blame God. That is what the world does. It is our own fault if we stand far off in the midst of illusion, hell, and darkness. Only if we stand in the shade of God's truth and act with His qualities and wisdom will we be sheltered. You must think about this.

My love you, precious jeweled lights of my eyes. Stand within His shade and receive His comfort. *Āmīn.*

93

If you take your dog out when someone else is walking his dog,
both will start fighting and end up full of scars.

Leave the Dog at Home

y love you, my grandchildren. Let us go for a walk. Look at those two dogs growling and barking at each other. They are enemies. Their owners let them out for a walk, but now they are rolling on the ground and biting each other. They will probably end up with cuts on their eyes or nose, or even lose a piece of an ear. They could be seriously injured. Eventually one will howl, "Oww, oww, oww!" and run away. Have you ever seen this happen?

My grandchildren, you are also raising a dog within yourself. This dog is filled with the qualities of jealousy, envy, selfishness, arrogance, hastiness, impatience, and the sense of I and you. If you let your dog out when someone else is walking his dog, both dogs will start fighting and you will both end up full of scars. Do not blame the other person's dog for the fight. A fight can only start if you also let your dog loose. Only if both of you leave your dogs tied up at home will there be no fighting and no murders. Then no one will be scarred.

It is because of these dogs within that one man bites and attacks another and the bitten one fights back. Men are not the enemies of men. It is the dogs within them that are the enemies. They bark, "He ate my food. He took my things. He is interfering." When people let these dogs run free, there are many fights and everyone is hurt. Then they all run away howling, with their tails between their legs.

Therefore my grandchildren, leave your dog tied up at home and go out alone, as a human being. Then no one will be your enemy, and no harm will come to you. No one will hate you. Instead of trouble, you will have peace and tranquility. You must think about this. My love you, my children. God has to give us this wisdom.

"O Sculptor, you are just a little man, and I am so huge!"

The Sculptor and the Rocky Mountain

My love you, my grandchildren, jeweled lights of my eyes. Do you see that huge mountain made of stone? One day a sculptor went to examine that mountain. He wanted to know if its rocks could be used for carving statues or building houses and other things. So he climbed up and began to chisel away at the mountainside.

"O man, why are you stepping all over me and standing on my head?" the mountain complained. "Why are you chipping away at me with your chisel? I am such a great mountain! Why are you doing this?"

"O mountain," the sculptor replied, "I have come to help you. You have so many cracks and crevices! If you didn't have these faults, I couldn't have used them as footholds to climb up here. I only want to make you more valuable."

"What!" the mountain roared. "I am already the greatest! I am the only immovable thing in the world! You are just a little man, and I am so huge! How could you give me any glory?" The mountain trembled and shook with anger as it spoke.

"That is true. I am very small," the sculptor agreed. "If you moved and made me fall, I could be hurt. But there is something much smaller than I that can control you, even though you are so big. If that tiny thing released its force on you, you would be completely destroyed. Look, this little stick called dynamite is right here in my hand, and it can blow you to pieces.

"O mountain, don't you realize that I have come to give you greater glory? If you had understood this, you would not have spoken to me in that way. No one really values you as you are now, in so massive a form. None of the trees or bushes respect you. Look how they grow in the cracks on your head and try to become taller than you. Don't you see that you are the only one who thinks you're great?

No one else thinks so. How can you be proud of your present state? You are just a huge useless rock! Only if I break you apart can you attain any glory.''

"Just try to break me!" shouted the mountain. "Just try!"

"All right, you have shown me what it means to be big, so now I will show you what it means to be small." The sculptor took his chisel, and with each blow of his hammer, it penetrated deeper into the rock. Then he placed the stick of dynamite into the hole and lit the fuse.

A huge explosion followed, and the top of the mountain split into four sections. "You have destroyed me!" the mountain cried.

"Don't think it is only your head that I'm after. I will break all of you, right down to your feet, and I will continue to break you until your arrogance and pride are destroyed!" the sculptor shouted. Then he chiseled another hole and lit some more dynamite. The mountain crumbled.

"You are so small," cried the mountain, "and yet you have broken me!"

"You were of no use to anyone before," the sculptor replied, "but now I am going to give you great value and glory. I will use you to make so many things."

So the sculptor carried away the stones from the broken mountain and used them to build fine houses, erect beautifully polished pillars, and put up handsome lintels. He even made statues with noses and eyes. Then he built temples for these idols so the people could come to perform their *pūjās,* their ritual devotions.

"Now do you understand?" the sculptor asked. "In your transformed state everybody bows before you. Every day they wash these idols made from your stone with milk and show so much devotion. They do all this for you. How does this compare to being a mountain? And how did you get this glory? Was it my smallness or your bigness that increased your value? Look at the difference between what you were before and what you are now. The houses and temples made from you are very valuable, and everyone praises you so much.

"O mountain of rock, this breaking down is good for ignorant people like you. Of course, other ignorant people will try to protect you so that you can remain full of pride. But those with wisdom will break you apart in order to create an open space and allow the air to flow where you once stood. Then everyone can breathe easily.''

My grandchildren, just as the sculptor blasted the mountain, a truly realized teacher, an *insān kāmil,* must shatter the rocky mountain within us. That mountain is the arrogance and ignorance of our minds. It stands in the way of our good health and our peace. Its massiveness conceals our splendor and beauty. That rock must be broken and removed. Otherwise we will remain useless.

This can only be done by a man of wisdom. First, with his wisdom, he must break the mountain of arrogance. Only by breaking that apart, can he make you beautiful and useful. Next he must dig deep and destroy the base of the mountain, which extends underground. That will clear the way so that peace and tranquility can be established in the world. Then he can build a city of peace on the clear open space. He can build the kingdom of God within us.

All the prophets transcended that rocky mountain of arrogance and spoke to God. This is the true meaning of the story of Moses ☺ climbing Mount Sinai and speaking to God. Prophet Muhammad, the *Rasūl* ☺, also climbed up that rock and went beyond, passing through the seventy thousand veils of illusion to meet God. We too must go beyond our mountain of arrogance if we want to speak with God and attain peace and tranquility.

Once that mountain within is broken, we will know the kingdom of God, and with the ensuing peace we can build heaven on earth. We will attain great glory and receive the joy appropriate to the children of God. Then the whole world will come in peace, bow down in obeisance, and worship the love found in that kingdom. We will attain the splendor of the son of God. This is the glory that comes through the sheikh.

My grandchildren, you will be so much more valuable in that state! Think about this. Do you want that mountain of arrogance to remain within you? As long as it is there, you will never attain freedom, peace, or serenity. You will never attain the glory the sheikh wants to give you. It's true that it might hurt a little when that mountain is chiseled and blown apart. But what is it that is hurt? The monkey mind, the dog of desire, and the five elements. Only if the sheikh breaks that mountain apart, level by level, can he discard the evil and give you the good. This is what a father of wisdom will do.

My love you. You must think about this. Realize with wisdom that the sheikh does this to help you receive the goodness, the splendor, and the glory of a life of freedom and health. Only then can you truly be the child of God. My love you. Think about this, my grandchildren.

True Love

y love you, my grandchildren. Do you ever listen to the radio? They are always playing songs about love. But what is true love?

Is it love to expect help in return for something we have done? If we love someone because we want something, can that be called true love? Do we only love God in order to attain heaven? No, it cannot be called true love when there is a selfish motive behind it.

God has spoken to us about love. His words are in the Torah, the Bible, the Puranas, and the Qur'an. "Love all lives. Respect all lives. Help all lives." Many great men throughout history have also told us this.

How does God love? He regards each creation equally and performs His duty toward them all. His love does not reject anyone. God gives each and every creation its own nature and form and its own place to live. He shows each one exactly the kind of love it needs. When He created the dog, He gave it a proper place and showed it the kind of love a dog needs. He even created satan and then created hell for him, as well as the kind of love appropriate to him. God cares for all lives as if they were His own life. He has the same love for dogs, foxes, cats, men, and all the creations.

God does not care if someone says, "There is a God," or "There is no God." He does not care whether someone praises Him or blames Him, whether someone worships Him or not. God still gives each person his proper place and the kind of love appropriate for him. This is what God's love is like.

Therefore, my grandchildren, if a man of wisdom dwells within the qualities and actions of God, if he melts within the love of God and disappears within the justice of God, then the appropriate place for him is within God. If he has wisdom and the absolute faith, certitude,

101

God regards each creation equally
and performs His duty toward them all.

and determination known as *īmān* and has understood God completely, he will be placed within God's protection. He will have no
accidents, no wants, no beginning, no end.

In the same way, those who go away from God will have a place
appropriate to their state. But wherever they are, God will still love
them. They will receive the same love as those He has placed within
Himself. God shows love to the lives outside Him and to those within
Him. He gives clarity to those with clarity. He shows light to those
with light, and He helps them to nurture that light. He shows darkness to those with darkness, and He helps them also. He helps each
creation according to its state. He never shows differences. There is
no fault in Him. His love feeds all beings. They all experience His
love. This is what God's love is like.

My love you. It is our duty to think about this. My children, you
must understand this. If you do, the state of being within God will be
yours and you will know peace. Until you understand this, it will be
difficult for you.

May Allah help you. You must resolve to live within Him. That
will be good. *Āmīn.*

*The young ones are so lovable, but look at the
mothers. Their qualities are very different.*

The Safari Park

y love you, my grandchildren, my sons and daughters, my brothers and sisters. Shall we go outside for a little while? Come, let's take a ride to a safari park where all kinds of animals live in their natural surroundings. Lions, tigers, leopards, and other meat-eating animals wander about freely, but they are kept separate from the deer, elk, elephants, and other plant-eating animals. The keepers have built a fence to divide these two groups.

Let's go a little closer. This is where the deer and the goats live. Don't worry, they are not dangerous. They will not harm or kill us. But we should still be careful and respect their boundaries, because the elephants also share this area. It will be safer if we stand outside the fence and watch.

Do you see the baby elephant? How white and beautiful it is. The deer and elk babies are lovely too, aren't they? The young horses, donkeys, and goats are also beautiful. Have you ever noticed how their baby fur changes color when they become adults? Look at the mothers. They no longer have that youthful beauty. The babies run and jump and play so happily when they are young, but the mothers are not happy anymore. They have changed. They just shake their heads and graze.

Oh look, that young goat has fallen into a hole! The other kids were able to jump over it, but that one fell in. "Baahhh! Bahhh!" it cries, and the mother comes running to help her baby. First she tries to pull it out with her mouth, but that doesn't work. Next she puts two legs inside the hole and tries to push it out with her head. Ah, that did it, and the baby goat runs off to play some more. Mothers are always busy with this kind of work. They're not free to play like the babies are.

Do you see those young fawns over there? Look, they are putting their noses up against the fence. Let's go talk to them. They are not afraid of people now, but when they grow up, they will run away from us.

Now let's walk around to the other side, to the fenced-in section where the leopards and lions are. Their babies are also very happy. See how they run and jump and chase and nip one another. They roll around together on the ground like little foxes and puppies! They are only playing, without hurting each other or any of the other creatures. The young ones are so lovable, but look at the mothers. Their qualities are different; they roar and threaten to kill others. The lion cubs will also be like that when they grow up. They will become just as ferocious as their mothers. Today they are happy, but later on the adults will teach the children their own qualities and actions. They will show the cubs how to catch and kill other animals and drink their blood in order to satisfy their hunger.

But for now all the children are playing together happily. The lion and tiger and leopard cubs come right up to us, make cute little sounds, and sniff at us. Do you see how their mothers watch to make sure we don't harm them? The mothers have a force that could destroy us, but you need not be afraid. As long as we are on this side of the barrier, we are all right.

My grandchildren, do you understand what we have seen? Think about it. This is a safari park, a place where you can find both peaceful and dangerous animals. The world is also like this place. There you find human beings and human animals. Can you tell the difference between the two by looking at them? No. It is easy to distinguish between a tiger and a deer, but you cannot see the difference between animal-men and true human beings. They all look alike. We know to run in fear when we see a full grown lion because we know it is dangerous. But when we see people, we cannot tell whether they are good or bad, whether they will hurt us or not. They all appear to be human but when evil qualities and actions come into them, they turn into dangerous beasts. It is important that we learn to recognize the difference. We must have that awareness in order to escape.

How can you tell whether a person is a human being or a beast?

Human animals will have many connections to the world. They will have selfishness, anger, jealousy, and envy. Such people will have no peace in their lives. They will have only doubt and suspicion, hastiness and impatience, resentment and pride. They will seek praise, titles, and honors and keep saying, "I, I, I!" They will be prejudiced against different religions, races, and colors, and even against certain kinds of prayers. They will have four hundred trillion, ten thousand spiritual differences and be filled with arrogance, karma, illusion, lust, and selfishness.

Everything these human animals do is motivated by selfishness, pride, and the arrogance of the I. They harm other lives, they create trouble and cause fights, they torment and torture and murder others. They create political differences which lead to wars. They fight racial wars, religious wars, wars for land, and wars for freedom. They fight wars between the I and the you. They destroy each other, and they destroy unity and love. They disrupt peace and oppose compassion at all times. Inner patience, contentment, surrender, and giving all responsibility and praise to God does not exist in these human beasts.

My love you, my children. You have seen people like this, haven't you? Such people tear others apart in the same way that an adult lion devours its prey. They try to destroy everything. Look how they destroy your unity, peace, and happiness. Their prejudice makes you feel sad. In a short time, they can make you very depressed. They say, "I am different from you. You have one God and I have another God. I pray to my God and you pray to your God." They won't let you have peace, even for one second.

My love you, my children, jeweled lights of my eyes. This is the way it is among men. It is a rare person who has peace. The majority of people are animals. This terrible karmic illness, this illness of arrogance and illusion, has caught hold of man.

My grandchildren, as small children, you now have a connection to God, and so you have peace. God plays with you and you play with Him. You play with the truth, and you feel tranquil. Your hearts are clear, your bodies are clear, your love is clear, and your peace is clear. This is the way you are now. This is the way all children are, whether they are white, black, brown, red, or yellow. Young children all speak one language and are able to communicate with each other perfectly. Some of you are still young enough to understand that one language, and when you speak, God understands. You are happy and tranquil and embrace everyone without noticing their color or any other differences. But the people who have those illnesses do not understand your language. Parents do not understand that kind of communication. They do not understand that kind of happiness, serenity, and peace.

My little grandchildren, strive to keep that beauty you have had since you were born. Cherish unity and good qualities and keep them until the very end. If you protect these qualities, you will always exist within the protection of God. You must establish this in your lives.

My children, my brothers and sisters, those of us who are older must analyze our own state and change back into human beings. We must find peace through God's qualities and actions. We must chase away those animal enemies within so that we can become true human beings. As long as these exist within us, we will never have serenity. We will never know the beauty and tranquility of our Father. We will never have that light and beauty and peace of the soul. We lose them all when these illnesses of arrogance, karma, and illusion grab on to us.

You and I must think about this and try to chase these things away. Then our Father who created us can live in peace with us, and we can live in peace with Him. We can regain our beauty, our light, our purity, and our perfection. And we can share the peace in our hearts and lives with others. One who does this is a true man.

My love you, my grandchildren. Let us think about this. May God protect us. May He give us unity and wisdom. May He give us a way to attain this peace with His grace. *Āmīn.*

The Kingdom Beyond the Earth's Pull

y love you, my grandchildren, my daughters and sons, my brothers and sisters. Come and look at the sky. We are standing here upon the earth and above us is the sky. There is a connection between these two worlds, earth to sky and sky to earth. The same five kinds of lives that dwell here on earth also exist in the sky: earth life, fire life, air life, water life, and ether life.

My love you, my grandchildren. Each of the elements is an enemy to the others. There is enmity between fire and earth; fire can burn the earth and change its color. There is enmity between water and fire; water can put out fire. There is enmity between water and earth; water can erode earth. And there is enmity between the rain and the air. Each element proclaims, "I! I! I am great!" Earth shouts, "I am the greatest!" Air shouts, "I am the greatest!" Fire shouts, "I am the greatest!" And water shouts, "I am the greatest!" Enmity also exists between truth and falsehood and between illusion and reality. Even illusion shouts, "I am great!"

These qualities of enmity will shout within you as long as you have a connection to the five elements and to arrogance, karma, and illusion. They will be the cause of enmity in your mind. Earth's magnet will pull you, illusion will throw a net over you, and torpor will drag you down to its level. Peace can never arise from the elements. As long as you have those five aspects in yourself, they will cause sorrow, suffering, and hardship. You will remain in a condition of enmity. You will think of other religions, races, scriptures, and languages as your enemies. You will feel hatred for other colors and for the gods of other people, and you will think you are better than others. But prejudice, magic, mantras, and hypnosis will remain in you.

My grandchildren, you must think about these different kinds of

*Even if you develop occult powers and learn to do miracles, you will
still be pulled by earth. You must go beyond that and be pulled
only by the power of God's kingdom.*

hypnotic attractions within you. Look at the sky and the upper ethers. There is light in the sun, the moon, and the stars. Each day of your life has been divided into light and darkness, day and night. The daytime is the great kingdom, the time of clarity, the time of the soul and wisdom. Wisdom is the sun, and when this dawns in you, the purity of the soul will shine forth from you. The night represents your connection to this earthly kingdom and the darkness of illusion. It is the dark time of birth. The beauty of illusion glitters in that darkness and pulls on you like the moon's gravitational pull on the earth. This will exist as long as you have no clarity, as long as you still lack wisdom and are connected to other things.

As long as these energies flourish within you, the earth will fascinate you. You will be like a corpse hypnotized by its power. Anyone who is intoxicated by the five elements and the five senses is like a drunkard who has no awareness of whether his clothes are covering him properly and no shame about exposing parts of his body. And just as the drunkard does not know bodily shame, the one who loses his wisdom has no shame about his prejudices. One condition is as intoxicating as the other. In that state of stupor, you will have no modesty, sincerity, respect, fear of wrongdoing, or good conduct.

But there is a greater power that exists beyond the elements. It is the power of God, His *qudrat.* It contains no earth, fire, water, air, or ether and has no connection to them. It exists in His kingdom, the kingdom of the soul, the kingdom of purity, as grace, as the radiant light of all souls. In that kingdom of mystery the soul is light, truth is light, wisdom is light, the qualities of goodness are light, and God is light. That power is the All-Knowing Father, the All-Pervasive Kingdom of Plenitude that rules itself.

In that higher realm, none of the sorrows which arise from connections to the earth and the ether exist. But if, instead, you remain at a lower level, holding on to those connections, you will be affected by rain, gales, and hurricanes, and the earth will continue to exert its gravitational force upon you. Even if you develop occult powers and learn to perform miracles with the elemental forces of earth, fire, water, air, and ether, those forces will still connect you to the earth.

111

No matter how high you fly, you will still be pulled down by gravity and experience torpor.

You must go beyond these miracles and occult powers. Then nothing in this world will be able to attract you. You must go beyond the earth's pull and cut the connection, the fascination, the prejudice, hatred, and separations that exist within you. When those connections are cut, you will be able to look upon all lives as your own. You will realize true unity and you will have the compassion which knows that the hunger, suffering, and sorrow of others are just like your own. Your compassion, your love, your justice, integrity, and conscience will come to life within you. Then you will be in another state. You will be connected to the power that exists beyond, the great kingdom. When God's grace comes into you and you acquire perfect wisdom, and when your soul, your wisdom, and your qualities attain the state of God's qualities, then you will be pulled only by their power. The radiant light of the soul will draw upon the great treasure which is Allah, and that power will pull you up.

My grandchildren, you must reach that treasure. You must not let it be destroyed in you. As you grow in your understanding, you will come to know these things. May God help us. *Āmīn.*

Flowers of the Same Color Are Boring

y love you, my grandchildren, jeweled lights of my eyes. Shall we go on another journey? The world is a huge garden and within it are many smaller gardens filled with flowers, plants, and trees. Let's visit one of those gardens today. Do you see the flowers over there? How lovely they are! Look at all the different colors and hues. There are white flowers, blue flowers, pink and yellow flowers. Some have petals with two or three colors. There are so many varieties of wondrous flowers, both large and small. How God loves them all! Everybody loves them! Their beauty makes everyone happy. Let us ask the gardener if we can go in and take a closer look.

"Please, may we see the flowers?"

"Yes, come in and look around."

All right, my grandchildren, let's go inside. Now we can smell each flower and see which kind is fragrant and which is not. Look, this one is called 'The Queen of the Night'. It has a lovely fragrance which fills the air all through the night. This rose also smells very sweet, and the fragrance of this jasmine flower is wonderful too.

Shall we walk to the other side of the garden and watch the workers planting seeds? Let's find out how the flowers are grown. Do you see all these wooden boxes? They are called flats. This is where the young plants are started. In the first flat all the flowers are red. In the next they are all white, and in the next they are yellow. Each flat contains only one color.

My grandchildren, are the flowers in these flats as pretty as those we saw in the garden? No, they are boring. We see whole sections of red, whole sections of yellow, and whole sections of white. They don't please our eyes or make our hearts happy, do they? And their smell is not as nice, either. Let's go back to the garden where so many

Are the flowers in these flats as pretty as those we saw
in the garden? No, they are boring.

different colors grow together and so many fragrances intermingle and fill the air. Isn't it beautiful when they are all mixed together?

My love you, my grandchildren. In God's wondrous flower garden of souls, everyone lives together in unity and harmony, just like the flowers in the garden we see here. God created everything in a state of unity, to exist together in harmony. God made the world of the souls, this world, and the next world in a beautiful way. All three kingdoms exist forever in unity.

So many colors grow next to each other in this garden of souls: black, white, yellow, red, and pink. One color complements the other. Some flowers might not be as beautiful as others, but when they are next to each other, they all look beautiful. Some are fragrant, some are not. But even the ones without any fragrance pick up the sweet scent of the others. This is what God's kingdom is like, a flower garden of unity and harmony, a flower garden of the heart.

Do you remember how the flats each contained flowers of separate colors? That is how man plants his gardens and ruins the beauty God created. He puts only one color in each area. That is what the mind of man does. It separates things. It always wants to keep things divided. The monkey mind, the dog of desire, jealousy, arrogance, and karma are the gardeners who separate the flowers.

How boring it is to look at flowers of all one color. Honeybees never hover around the flats where they grow. Only viruses and diseases are attracted to those flowers that are grown separately. But where many different plants coexist, viruses cannot survive, because certain flowers and herbs contain antidotes which can kill the viruses in the others. When all are mingled together in unity, they can counteract the harmful things in each other. Certain plants and herbs have these healing properties and are able to protect each other. But when they are grown in separate areas, the wind can spread the viruses and easily destroy an entire section.

In the same way, a whole race can be destroyed by the virus of prejudice. Men are murdered because of the differences and separations in their monkey minds and by the four hundred trillion, ten thousand so-called spiritual qualities which spread these viruses. And when colors start to kill each other, they end up destroying themselves, their freedom, and their own souls. They destroy their worship of God, their faith in God, the truth of God, and the wisdom of God. They destroy the peace and harmony God gave them.

In a garden where all grow in unity, the healing herbs of truth, wisdom, and God's qualities work together to protect the flowers. But in a garden where separation and division exist, there is no such natural protection.

My love you, my children, jeweled lights of my eyes. We have to dispel those viruses and attain unity in this flower garden of the heart. We have to nurture God's qualities in our inner garden so that we can smell their sweet fragrance and see their beauty, unity, and love everywhere.

Such beauty can never be acquired by makeup and outer actions. Man cannot acquire the beauty of God's qualities simply by going to the church, mosque, temple, or synagogue. This beauty must grow within the heart, like the fragrance within a flower. Only when unity and harmony exist within the heart can beauty and fragrance be known on the outside.

My love you. You must search for that beauty. You and I must learn, know, and understand the explanation of each and every thing within ourselves. We must consider our lives very deeply. My grandchildren, God is love. He understands every creation before He brings it into being. He understands the food, water, fertilizer, and habitat needed for each creation before He creates it. He never does anything without understanding. We too must understand every point before we act.

You and I must try to attain this state. May God protect us and give us great beauty and peace. My love you. *Anbu.* Please search for this with wisdom and awareness. *Anbu. Āmīn. As-salāmu 'alaikum wa rahmatullāhi wa barakātuhu kulluhu.* May the peace and blessings of God be upon all of you.

116

The Temple Priest Who Collected Karma

y love you, my grandchildren, my brothers and sisters, my sons and daughters. There once was a priest whom the whole world praised. They called him a sincere devotee of God because he had performed his rituals and *pūjās* in the temple for nearly eighty years.

One day the priest had a pain in his leg, and he cried, "O God, *Kadavul,* Allah, my Lord! I have dedicated eighty years of my life to You. I have given all my possessions, my body, and my soul to You. Why should I suffer from this pain? Why should I be tormented this way?" He cried and cried in his pain, all the while complaining to God under his breath.

At long last God answered him. "O man, O devotee, you have never seen Me and you cannot see Me now. How can anyone serve Me if he cannot see Me? For the past eighty years you have seen only yourself. Just being in this temple does not mean that you have seen Me. Who did all this duty you speak of? It was I who worked for you for eighty years. You never did anything for Me.

"You did your own duty, not Mine. If you had done My duty for even one second, you would have seen Me in that second. All your effort was for your own sake, taking care of your own *pūjās* and worship. And now you are blaming Me for this little illness.

"Have you really looked at yourself? Was all that duty for Me or was it for you? Look at all the karma this person brought and that person brought; look at the evils and demons people brought. Because you took the responsibility for all of them upon yourself, you experienced them personally. If you had seen Me just once, you would not have taken even an atom of their karma into yourself. You would have been searching for Me and My qualities.

"Instead you searched for and took what other people were trying to give away. You took all of these karmic illnesses, thinking that you

There was no contribution or offering that the priest
had not tasted or taken for himself.

had the power to destroy them. But I forgave you because you were so full of ignorance. The little illness you are now experiencing in your leg is only a small portion that went beyond My forgiveness. It is only a small pain, and yet you are finding fault with Me, wondering why I am doing this to you. But I am wondering what you would do if you had to experience the full pain of all the karma you have taken on over the years.

"O priest, it was your ignorance that complained to Me. You have not understood your own faults and so you find fault with Me, crying, 'O God, I have done so much for You. I have dedicated my body, my soul, and my possessions to You, and look what I get in return!'

"O man, take a good look at yourself," God advised him. And when the priest looked, he saw his whole body, his skin, and his blood filled with all the illnesses, poisons, snakes, and scorpions which had come from all the karma that people had brought to him over the years. He had taken all their sins upon himself, but he had also taken fruits and flowers that the people had placed in the temple to help atone for their sins. There was no contribution or offering that he had not tasted and taken for himself—the mangoes, the coconuts, everything. He always took three shares, two for himself and one for the others who worked in the temple.

"O priest, you took for yourself the food offerings that were brought to Me. And in your ignorance you turned Me into a temple filled with statues. It was not Me you were worshiping, it was the hunger of your stomach. O devotee, do you understand your devotion better now? If even an atom's worth of the work you did had been My work, you would not have kept all the things that people brought.

"O devotee, understand this and act accordingly. If you perform My work for even a second, you will see Me. And once you see Me, your connection to that karma will leave you. But some time must still pass before you can reach that state. When that time comes, it will only take you a second to understand. Meanwhile you must do your duty correctly." This is what God told the temple priest.

Then the priest became a true devotee. He looked deeply into his own state and his own body and begged, "O Father, my God, forgive me for what I have done! Forgive me. Save me, my Father, my God, my Allah!"

Children, we too must constantly think of what kind of duty we are doing in the world and of how we should show our devotion to God. If we go to temples and places of worship and pray with selfish thoughts in our minds, we will only gather sins. As long as we dwell upon our karma, we will have illness and disease.

We must give the responsibility for our hearts, our souls, and our love to God. Then we will see Him and our karma will end. Then our sins, our anger, our poverty, and our illnesses will not touch us. We will attain freedom for our souls, and we will know peace, serenity, and justice in ourselves and in others. We will know the love which is compassion. We will be filled with the wealth of God and the wealth of grace and wisdom, both in this world and in the next. When we receive those treasures, we will attain triumph and victory in our lives.

Very precious children, jeweled lights of my eyes and my soul, we must think about this and realize ourselves. The mirror of wisdom, perfection, and purity is within our innermost heart, our *qalb*. Within that mirror we will see and understand all the thoughts we have while performing our duty. We will see our lives, ourselves, our beauty, and our forms. The ability to see all that is within us.

My love you, my grandchildren. If we search for wisdom and God's qualities, we will know ourselves. This is what the prophets have told us. It is the word of God. Therefore, let us think about this and perform the duty that we have to do in our lives: our duty to God, to the people, to the world, to the soul, and to the sheikh. We have to know what these duties really are and how to do them correctly.

O God, do not allow the sins that we ourselves gather and the sins that come from others to collect in us. Save us from our karma and from all the evils that surround us. Do not let them touch us. Cut them away and help us to put them aside. *Āmīn.* Please give us wisdom, good qualities, and tranquility. *Āmīn.*

A Visit to the Communities
of Good and Evil

y love you, my grandchildren. Today we are going to visit two very different communities that exist inside of us. One is evil and the other is good. Look how crowded this first community is. Who lives here? Arrogance, pride, jealousy, anger, hastiness, impatience, and the egoism of the I. Doubt also lives here. And what does doubt do? It takes away your peace and in its place gives you suspicion. One small thought or doubt can torture and torment your life. It will invite vengeance to join you, to beat and murder you.

Many sins like these live within you. Do you know what they do? They strike everyone in their path. They crush everything. They commit murder. Can anything good ever come from these evils? Will any of them ever help you? No, they will only harm you and others in countless ways. They will never do anything good or decent. Their only purpose is to destroy.

That is what the bad people inside us are like. We should never depend on their help for anything. We should not provide them with any food that might nourish them. If we allow them to live within us, they will destroy us.

Come, my grandchildren. Now let us look at the other community within us. Who lives here? Love, patience, tolerance, peace, contentment, compassion, truth, justice, conscience, integrity, and all of God's qualities. Will these people hurt anyone? No. Love never kills anyone. Unity never harms anyone. Peace never torments anyone. Compassion never causes difficulty or danger to any life. Truth always protects. God's beauty and His three thousand qualities of grace give tranquility to all lives.

My love you, my grandchildren, my sons and daughters, my brothers and sisters. All the evil qualities of satan, which crush and destroy the self and others, live in the first community we visited. But the qualities of God's grace live in the second community, giving peace to all lives. We should think about these two communities within us. Which one brings goodness and which brings destruction? Who should we love and nourish, and who should we chase away? We must chase away this satan who seeks vengeance, commits sins, and destroys and crushes others. We must nourish the One who protects everyone, the One who gives love and compassion. We must nourish God within us.

My love you, my grandchildren. Think about this. Chase away the evil things which come to destroy you and others. Beat them with wisdom. Then only the one community will remain, and all the good qualities will dwell there together in peace, tranquility, and serenity. My love you.

Did a Fish Ever Go
to Heaven on a Rainbow?

y love you, my grandchildren. Look at the beautiful rainbow way up in the sky. Its seven colors form an arc which rises from one side of the sky and bends all the way over to the other side. When one end is in the ocean and the other end is in the river, it draws the moisture up into the sky and distills it in the atmosphere. The rainbow even has the power to pull up fish, crabs and other things from the rivers and oceans.

What happens to those fish? Did a fish ever go to heaven on a rainbow? No, after the rainbow pulls them all up into the sky, they are scattered throughout the clouds, and they die. Eventually the moisture that collects in the clouds comes down as rain, and the crabs and fish fall down with it. The magnetic force surrounding the earth draws them up into the sky and the gravitational force of the earth pulls them back down. They rise from earth and they return to earth.

My love you, my grandchildren. Miracles, occult powers, and the ego operate in the same way. They are pulled by the illusory energy of the ether and the magnetic force of the atmosphere. They appear to be miracles, but they cannot go beyond a certain height before the gravitational force of the earth will pull them down again. Anything that is pulled up by the five elements, mind, and desire is dispersed in the clouds and then falls down. Illusion pulls them up and the earth pulls them down again.

Like that, if you are pulled by illusion, you will also have to fall. If your five elements, mind, and desire are dispersed in illusion, you will have to die. Your mind will suck you dry.

This is how these miraculous powers work. You rise to the skies with the energy of illusion, but ultimately you return to the earth. You fall down, flop around, and die, like the fish and crabs. The state that

123

*The rainbow pulls fish up into the sky, but eventually
they fall back down with the rain.*

you were in before you were pulled by illusion is gone, and the state that you were attempting to reach is gone as well.

Earth, fire, water, air, ether, mind, and desire are represented by the seven colors. Like the rainbow, they have a connection to both the earth and the sky. Anything that goes up into the sky will fall down again to the earth, pulled by the force of gravity. These energies of illusion, these decorations and worldly beauties can never reach great heights, but still they do attract you. This is the way these *saktis,* or energies and elemental miracles, work.

My love you, my children. Look at the powers human beings have. They have feeling, awareness, intellect, a sense of judgment, subtle wisdom, analytic wisdom, and divine luminous wisdom. The first three levels of feeling, awareness, and intellect can reach only so far, but judgment can go a little higher.

My children, with your sense of judgment you must recognize your limits. You have to understand where you came from, where you have come to, and where you will go after you die. You have to under-stand what illusion is, what energy is, and the height each thing can reach. You have to carefully distinguish each aspect. Then with your subtle wisdom you must understand the correct foundation for your life. Once you have understood that foundation you must analyze it with analytic wisdom, extract what is right, and finally look at it with divine luminous wisdom. Then you will see that everything is unreal; it is all illusion, maya. All that exists in this creation, all the miracles, all of everything is made from the energies and forces of the five kinds of lives. Is there anything beyond those energies? The soul of man, the soul of light transcends all these *saktis.* That is the kingdom of God. That is the treasure which belongs to God. That is the son of God, the light which comes from Him.

Through your analytic wisdom, your divine luminous wisdom must understand the clarity and subtlety and limit of each thing. You must distinguish what is right and what is wrong, what is heaven and what is hell, what is good and what is evil, what is true and what is false. As you understand these things, the splendor of patience, con-tentment, trust in God, and praise of God, the splendor of *sabūr, shukūr, tawakkul,* and *al-hamdu lillāh* will dawn in you. Wisdom, resplendence, and the one point which is God will dawn in you.

Allah has no birth or death, no shape, color, or hue, no wife or child, no livestock or property, no house or possessions. He has no hunger, old age, disease, or death. He has no form. He is within everything, but He does not possess anything. He is the power called God, Allah.

When you form a connection with that power, when you form a relationship with the soul, then you can go on the direct path and transcend mind, desire, and the five elements. You can burst through these seven and go beyond, passing through all the energies. At that point you must go quickly. If you can do this, you can establish a good connection with your Father. However, you cannot go with a form that has to come back. You must exist in that state beyond everything.

God exists here and there at the same time. He is that Unfathomable Ruler of grace, the One who is incomparable love. He is within love and beyond love. He is within wisdom and transcends wisdom. He is within your innermost heart, your *qalb*. He is understood within your soul and within your wisdom.

When you reach that exalted state, you will be within Him and He will be within you as a great resplendent light, an all-pervasive radiance. The clear treasure of wisdom within wisdom, the treasure of the soul within the soul, the treasure of the *qalb* within the *qalb*, and that radiance will all be seen at one time, in both this world and the next. You will know the clarity in life which comes from the liberation of your soul. Understanding that state will be purity for your soul. That is the *gnānam*, the wealth, the grace, and the true miracle of God. Nothing can cause it to waver.

If you know yourself, you will know your Father. If you understand yourself, you will understand your Father. If you exist in the kingdom of your Father, He will exist in the kingdom of purity within you. Then you will have no birth, no death, no karma, and no relationships here. You will have cut off your connections, your karma, all your questioning, all your sins—you will have overcome it all.

If you establish this state within you, then you will be the son of God. Man will be within God and God will be within man. The two will shine as one soul, as the soul within the soul, as wisdom within wisdom, and the truth will radiate there.

My love you, my grandchildren. The rainbow's power to draw up fish is not a miracle. Occult powers are not miracles, either. You have to understand what constitutes a true miracle. When your arrogance, your karma, your illusion, and your sins are cut off, that is a miracle. To understand truth is a miracle. To understand the Ruler who is your Father is a miracle. There are no other miracles. Think about this and know this state. When you attain it, you will be a true human being, an *insān kāmil,* a perfected, God-realized being.

My love you, my children, my sisters and brothers, my sons and daughters, my grandchildren. Strengthen your faith and search for wisdom and God's qualities. May God help you to do this. *Āmīn.*

The two biggest frogs both claim to be the greatest. They
are full of pride and the qualities of the I.

The Arrogance of the Puffed-Up Frogs

y love you, my grandchildren, my brothers and sisters, my sons and daughters. It is twilight now, and the sun is low in the sky. Shall we go out for some fresh air? Come with me. This park is a very nice place. Everybody comes here to breathe in the fresh air and feel healthy. Do you see the well over there? People can draw water from it when they are thirsty. Let's go closer and look inside the well.

Oh, look at all the frogs down there! They eat the germs and bacteria in the water, making it cleaner for drinking. Look at them jumping up and down, leaping here and there, and pulling on each other. They seem to be fighting. But why? Are they fighting over food? Are they competing for insects? Let's watch some more and see if we can discover why they are fighting.

Ah, there is the cause! It's not food they are fighting over. The two biggest frogs are both claiming that they are the greatest. Each one thinks he should be the leader. All the other frogs are frightened by their size and are diving deeper into the well to escape. But the two big frogs are challenging each other. They are full of pride and the qualities of the I. Look, my grandchildren, they are trying to swallow each other! But both of them are the same size. What do you think will happen? Let's watch and see. Don't chase them away. If we break up the fight now, they will only start another fight later. Let them finish their quarrel, or they will never have any peace.

Look, the first one has a good hold on his opponent and has swallowed his front legs. Do you see how his stomach is beginning to swell? But the second one has also swallowed the hind legs of the first and he too is puffing himself up. Now both of them have lost all the strength in their free legs, which are tiny and useless in comparison to their inflated bodies. Neither of them can jump any more. Each frog has swallowed half of the other, and they can't breathe.

Oh, no! Both frogs have died! They tried to swallow each other, and as a result both have suffocated and are floating belly up in the water.

My grandchildren, sometimes men also try to swallow each other, like these puffed-up frogs. And just like the little frogs who dove deeper into the well, good people become afraid and try to escape when they meet a man who is puffed up with pride and the arrogance of the I. It does not take long, however, until another arrogant man comes along to challenge him. They each boast, "I am the greatest!" Then, just like the big frogs, each man catches hold of the other and swallows half of him. They torture each other, and in the end they both die.

Frogs challenge each other out in the open, one on one. But men torment each other in a devious, vengeful, and jealous way. One person kills another, then a third person attacks the winner, and soon they all die, just like frogs.

My grandchildren, a female frog lays so many millions of eggs, and hundreds of thousands of them hatch. They all live together, but then, because of their arrogance, they fight with each other and die. Like this, animals and human beings have been slaughtering each other for two hundred million years. And this destruction has been growing worse all the time. You have seen this fighting, haven't you? You must be very careful not to catch this disease. Do not be arrogant or conceited. Do not be jealous of others. Do not let doubt creep into you. Do not become vengeful. Do not plot against others. Do not lie. All these qualities are destructive, deadly diseases. Each man causes his own death by letting them grow inside himself. Eventually, someone else with the same disease will come looking for him, and soon both will die from their arrogance.

When you see arrogance, do not confront it. Why should you point out people's arrogance to them? Their time will come, and they will destroy themselves.

Those with wisdom who are devoted to God and trust Him must hide from the karma, arrogance, illusion, and pride of the world. Like the little frogs who dove deep into the well to escape from the big frogs, you have to hide. People with wisdom must dive into God, truth, and wisdom. They must escape by disappearing into love, peace, and tranquility.

This is what you must do in your lives, my grandchildren. Become human beings and search for the qualities of peace. Arrogance will always take on new forms, so you must be alert and do your best to escape. Hide in the truth. Hide yourselves in the qualities of the One who is unfathomable grace. Take on the natural and beautiful light form which is God's compassionate, just, and loving form. Reflect wisely and try to fill yourselves with good thoughts. You and I must try to live in God's protection.

My love you, my grandchildren. God is sufficient for us. He will protect us. *Āmīn. Āmīn.*

131

The bananas live together in such unity, sharing the same
nourishment, the same taste, and the same color.

The Unity of the Banana Tree

y love you, my grandchildren, my sons and daughters. Come and look closely at this banana tree. It looks like a hand, doesn't it? See how the leaves are just like fingers. Do you know how a banana tree grows? When a young tree sprouts from the mother tree, first one leaf emerges, then it bends down and another appears. One after another, eight, nine, ten, or even more leaves emerge in this way. And as they continue to sprout from this one central point, they grow closer and closer, overlapping like pieces of paper all glued together. How much unity and symmetry these leaves have!

The bananas also grow clustered together, emerging from a single stem and forming into bunches. They live in such unity, sharing the same nourishment, the same taste, and the same color. But then we pick them and break them apart, one by one. That is something to think about.

My grandchildren, all of God's creation is like this banana tree. God created Adam and Eve ☺ from just one point, and from this point emerged twenty-one sets of twins, or forty-two children. They had one mother, one father, one family, and one God. They all started from one point in such unity, but then they separated into many religions, races, and societies, and so many differences developed.

God and God's family, the community of mankind, all came from one point. The whole society of mankind is one family. They all emerged from one God, one truth. God has told us that we are all different parts of the same thing. No matter what our external differences may be, we are all one. We are all one.

When wisdom comes and we understand this, then differences, murder, and sin will not exist among us. We will live in unity. Think about this. My children, through the example of the banana tree, God has shown us what unity can be like. My love you. *Anbu.*

The mother crab used to live in this shell, but her babies have eaten her.

Baby Crabs

y love you, my grandchildren, my daughters and sons, my brothers and sisters. May God protect our hearts, our lives, our certitude, our faith, our determination, our wisdom, and all His qualities within us.

Come, let us walk along the banks of the rice paddies and watch the crabs in the irrigation canals. Ooooh, look at that crab. Is it dead? It's not moving. Its eyes are open, yet it seems to be dead. Let's pick it up and see.

Oh! You can flip open the shell just like the hood of a car. Look at all the little babies inside. The mother used to live in this shell, but the babies have eaten her. Even though they were formed within the mother, they ate her. And look how happy the children are now!

My grandchildren, we too are like this. Our attachments, our blood ties, our possessions, our property, all that we love, all that we desire, and all the relationships which bring us pleasure are like the baby crabs. When these relationships establish a connection in our hearts and minds and grow within us, what happens? They hatch and then devour our truth and wisdom, our justice and integrity, our tranquility, our compassion, our unity, our conscience, and the qualities of God. They eat away at our very life, nibbling from within until we can no longer move. Then the ants, rats, foxes, dogs, and cats eat what is left over. We must think about this.

My grandchildren, have you noticed this? At first our children and our money seem to make us happy, but that happiness itself eventually consumes and destroys us. Like that, if we are attached to lust, hatred, mind, and desire, they will eat away at our souls, our wisdom, our truth, and our goodness. Our lives are devoured by these attachments. We must recognize the difference between a wrong attachment and a right attachment, and then nourish only the relationships that will neither cause us pain nor destroy us.

The only right relationship is to God and His qualities, to the subtlety of wisdom, to peace, tolerance, truth, justice, integrity, tranquility, patience and contentment. We must form this relationship, trusting in God and giving all praise to Him. Such a relationship will nourish us without causing any pain. All other attachments are to the world, like the relationship between the baby crabs and the mother.

We have to think about this. Which relationship will help us? Which attachment will kill us? We have to know what is right and what is wrong in our lives. If we know what is right and follow it, that relationship with goodness will protect us in all three worlds. But if we establish a close relationship with those crabs, they will gobble us up.

My love you, my grandchildren. Please understand this. Nourish and love those things which can protect you. Nourish and love truth, faith, certitude, and determination. That will be good. Then you will escape from the baby crabs. May God protect you and establish for you a good relationship with Him. *Āmīn.*

Who Can Fly As High As the Eagle?

y love you, my grandchildren, my sisters and brothers, my daughters and sons. It is early morning. Shall we go for a walk? Look! A family of eagles is sitting on those trees that overlook the ocean. They have white-feathered necks and their bodies are the color of earth. Some are gazing intently at the nearby pond, and others are peering out toward the ocean. They are searching for food.

Do you see that lone eagle perched way up there on the highest branch? "O eagle, please come down. We want to talk with you.

"You fly so high, with such beauty and majesty. You can fly better than all the other birds. But what do you think about as you soar through the air? You think about killing other lives and eating them. Is that good? Is it right to kill? Please tell us why you do this."

My grandchildren, listen carefully to the eagle's answer.

"O wise one, what you say is true. We eagles build our nest up high and fly way up in the sky in order to protect ourselves. For if we remained close to the earth, man would not spare us, nor could we spot our prey. God created us with a stomach, and so we must circle around and around, way up high, searching for food to satisfy that stomach.

"But even as we soar through the air, we have to be alert to certain dangers. We must pay close attention to the direction of the wind and avoid flying against its currents. That could break our wings. Only if we fly with the wind can we fly safely. There is so much we have to think about. When there is too much wind, we must turn around and escape, and when there is not enough wind, we have to flap our wings to keep our balance. At all times we must be very careful to maintain that balance.

"Other birds try to imitate us, saying, 'I can do what the eagle does!' But they always fail. They have not attained our skill in flying.

"O eagle, what do you think about as you soar through the air?"

In one short second we can swoop down, seize our food, and then climb back up again. The other birds do not have the breath to do that. And because they cannot adjust their flight to the winds and currents, they meet with accidents. God has given us this special flying ability, as well as the feeling, awareness, and intellect to know how to escape.

"But, even though we have faith in God, we do not know right from wrong or good actions from sinful ones. So why do you criticize us for killing? We only act according to the limited understanding of our intellect. For example, we will sit anywhere, even in the midst of thorns or stones. We don't know any better. You human beings would never do that. You have the awareness to clear a smooth space before sitting down.

"O great one, O wise man, God made us the way we are. We only kill in order to satisfy our hunger. But you men bring danger to so many lives! You descend deep into the earth and rise high up into the sky. You fly everywhere, to all different countries. You have no wings, yet you dare to fly far beyond any place we could ever reach. But do you ever try to rise up in order to reach God and the truth? No, instead you fly to evil places.

"Although we eagles may not know good from evil, at least we are able to escape from danger with our sense of balance. But you don't have that ability. You have lost your balance, and thus you meet with dangers and accidents far worse than those we face. Think about that. Instead of asking us about our behavior, perhaps you should tell us why men do the evil things they do. You should correct them for the way they act!"

My love you, my grandchildren. Did you listen to what the eagle told us? Everything he said was true. The mind of man flies faster than the wind, but it lacks balance. When gales and storms strike, man does not know how to use his wisdom to adjust himself and escape. Instead, his mind flies everywhere—over oceans, lands, and mountains, into caves, and even into space. Unbalanced and uncontrolled, it flies all over the world. Man has not understood the four steps of surrender, focus, balance, and grace-awakened wisdom, or *gnānam.* And he lacks the virtuous qualities of modesty, reserve, good conduct, and fear of wrongdoing.

The eagle at least has a sense of balance that can operate within the limits of its intellect. But man doesn't have even that. He fails to glide along, calmly and quietly. Instead, with his ego he flies directly into storms and then is unable to turn back and reach safety when he needs to. As a result, he eventually breaks down.

The eagle carries only the hunger of its stomach, but man carries the weight of the whole world, while he searches for food to satisfy his soul. He searches for God, for *gnānam,* and for heaven. But at the same time he also seeks food for the ego of the I. He thinks he can manage both God and the world. He carries the added weights of magic, mesmerism, and miracles. And no matter how high he flies, those heavy weights eventually pull him back down.

The eagle glides down and lands smoothly on a rock, but man plummets down and crashes into hell. He cries and cries and tries to climb out, but the dog of desire pushes him back down again. Torpor, the currents of illusion, the darkness of ignorance, and the monkey mind all drag him down into the worst of hells.

My love you, my grandchildren. This is how the mind of man works. It flies all over the world, but fails to be of any benefit to him. At least the eagle finds food. All man finds is hell. He does not know peace for even one second. The sorrows and sufferings of the winds of the world batter him constantly. Man must learn to maintain his balance by using God's qualities. If he cannot do that, then he must at least have enough wisdom to avoid the storms. But instead, man flies in the sky saying, "I am great. I will go to heaven. I alone will see God and speak to Him." He tries to mimic the eagle. He tries to fly without wisdom or the right qualities, without understanding the ways of God or the ways of the world, and without understanding the soul.

While he is in this state, so many winds strike against him: the winds of illusion, darkness, arrogance, karma, mind, and desire, as well as the winds of differences between races, religions, colors, and languages. Battered by all these gales and storms, he somersaults and plummets to the earth. No matter how high he flies, the currents of illusion drag him down and he falls. He sees only illusion and hell. He never sees heaven.

Only one who has God's grace and God's qualities, only one who has true wisdom, certitude, and balance can fly higher than all the others. At that great height there is nothing for him to rest upon, not even a tree. So he breathes in God's air and balances in that air. Flapping his two wings of *Lā ilāha* and *ill-Allāh,* he balances his life with the qualities of God. Then he gazes about in all four directions, and using his wisdom, he observes all that is there. He sees the world. He sees ignorance, illusion, darkness, the elements, ghosts, and the four hundred trillion, ten thousand spiritual energies. He sees God, the sun, moon, and stars, hell and heaven. He surveys truth and falsehood, good and bad, hunger and disease, wealth and poverty, the perfectly pure soul and the impure soul. With his wisdom he researches all of these, and with his balance he turns, leaving behind his weighty connection to earth, mind, and desire.

After analyzing all these things from on high, he understands where God's grace is and dives into that grace. Unlike the eagle, who must come down to the earth for its food, the man of wisdom looks down and realizes that his food is not on the earth, and he takes the food for his soul from God.

Then with faith, certitude, and determination, he rests upon the high branch of God's wisdom and surveys the entire earth. Now, when he looks with wisdom, the distance between earth and sky does not seem great. He can use that wisdom like a mirror, turning it from side to side. One side will reflect heaven, the other will reflect the world. Or he can use his wisdom like a telescope that he only needs to focus to see everything in this world and in the hereafter, either from a distance or at close range. His wisdom can also be used as a microscope, enabling him to enlarge even the tiniest thing and examine every atom.

With this divine analytic wisdom there is nothing he cannot do. If he understands what he sees and discards what must be discarded, then only one thing will remain—light, the resplendence of the wisdom of the *Nūr.* Whether he is dwelling in this world or in the hereafter, in *ākhir,* the world will no longer be within him. Only *ākhir* will be within him, and he will be dwelling in heaven.

The one who has that wisdom, that balance, those qualities and actions, and that perfectly pure soul is an *insān kāmil,* a perfected

141

human being. God is the Protector of his balance and his wisdom. This *gnāni,* this wise one, leaves all else behind and says, *"Lā ilāha ill-Allāh.* Other than You, we have no help. You are the only One." Very rarely does anyone maintain that balance and reach the light in heaven. Such a one flies in the heaven of grace where the crown of Allah is found. His food is the grace of God, the peace of God, and the freedom of his soul.

My grandchildren, when other men see an *insān kāmil* flying, they think that they can fly too, just as other birds try to imitate the eagle, even though they do not have the balance to do so. The only one who can fly in the sky is the one who has God's wisdom and actions, the one who has faith, certitude, and determination. Only when a man surrenders to being pulled by that power can it pull him up, and only then can he fly. Such a one has succeeded in his journey. God will accept him as His son, as His child, His messenger, and His representative.

My love you, my grandchildren, my brothers and sisters, my daughters and sons. Think about what the eagle told us. Man flies everywhere without wisdom, and this is why he meets with accidents and falls down. The eagle flies only to hunt for food, but man flies for praise, for fame and titles, for the I and the you.

My grandchildren, you must not fly in that way. You must prepare your qualities while you are here. You must have the ideal of God within you and do His duty. Leave all those weights behind and carry the qualities of God instead. Search for wisdom and acquire balance.

My precious grandchildren, wherever you may go, you will only know the secret if you go in His state. You must understand this state while you are here on earth. Then you will know the explanation of the creations and the meaning of heaven and hell. You will understand truth and falsehood, good and evil, and all of everything. Have faith and certitude that there is none other than God. Focus on Him and pray to Him in this state. Then you will receive your Father's treasure, the freedom of your soul.

O my God who creates, protects, and sustains us and who guides the soul, O Allah who is plenitude, You are the only One who has the heart that never forgets us, no matter who else may forget us. You are the Mighty One who protects all lives with that heart. *Ill-Allāh.* You are the only One who is Allah. May You give us Your qualities, Your actions, and Your state. *Āmīn. Āmīn.*

Take Only As Much
As Your Cup Can Hold

y love you, my grandchildren. Are you thirsty? Would you like a cup of clear, refreshing water? Come, let's get some, but be careful not to pour too much into your cup. If you try to take more than your cup can hold, it will spill over the rim and be wasted. All right, now fill your cup. Be careful! Oh no, you spilled some! Now neither you nor anyone else will be able to drink it. So always take only as much as your cup can hold. If you need more you can take another cupful later. There's no need to be greedy. You can refill your cup over and over again.

My grandchildren, mind and desire are always greedy. They want wealth. They want to rule the entire world and grab everything for themselves. They both want things that go beyond the safe limit. But as soon as they take on more than they can handle, they cry, "This is unbearable! Someone must carry this for me. Help me, I can't manage!" They cannot stand it. Mind and desire search for help on all sides, but in the end they are crushed by the weight of their burdens. And anyone who tries to help them will also be crushed.

My grandchildren, that is the work of the mind, always collecting more than it can carry. If you take too much of anything it will kill you. Any food or water, titles or honors that are beyond your ability to carry will crush you.

And whose fault will that be? It will be the fault of the person who reaches beyond his capabilities. If you accept a title that is too heavy, if you own ten houses, if you have too big a family, or if you try to carry burdens that are beyond your ability, you will experience only difficulties and suffering. You won't be able to sleep day or night. You won't be able to eat. You won't be able to do anything.

Whether it be worldly possessions or the wealth of grace or the wealth of wisdom, you can only take as much as your cup can hold.

143

*If you try to take more than your cup can hold,
it will spill over the rim and be wasted.*

You can only handle as much as you are capable of, as much as your wisdom can grasp. If you look for something beyond your capacity in any of these realms, you may go crazy, because you have no way of holding on to what you've taken. If you don't have wisdom, if you don't have purity of heart, and if you don't have a clear life, you cannot contain these things and you will find it difficult. So, it is best if you just take what is needed to satisfy your hunger at each particular time, and then take another portion the next time you are hungry.

This is how to live your life. This is how you can sleep peacefully and be happy. Then you will not suffer or be sad. The monkey mind will not jump about in the jungle causing trouble, and the dog of desire will not run around and bark.

My love you, my children. You have to dig deeper and become clearer. As you dig deeper and deeper you can handle more and more and fill yourself with more refreshing water. Then there will be ample room for wisdom and good qualities, and you can gather more and more goodness, grace, love, compassion, justice, and good thoughts. These qualities are not heavy at all. But desire for the world, land, women, and gold is very heavy. They are the burdens of hell, and if you try to hold onto them, you will bear all the weight of hell. If you understand this, then even if you have to live in that hell, you can carry only the necessary weight and try to escape from the rest.

Therefore, my grandchildren, my sons and daughters, my brothers and sisters, think about this a little. Take on only as much as your cup can hold. Attain clarity in your lives and search for wisdom and good qualities. That will be good. My love you.

The Light That Guides Us

y love you, my grandchildren, my sons and daughters. It is night now. Will you come with me on a journey across the ocean? First we will have to make a raft by tying together five wooden planks. Then, riding on this flat boat, we must cross over to the other shore where we will see many wonders.

Now let us climb aboard and begin our journey. Be careful! The water is under us, all around us, and splashing over us. But even if the waves toss us about and the water rises up and gushes over the raft, we must cross with certitude and steadfastness. We cannot sit down even for a moment. We must stand firm.

My grandchildren, so far we have traveled almost four miles, but we have still eight more miles to go before we reach the opposite shore. It is so very, very dark. Wherever we look, all we can see is endless space and the wide-open sea. It is too dark to see the distant shoreline. There are many, many dangers out here on the open sea. Gales and windstorms can arise and blow us about. The waves can easily wash us overboard and there are dangerous sea creatures all around us. We must travel with great care if we wish to reach the shore. We must cross this sea with attentiveness and concentration.

Even though it is so dark, we cannot carry a lantern with us, for the waves might pound against it and crack the glass. Some other dangers could also threaten us if we carry a man-made light. There is a kind of fish which has a nose like a needle six to twelve inches long. The moment this fish sees any light, even from a great distance away, it will rush toward it and lunge right at it. Its long needle nose could pierce through someone's stomach and go right out the other side.

Look how vulnerable we are to this fish. All four sides of our raft are open to attack. We would be protected if we were traveling in a covered boat, but standing out here in the open, we have to be very careful if we want to survive. We must not carry any kind of light that could attract these dangerous sea creatures. The only light that will be safe to use is the one hidden within, the light of wisdom. This light will help us, but by itself it is not enough to take us safely across. In addition to this inner light, we also need a natural light to guide us in this darkness, a light created by God. Look up at the stars in the sky. These are the natural lights that God gave us. By studying them, we can determine the time as well as the direction of the shore. Look! That star rises at midnight. That one at three o'clock. That star appears at two o'clock and that one in the early morning. If we know which star appears at which time, they can be our guides. And once we arrive safely, we will experience great joy and comfort.

Do you understand, my precious jeweled lights of my eyes? This ocean represents the illusion of our lives. We have to cross it, riding on the raft of the five elements: earth, fire, water, air, and ether. It is the soul that must ride on this raft and wisdom that must guide it.

On this journey, there are many currents, whirlpools, and energies that will threaten to pull us under. We must have the strength of faith, certitude, and determination to stand firm when these waves and storms toss us to and fro, roll us about, and pull us up and down. There are many of God's creations within this sea of illusion that can cause us trouble. Some of them are huge! If we try to use any light of our own making, these dangerous creatures will be attracted by it and attack us. We must use the inner light of wisdom.

Children, if those creatures do leap out of the sea and lunge at us, we must show compassion and love to them. Even though we know they are evil, we must not hurt them, we must simply protect ourselves and escape. We must not destroy those beings just because they are jumping at us. We have to understand their joy. We must tell them, ''All right, you go your way and I'll go mine,'' and then carefully knock them off the raft, allowing them to return to their natural places. There is no need to hurt them. If we hurt them, they will hurt us.

My grandchildren, we need to develop and nurture His *sabūr,* His patience. The light of wisdom and God's qualities must be with us to

*My grandchildren, once we have crossed the ocean
of illusion, we must leave this world and go beyond.*

guide us safely across the vast ocean of illusion in our lives. To cross to the next shore in the face of so much suffering, we need determination. This is how we must proceed through all these hardships.

When we reach mid-ocean in our lives, we will be surrounded by darkness. As we look around in all directions we will see so many glittering things glowing in the water; the crests of the waves rise white and luminous. We must look at these many glitters with wisdom, for without wisdom we cannot see anything clearly.

My grandchildren, let us travel a little further in this sea of darkness. We have to be very careful at this point. We must have the quality of surrendering ourselves to God with love. That is what will help us reach the shore. We must not lose our balance. The gales and storms of life are tossing us about, so we must be cautious. At all times we must be attentive and turn our hearts to the right point and surrender the self. That is the point.

The light of wisdom will guide us, and God has also given us the light of the *olis*. Like stars in the sky, these lights of God will help us to determine the direction of the shore we are striving to reach. We started out in the east, and we are traveling toward the west, toward the section of Allah. We must go in that direction and reach the shore of His plenitude. There we will find the freedom of our souls and we will see wonders which mind and desire have never seen.

Now we are drawing closer, we are almost there. Look! We can see Him. We can see Allah! Slowly, little by little, we are coming to the shore of His kingdom, the kingdom of purity where we will see only His resplendence.

At last we have landed! We have come to see our Father's home. Now we must research into the kingdom of our Father. Let us explore this place that has no end and no beginning, the realm of limitless grace, incomparable love, and undiminishing wealth. Here we will find the wealth of the three worlds, the wealth of grace, the wealth of the grace-awakened wisdom of *gnānam,* and the wealth of the divine knowledge of *'ilm.* This is our Father's treasure. We must decide what we need from it and take it. We must try to understand and re-

149

ceive that wealth which can only be given to those who have crossed the ocean and reached the shore.

My love you, my grandchildren. Once we have crossed the ocean of illusion, we must leave this world and go beyond. We need to understand what will happen before and after this journey. It is important that we learn this in our lifetime. We have to make the effort with God's qualities and with wisdom, conducting the journey of our soul in a good way. We must make this journey.

Allah is sufficient unto all. May He protect us all. My love you, my grandchildren. May God help us.

Don't Pour Mud on Your Head Like an Elephant

y love you, my grandchildren. Would you like to see some more of the jungle? Let us climb up this rocky mountain and look around below us. Ah! Do you see that herd of elephants? Two or three appear to be leading the herd into the pond. Look how they roll in the water, then draw it up into their trunks and spray it all over themselves. They love to play in the water and spray each other. Let's sit down and watch for a while. Don't go too close, because elephants will turn on you if you frighten them.

The bath seems to be ending now. They have cleaned themselves and are leaving the pond. But look, they are lifting their trunks high into the air and blowing dust and dirt all over each other. Oh no, they are all muddy and sandy again! They are even dirtier than they were before! It doesn't look like they have washed at all, does it? But they have finished their bath, and now they are happily leaving the pond. Listen to them trumpeting and calling to each other.

My grandchildren, did you see how the elephants behaved? Man also acts like this. He lives in a jungle without any light, the dark jungle of his mind. Even though that mind is fanatical and arrogant, man wants to believe in God, trust in God, and bathe to purify his soul. And so he searches for a way to attain that purity of soul.

People of every race, religion, and color, and people who follow the various scriptures and creeds—all want to trust in God and make their souls pure. This is how people are. They go to temples, churches, mosques, and other places of worship, seeking freedom for their souls. Yet when they get there, what do they do? They bathe like the elephants and spray the mud of hell all over their heads. They think of revenge and murder while they pray. They want to kill some-

Elephants love to play in the water and spray each other.

one or win something from someone or ruin someone's business. They take the mud of each evil thought and splash it all over their heads.

Sometimes they even ask God to kill someone. They pray, "O God, that man is my enemy. Destroy him. Destroy my competitor and grant me wealth. Destroy the man who has taken my house." People have such thoughts within them. They want to hurt others. But after praying like this, they are dirtier than they were before entering the church. They put the mud of selfishness, anger, haste, and impatience on their heads and then blame God. With their arrogance, karma, and illusion, they take all the sins of the world and dump them onto their heads. They are just like elephants.

Any man who lives in the dark jungle of the five elements, ignorance, and desire is like this. He enters a place of worship with a little bit of devotion and a sense of awe, but he is really looking for miracles and powers. He comes to purify his soul, but instead while he is there he thinks about attacking others or about fulfilling his own desires. And when he leaves he is dirtier than when he came.

What difference is there between man and elephants? Man can walk through the jungle where the elephant lives, but no one can enter that dark jungle of the mind of man. At least we can protect ourselves from elephants most of the time, but it is a very different matter to escape from man and his dark jungle. Man is even more arrogant than an elephant.

My love you, my grandchildren. If we want purity and freedom for our souls, we must understand this and gradually try to escape. Then our souls can be free. My love you, my grandchildren, think about this.

Even though the peacock is so exquisite, when he looks at his skinny black legs, he cries, "Why are they so ugly?"

Depressed As a Peacock

My love you, my grandchildren, my brothers and sisters, my sons and daughters. Let us go for a walk in the jungle.

Look at that beautiful peacock dancing like an open flower. He is performing for the peahens. His long, beautiful tailfeathers fan out to a height of nearly five feet. Isn't he lovely? His feathers have only five different colors, but when the sunlight falls on them, the colors seem to multiply. They glisten in a full spectrum of green, blue, turquoise, hues of fire and earth, and the deepest black. Look at all those beautiful colors!

But even though the peacock is such an exquisite bird, when he looks at his feet he feels sad and cries, "Why should my feet be so ugly? God made my body nice and plump, but He gave me skinny, black legs. Why didn't He create my legs to match the rest of me?"

My grandchildren, look how worried the peacock is about his legs! Why should he be sad about this thin layer of black skin that covers his legs? Underneath the skin his legs are not black, but the peacock does not realize this. He dances so beautifully, showing off his lovely colors, but afterwards, he hangs down his head and is depressed.

My grandchildren, God also created man in many colors and hues. Look at all the colors in his eyes, in his face, and in his skin! Look at the beautiful hair on his head. Even his fingernails are pretty. Man has so many different kinds of beauty. Listen to his voice. Listen to all the words he can speak and the sounds he can make. Look at his teeth and tongue. He is the most beautiful of all creations.

Man has five colors, just like the peacock. He contains the colors of earth, fire, water, air, and ether. Strutting like a peacock, he dances upon the world in a lovely way. But his mind is black. And just as the peacock feels sad about its legs, man becomes depressed when he looks at his mind. Although he may praise his physical beauty, he becomes depressed when he looks at the sadness, the sorrow, and the differences his mind creates.

Man must realize that he is truly beautiful. If he can dispel the blackness of the mind, he will no longer be depressed. Everything within him will be beautiful, clear, and happy. All that is wrong will have left him.

His black mind is what is wrong with him. Mind, desire, ego, anger, haste, pride, jealousy, envy, resentment, doubt, trickery, deceit, illusion, and so many other bad qualities cause this darkness. If a man can dispel these, only the beauty of God will remain. What wonder, what beauty that will be! Everyone who sees it will be truly amazed.

This really is just a small job, my grandchildren. The mind that covers your heart is just like the skin pasted onto the legs of the peacock. If you peel the skin off the peacock's legs, they will not be black anymore. And if you peel off this thin layer of the mind, you will be very beautiful. Unlike the peacock which sees only its outer beauty, you will see the beauty of God both within and without.

My love you, my grandchildren. Think about this. Peel away and discard this blackness of hell. Then you will never feel depressed again. You have to cut away these dark qualities. Then you will know peace, tranquility, equality, justice, unity, grace, compassion, and the qualities of God. Then you will have a life of freedom in this world, in the world of the soul, and in the kingdom of God. Make the effort to learn what is right and wrong, and peel away all that is wrong. That will be good. *Āmīn. Āmīn.* Allah must help us.

Peacefulness at Dawn and Twilight

My love you, my grandchildren. Shall we go out for a while? It is about six in the evening, and the heat of the day is gone. It is twilight now, a happy, restful time. This is a good time to go to the seashore, for even the ocean is calm and cooling now. Twilight is also a good time to begin a journey or to pray, for at that hour you do not feel tired. The air and the light in the sky bring a little peace to your blood and your mind. The same is true around four o'clock in the morning, just as the day is beginning to dawn. That too is a cool, clear, and peaceful time. But shortly afterwards, when the sky turns red from the rays of the rising sun, the day grows hot and you feel tired.

My love you, my grandchildren, my brothers and sisters. When we dawn in this world, we are peaceful for a short time, just as we are peaceful from four to six in the morning. But after a few years, the red color of blood ties and the heat of our karma begin to affect us. From that time on, for so many years, we suffer and suffer. Then, as our sun is setting, it becomes red for a while, and in the twilight of our old age we may find a little peace again.

My love you, my grandchildren. The only times in life that we may know some peace are right after we are born and just before we die, during the dawn and twilight of our lives. At these times, we may enjoy some silence from the rest of the world for a little while. It is even like that for a man of wisdom. He may have known a small degree of peace as a baby, and he becomes somewhat peaceful again when he is old. But all the years in between are very difficult and full of suffering.

My grandchildren, in order to attain peace in our lives, we have to smooth things over with patience, contentment, trust in God, and

For a little while we may enjoy some silence from the rest of the world.

praise of God, with *sabūr, shukūr, tawakkul,* and *al-hamdu lillāh.* During the time that we suffer from the heat, these qualities must be within us. We must surrender all responsibility to God and try to make life easier for ourselves. We have to do what we can and leave the rest to God. That is how we can attain tranquility in our lives.

Think about the peacefulness we feel at dawn and at twilight. And the rest of the time, we must have inner patience, contentment, surrender, and praise of God. We must place everything in God's hands. That will be good. May God help us. *Āmīn.*

The Story of Abraham and Ishmael (*A.S.*)

y love you, my children. Today I will tell you the story of Abraham and Ishmael, may the peace of God be upon them.

Abraham ☺ was sent as a prophet to show the people God's good actions and His power, His *qudrat*. And when Abraham ☺ was thrown into the fire, he demonstrated the strength of his *īmān*, his absolute faith, certitude, and determination, to the people, to the angels, and to the other prophets.

Then one day God gave him a son named Ishmael ☺. Abraham ☺ had much love and affection for his son, and his attachment grew stronger and stronger every second.

Allah looked at that attachment and said, "Abraham, you must sacrifice your son to Me. I will tell you exactly how to do it. Your eyes must be unwavering, your body should not tremble, and your heart should not waver. Your eyes and nose should not even become moist. Your face should not become drawn. You must make this sacrifice with a very happy face. You must look directly at your son, and your son must look at you. First sprinkle a little water on him and say, *'Bismillāhir-Rahmānir-Rahīm*: You are the Creator, the Protector, and the Nourisher.' Then, while looking into your son's eyes, you must take the knife, place it at his throat, and draw it across his throat three times.

"As you are wielding the knife, your hand should not shake, your fingers should not tremble, and you should not hold on to anything for support. Your heart must not beat any faster. You must have a very blissful smile on your face and then kill your son." God gave him all these conditions to abide by, saying, "Abraham, this is the way you must sacrifice your son to Me, and you must understand the meaning of this sacrifice."

Abraham ☺ felt disheartened as he thought of what he must do, but his son said, "O father, no matter how long I live, I may never again come to a state in which God will accept me. If I do not go to Him the moment He calls me, I may never receive such a chance again. Therefore put aside your sorrow, and sacrifice me according to the word of Allah. If you do not, I will sacrifice myself to Him." This is what Ishmael ⨀ told his father.

When Abraham ⨀ saw the determination, certitude, and faith in his son's heart, he said, "All right, Ishmael, I will sacrifice you according to the will of God. I will take you to the mountain where He said the sacrifice must be performed." And so together they climbed the mountain.

Just then satan came. "Abraham, are you a man? Are you a father? Don't you have any mercy? God may be God, but this is your own born son. How can you kill him? Don't you have any compassion? What kind of God would ask a thing like this?"

Abraham ⨀ shouted, "Go away, satan!" and threw a stone at him. But satan came back, so Abraham ⨀ threw another stone at him. He came back a third time and again Abraham ⨀ threw a stone and yelled, "Go away, satan!"

Then, as Allah had commanded, the father sprinkled water on his son and prepared to sacrifice him with a smiling face. Suddenly he heard the sound of Allah commanding him, "Stop, Abraham! I have now accepted your son Ishmael. I am sending you a lamb to sacrifice in his place." And so Abraham ⨀ sacrificed the lamb instead.

My grandchildren, we must understand the meaning within this story. You can read about this in the Qur'an, in the *hadīth,* and in the Bible, but these are only outer meanings. We have to go much deeper. We have to understand the reason why God told Abraham ⨀ to cut his son's throat. We have to understand this with *'ilm,* with the divine knowledge which is the wealth of God. We have to reflect upon it with the *'ilm* within *'ilm,* and with the wisdom within wisdom. We must understand the meaning of God within God, the soul within the soul, and duty within duty. We must understand these inner meanings. God created man as the most exalted creation, as the one capable of understanding. He has said that man will know things

Then, as Allah had commanded, the father sprinkled water on his son and with a smiling face prepared to sacrifice him.

which even the angels will not know. And because he has been endowed with this wisdom, man must always look for the inner meanings.

My love you, my grandchildren. Look at this story with your wisdom and think about it more and more deeply. Is God a torturer or a killer? Would He want human sacrifice? Would He ever tell us to sacrifice the lives of others? No, Allah is not a murderer. It is not His duty to accept sacrifices. He is the life within all life. He is the wisdom within all wisdom and the love within all love. He is compassion within compassion. He is the Father who protects all lives. *Bismillāhir-Rahmānir-Rahīm:* He creates, protects, and nourishes. That is His duty. He dwells in all lives. Would the One who dwells within all lives be a murderer? If He were, He would be killing Himself, because He truly is within all lives. Is God going to commit suicide? No. This is only a story, an outer example. The inner meaning is very different.

If we ponder with our wisdom, we will understand that Abraham ⊕ was the messenger of God, His representative on earth. There was no other prophet at that time. God sent this one prophet at that particular time for all the children of Adam ⊕ in all four directions: east, west, north, and south. And as the one prophet to all, it was important for the sake of justice that he see all lives as equal to his own. He had to love all lives as he loved his own, to feel all hunger as he felt his own, to treat all illnesses as his own, and to know the sorrow of others as he knew his own. He had to be able to give God's love and justice equally to all.

But Abraham ⊕ grew more and more attached to his son, even more than he was to God. He developed this selfish attachment, and because of it he was unable to be impartial if someone fought with his son or became his son's enemy. He could not settle such a dispute with real justice. He loved his son so much that he was unable to consider all lives equally. He saw others as less important than Ishmael ⊕. He could not see the worth and plenitude of other lives, and he was no longer able to love God in the proper way. Thus his justice, affection, good conduct, and equality toward others was diminishing.

Through his attachment to his son, Abraham ⊕ was beginning to form a connection to the world, to karma. Illusion and blood ties were starting to change him so that he could no longer act according to the justice and qualities of God. This is why God demanded that Abraham ⊙ make a sacrifice. But it was not really his son that was to be killed, it was his attachment. "O Abraham," God said, "you haven't seen the sorrow of others as your own sorrow. I have sent you as My prophet, and yet I do not see any difference between the relationship you have with your son and the relationship an ignorant man has with his son. Because of this favoritism, you will swerve from justice. This is why My commandment came, in order to cut your selfish love. You can only show justice if you have no attachment for anything but God."

My grandchildren, if you have the qualities of God and if you love all equally, you can be just toward all lives. But if you have blood ties, you cannot be just. This is why God asked Abraham ⊙ to sacrifice his son. As soon as that state of readiness came within Abraham ⊙, God said, "O Abraham, I accept your son. I am sending you a lamb, which represents all the joys and sorrows you have gathered on earth through your attachments. These would have gone ahead of you and awaited you on Judgment Day, but I am sending them in the form of this lamb. Now sacrifice those joys and sorrows. Be ready!"

Thus, in order to correct him and to reestablish God's qualities, His justice, His peace, and His equality within His prophet, God told Abraham ⊙ to cut away his attachments, his karma, his blood ties, his love, and his selfishness. Only then could he reach a state of peace where he could show equality toward all lives.

My grandchildren, think about this story. If you are in a state of selfish attachment, your verdict in any situation will be contrary to justice. If you are a judge and your wife has a fight with a neighbor's wife, you will always be on your wife's side. If your son fights with a neighbor's son, your decision will favor your son. In a conflict between your mother and someone else's mother, you will not be able to use that sword of justice. No matter what situation arises, you cannot be just if you have such attachments.

That is why Abraham ⊙ had to learn this lesson. He was not really asked to kill Ishmael ⊙, he was asked to kill his own attachment. Once he did that, God accepted Ishmael ⊙ who had reached a perfect state.

This story explains true justice. Is it right for a prophet to be unjust? Is this not contrary to how a prophet should act? Should a messenger of God show favoritism? If he did, how would he differ from anyone else? How could God's justice be conducted? What would God's love be like? How could the qualities of God be given to the people? We must really think about this. We have to understand the meanings within the story. This happened to Prophet Abraham ☺ in order to cut something away and take him beyond it. He had to keep what was good and discard what was bad.

My grandchildren, this is true for a judge, an ordinary man, a man of wisdom, or anyone. This story can teach you to cut away your own mistakes, so that you can go beyond your present state to a higher one. That is the lesson in a story such as this.

My love you, my grandchildren. Once we begin to understand the commandments of God and the actions of a prophet, we have to try to rise up to the level of God. Like that, as we begin to understand the words of a wise man, a *gnāni,* we have to see the state that he is in and try to attain it. Unless we are in that same state, even if we know everything from sunrise to sunset, we cannot fully understand anything. As long as we are not in his state, we must take ourselves back to the time and situation in which he spoke, and consider the circumstances very carefully. Then the meaning will come to us. This is how we must study the explanation of divine knowledge, of *'ilm.* Without doing that we will not understand the words of a wise man.

My grandchildren, my love you. We must understand this. The world has many different opinions about what has happened to the prophets. And some people have lost their faith in the prophets because of these interpretations. The words of the prophets and the words of God are such that we have to consider the time and the place in which they were spoken and the circumstances under which they occurred. We have to actually put ourselves there and try to find the inner meaning. Otherwise we will not understand. My love you, my children. May God give you good thoughts and good wisdom.

Come my children, we can cross at this point.

You Cannot Swim Against the Floodwater

y love you, my grandchildren. Look, the water is rising! A terrible flood is coming! Do you see all the people running? The floodwaters are rushing up behind them, and they are being pulled into the water. They are trying to escape to the other side, but not knowing which way to go, they are drifting toward the center where they will die. Because they don't understand the tremendous force of the current, they are trying to swim against it and are being pulled under.

My grandchildren, watch out! The flood is rushing toward us! How can we cross to safety? We have to swim with the current and proceed carefully. We can't just plunge in and swim against the rushing water. Did you see how the others fought the current and died? Only if we are careful to move along with it, inch by inch, little by little, can we reach the other shore.

My grandchildren, I will go in front. Follow behind me and do exactly what I do. Be in the same state that I am in. We must use our subtle wisdom. Follow me, and we can escape by drifting with the water until we reach a place where it is not as forceful. Come, my children, here the force is less! We can cross at this point. Oh, good! We have escaped and reached safety.

My children, do you understand? Just as the force of this floodwater causes destruction, in the same way the gales of illusion, the storms of arrogance and karma, the five elements, satan, demons, ghosts, the connections of four hundred trillion, ten thousand storms, and all the magics also rise up to destroy the whole world. We must escape from this destruction, but to do that we need wisdom. We cannot oppose the forces of the world all at once. We must go along with them and overcome them little by little.

Religions, races, and color differences will rise up with force. Blood ties, relations, elemental miracles, the arrogance of I and you, titles, status, money, and property—all these rolled together will come at us like a flood. The world will attack us in one huge force. So we must move slowly. We have to gradually fall into it and flow along with the current. Then slowly, very slowly, we can cross over.

My love you. Look, I am showing you the way. You appeared in the east, the place of your birth, and you must go to the west, to your Father where there is no birth. You must cross from east to west; you cannot go from west to east, for you will meet with opposition. You must cross over karma and all the other forces very, very slowly and go beyond to the other shore. You cannot plunge straight in. If you oppose them saying, "I must have wisdom now!" these four hundred trillion, ten thousand waves and storms will toss you about and destroy you. Go along with them, and little by little conquer mind, desire, and karma. Go along, overcome the world, and then reach His shore. That is the subtle way of doing it. That is wisdom.

My love you, my precious children. This is how you must conquer your birth. You cannot fight frantically saying, "I'm in a hurry! I must escape! I must see God now! I must receive wisdom now! I must escape from this right now!" That cannot happen. You will be rolled and tossed about. Think about the path you are on, and slowly, very slowly, go along with the forces and escape. This is using your judgment. This is subtle wisdom, divine analytic wisdom, and divine luminous wisdom.

This is how you must cross the karma of the world and cut the connections of this birth. You need faith in God. You must have the wisdom, certitude, and determination to swim in this ocean. Then you can attain freedom.

My love you, my grandchildren. Understand this. God must protect us.

The Sounds of Creation
and the Sounds of God

y love you, my grandchildren, my granddaughters and grandsons. Did you ever tap on silver, gold, or other metals and listen to the different sounds they make? You can produce an even greater variety of tones by combining different metals. If you mix silver with iron or gold, each new combination will produce a different sound. You can even arrange metals in a particular order and tap on them one after another to make a melody. This is called music.

God created a natural sound within each metal, and men arrange those sounds into melodies that are beautiful to the ears and to the mind. Everyone is attracted and mesmerized by them.

My children, these sounds exist inside of you as well as in the outside world. Just as metals can produce sounds, there are four hundred trillion, ten thousand spiritual qualities within us, and each one makes its own noise. These qualities and hypnotic sounds exist in every nerve and piece of flesh. And whatever is inside is then made into forms on the outside. On the inside they exist in the forms of ghosts, demons, and the elements, and on the outside they take form through speech, melodies, and sounds. These are only the sounds of creation, my grandchildren, but man is mesmerized by them.

Man has ninety-six abilities which are natural to him and enable him to do anything. But instead of utilizing those abilities, he turns to the melodies, voices, rhythms, and harmonies of the sixty-four arts and sciences and the sixty-four sexual games, and to music, magic, mesmerism, and the thirty-six abilities natural to animals. These elemental energies, these *saktis,* the senses, and the mind can evoke desire and thus mesmerize you. The mind puts all these things together, plays upon them, and then lies there hypnotized as each thing

169

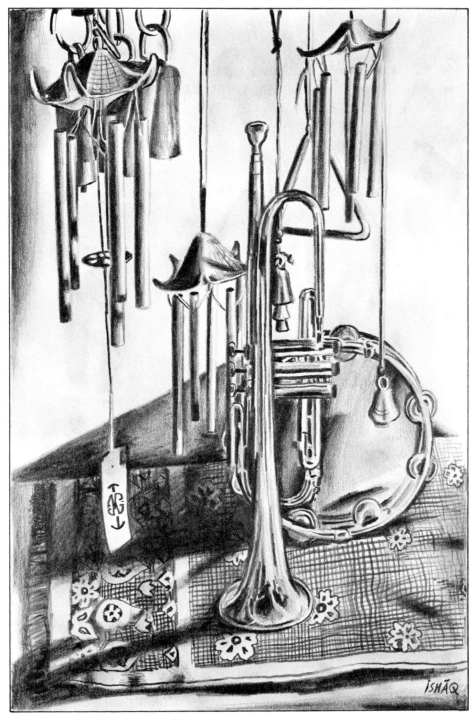

Within each metal God created a natural sound.
Men arrange these sounds into beautiful melodies.

displays its own sounds and qualities. The five elements, the five kinds of lives, and the five senses all sing, "Aaahh, eeeee, ooooo," and man lies there in torpor.

My grandchildren, metals were created by God, but they are not indestructible. Most of them can be melted by fire, and with the exception of silver and gold, most of them can rust and corrode or be consumed by the earth. Others can be eaten away by acid. In one way or another, they all can be destroyed.

In the same way, if you apply the acid of wisdom to these four hundred trillion, ten thousand energies, then seventy-five percent of them can be destroyed. And what wisdom doesn't destroy can be destroyed by the acid of God's grace. The only things that will not be consumed by these acids are justice, truth, light, and the qualities of God. Those qualities are golden, and your wisdom is silver.

My love you. You must use that acid of wisdom with the faith, certitude, and determination called īmān. Then the thirty-six abilities, the sixty-four arts, the sixty-four sexual games, and all the mesmerizing sounds will be completely corroded and consumed.

If you understand and do this properly, you can create the music of your Father's grace. His resplendent, radiant light will be perceived as music. That sound, that melody and harmony will be heard by all lives on the earth, and in the sky, in the sun, moon, and stars, in stones, trees, and rocks, and in the ocean or on land. As soon as they hear that melody of love, they will say, "My God, my Father!"

Precious children, pay attention, because that beauty is the original bliss which has no torpor. Try to imbibe this state of truth so that you can realize your ninety-six natural abilities. Once the demons and ghosts are destroyed, all that remains will be the natural abilities of the grace of Allah, which you can evoke in your speech and in your actions. This is wisdom. But if you do not understand, these abilities will be buried in maya, in illusion, and they will be corroded and consumed by the acid of earth, air, fire, water, and ether.

My grandchildren, wisdom has no sound. When it comes to you, when truth, love, and the gold of good qualities come to you, you will hear only the sound of God. You will hear only His speech. When that state comes to you, you will become the son of God. Your Father will be the plenitude, the completeness, and you will be one with Him.

171

Your body will be golden, your wisdom will be light, and you will understand everything.

My love you, my grandchildren, my sons and daughters, my brothers and sisters. Think about this. You must try to understand so that you can attain what is good.

May God grant us His grace. *Āmīn.*

A Lesson from the Woodpecker

y love you, my grandchildren. Look over there at that tree. Do you see the exquisite white-breasted bird with a colorful red throat and beautiful feathers? Observe the beauty of its head, its throat, and its legs. It is such a lovely bird, isn't it? I think it's a woodpecker. Yes, look how it uses its unusual beak to peck at the tree bark. Do you know why it does that? It is searching for insects within the wood.

Unlike other birds, the woodpecker can walk straight up a tree. It can walk up or down, to one side or the other, circling round and round the trunk, pecking away in search of its food. When people want to climb a tree, they have to put their arms around the trunk and grab hold firmly. But the woodpecker walks upright, hardly touching the bark. If the woodpecker had to hug the trunk as man does, it wouldn't be able to peck and extract its food from within the wood.

No other being can do what the woodpecker does. This behavior is a very rare thing to see. You will not find it in other birds.

My love you, my grandchildren. A wise man is like the woodpecker, and the world is like a huge tree. With faith, certitude, and determination, a wise man, an *insān kāmil,* can do what no one else can do. Like the woodpecker, he can easily climb upward, pecking at each and every point. As he circles the world without grabbing hold of it, he pecks with God's qualities and extracts the truth necessary for his nourishment. He extracts love, wisdom, compassion, tranquility, and God. A wise man doesn't cling to the tree of the world or attach himself to mind and desire. The world is not difficult for him, because he is free to move in any direction he wishes. Life and its relationships are not heavy for him, because he has the faith, certitude, and determination known as *īmān.* He only takes the truth, the point,

Do you know why it pecks at the tree bark?
It is searching for insects within the wood.

from each thing. This is natural for him.

Most men, on the other hand, stick their noses into each and every business of the world and try to grab it all. Because of this, they meet with many difficulties as they try to climb that tree. Do you understand?

The woodpecker is a subtle bird, and a wise man is a subtle being. If a man does not become wise and subtle, he will continue to grasp the world a .d will be unable to climb or fly. It will be difficult for him to extract the truth. It will be difficult for him to have good qualities or to know love or to attain the freedom of his soul. This is why he suffers and falls.

My love you, my grandchildren. Do you understand how the wise man lives in this world without holding on to it? It is so easy for him because he has faith, certitude, determination, and wisdom. Think about this. If you also learn how to do this, you will be more beautiful than the woodpecker. God will place His magnificent crown on your head and give you the two wings of wisdom and *īmān*. Your eyes will be beautiful and your heart will be pure white light. Your life will be complete, and you will have peace.

This is what a wise man is like. All others, all those without wisdom, are in pain. Even though they need God and wisdom and love, they hold on to the world, and so they suffer. My grandchildren, the more you cling to the tree of the world, the more you too will suffer.

My love you. Please think about this. May God give you wisdom. *Āmīn.*

175

Giants, Fairies, and Jinns

y love you, my grandchildren. Do you see that high mountain of solid rock? Giants, fairies, and jinns live there, but it is uninhabited by people. Sometimes we can learn things about man in a place where no men dwell. Shall we go there together?

Come this way. Oh, look at those three giants, one behind the other! Each is bigger than the next. The first one eats people. See how he peers all around. He has the face of a blood-sucking demon. The giant behind him looks like a lion and has the force of a lion. And the third giant has a face that keeps changing its shape and color every time you look at it. One moment it seems to be the face of a dog, then it changes to the face of a donkey, then to the face of a jackal.

My grandchildren, can you see how evil these giants are? Do you know their names? They are called *Tārahan, Singhan,* and *Sūran.* They split the mountain apart and emerged from inside the rock. The first to come out was *Tārahan.* His form is huge and black and filled with evil forces. He drinks blood and commits many evil acts. The one with the lion face is *Singhan,* and the one with many faces is *Sūran.* All three are horrible. Do you see how they are peering all around? Look! That one is turning in all four directions and drawing people into himself with his breath. Nothing is discarded by him. He has only to inhale and he draws in everything, even hell. Then he retreats within the rock. Did you watch him? He is very evil. You must be extremely careful, so he won't catch you!

These three giants emerged from the rock of arrogance, the rock of the mind, which is within man. They are the offspring of maya and have the forms of karma. They are the energies of hell and the forces of illusion. Be very careful! Do not let these forces enter you. They dwell in the man who is without compassion, love, or wisdom. Such a man is always saying, "I, I, I." He has a heart of stone that will not melt for anything.

Now look again. Do you see those beautiful heavenly beings coming out of the rock? The little winged ones are called fairies. The giants came out of the left side of the rock, but the fairies are flying out of the right side. God has given one of His rays to the fairies, and their beautiful faces shine with the qualities of God. They trust in God and are pure. They have a fondness for the children of Adam ⬚. Generally, fairies do good, but they do have the ability to kill someone who intends harm. They can appear and disappear. Just before they disappear they assume one form, and by the time they reappear they have changed into another. Fairies can travel around the entire world in one second.

Look, jinns are also coming out of the right side of the rock. God created the jinns out of fire. There are two kinds: demonic jinns who arise from the connection to maya, and light jinns who have accepted God and Islam. The demonic jinns sacrifice humans and drink blood, but the light jinns do only good. The light jinns have the ability to destroy, but they will never do anything evil. They are capable of doing many things. They can even fly about assuming different forms, many of which are very beautiful.

Men can control jinns. If you catch them, they will do whatever you ask. If you want to make a tree, or even if you want to turn the land into an ocean or the ocean into land, you can do it all through jinns. They can give you food and water where there is no food or water; they can give you fruit where there is no fruit; they can give you gems where there are no gems; they can make money where there is no money; they can build a house where there is no house.

Jinns can perform so many miracles for you. But you cannot reach God by means of these beings of fire. They are energies which are associated with the seven base desires of man. They emerge from only the first three levels of wisdom—from perception, awareness, and intellect. They will bring you almost anything you ask for, but they cannot bring you the grace of God. They cannot bring you *Allāhu.* They cannot bring you heaven. They cannot give you that perfect

God has given one of His rays to the fairies,
but He created the jinns out of fire.

wealth or freedom for your soul. They cannot give you God's power, His *qudrat*. They cannot give you the wealth of His grace, the wealth of the hereafter, the wealth of divine knowledge, or the wealth of grace-awakened wisdom. You cannot obtain any of these things through jinns. Such things can only come directly from God.

Moreover, even though we can control these jinns, if we allow them to exist in our innermost heart, our *qalb,* they become idols. They become veils between ourselves and God. If we rely on their help, we will not have a direct vision or a direct experience of God. Instead we will have built a huge mountain between ourselves and God. We will not be able to see God; we will only be looking at these jinns. And in the end, on Judgment Day, we will experience the torment of separation from God.

Man can make the fairies serve him, too. He can even control demons and ghosts for his own purposes, but he will receive no peace from that. The demons and ghosts will take him to hell. If he relies upon anything but God, that thing will become an idol for him which will separate him from God and deprive him of the benefits of divine knowledge and wisdom. Man must obtain wisdom from his Father directly.

The only real miracle you can ever know is the direct connection between yourself and God. You may perform worldly miracles, but they are useless. You may acquire all the wealth of the world, but ultimately that too is worthless. The only way to make that true miracle happen is first to understand yourself, and then to die within God and imbibe His glory.

Allah made Solomon ⓐ, the son of David ⓐ, the king of all creations and commanded him to guide everyone onto the good path. God gave him all the jinns and fairies as his disciples, and they served Solomon ⓐ in whatever way God told them to. You too may be carried aloft by jinns and fairies, just as Solomon ⓐ was carried from east to west and from north to south. But they did not have the power to carry him to heaven. For that journey, Solomon ⓐ relied upon Allah alone.

You must understand this, my grandchildren. Do not involve yourselves with such beings. All the jinns, fairies, satans, demons, and giants that you saw on this mountain might arise from within your own heart. Maya, darkness, and satans might emerge from the left side, while fairies and jinns might come from the right side. Do not ask them for anything. If they offer you something, say, "Thank you, you are very good, but continue with your duties. I must go." And then go to God. Do you understand?

Some people want to perform miracles to obtain whatever they desire. Others think they can rule the world. Do not think like that. You are not the ruler of this world or of any of the eighteen thousand universes. Allah is the only Ruler. You are not the one who gives to others, only Allah can give. You cannot give anything, for Allah is the Creator and the Cause of all things. You must accept Him with the faith, determination, and certitude known as *imān*. You must search for His truth, His qualities, His wisdom, His tranquility, His love and compassion, His patience and tolerance, His peace and justice. That is the true wealth. That is the wealth of grace-awakened wisdom, the wealth of *gnānam*, which you must obtain.

My grandchildren, my sons and daughters, my brothers and sisters, my love you. Think about this. Have you ever seen any of these beings we talked about? They are all within you. All these mysteries exist within your secret heart. You must seek to understand them.

Children, we must leave this rocky mountain now and go on. My love you.

Hunger

y love you, my grandchildren. Do you know how much trouble you undergo just for the sake of this one-span stomach? It constantly demands to be fed. Even though it is very small, you spend your entire life feeding it. You run about under all kinds of circumstances searching for food. Somehow you manage to feed it, even if you have to steal or lie or use deception and trickery. All this effort is made to satisfy the one-span stomach.

But there is also another kind of hunger, a hunger of the soul, a hunger for that complete treasure which is millions of years old, a hunger for life, a hunger for wisdom, love, and compassion, a hunger for justice and good conduct, a hunger for the kingdom of God. This is an enormous hunger.

My grandchildren, if you strive to appease this hunger of the soul, then the hunger of the one-span stomach will leave. If you can satisfy the hunger of the soul, it will redeem you from slavery and give you the absolute liberation of your soul. Your troubles, your difficulties, and your sadness will leave you, and you will attain peace. If the hunger of the soul is satisfied, all other hungers will end. But you have not worked toward that goal.

Children, do you know how to cut down a tree? You cannot just remove its branches. You must cut the trunk off at ground level and then dig down into the earth and cut the roots. In the same way, in order to end your soul's hunger, you must sever the roots of your karma, with wisdom. If it takes too long to uproot your karma, then at least try to cut off desire. At least separate the trunk of mind and desire from their connection to the earth. It will take a long time for them to sprout up again, and in the meantime you can do whatever needs to be done and accomplish a great deal of work. But never stop trying to uproot those deeper connections. If you remove only the

If you strive to appease this hunger of the soul,
then the hunger of the one-span stomach will leave.

branches and let the roots remain, you will never be able to complete your task. Eventually karma must be totally uprooted. That can only be done with wisdom.

My love you, my grandchildren. You must consider the reason for your hunger and then control it with wisdom. You must understand which hunger you need to appease before you can control anything else. That is the only way to attain peace in your life. May God help you. *Āmīn.*

The Wondrous Margosa Tree

 y love you, my grandchildren. Today let us go to a place nearby where there are many different kinds of fruit trees. Do you see that beautiful, big tamarind tree? Here, taste one of its fruits. The tamarind has five different tastes in all, but many people prefer the sour ones. These trees can grow to be five hundred to a thousand years old. Their branches spread out very wide and provide so much good shade. Look, stones have been placed under it for people to rest upon.

Over there is a woodapple tree. It doesn't live as long as the tamarind tree. It has a life span of only one or two hundred years. Do you see any stones to rest upon under this tree? No, because it doesn't have enough leaves to provide any shade, but it does have many fruits. Like tamarinds, woodapples also have five tastes. Some are sweet and some are sour, and sometimes they are so sticky that they cling to your tongue and throat.

My grandchildren, people do not realize that both of these trees, the tamarind and the woodapple, have the energies of the five elements within them. If a man sits beneath their branches, the air will make him ill. And if he falls asleep, when he awakens his eyes will be burning, his head will ache, and his whole body will feel like it's on fire. The fat in his body will have changed and he will feel as if all the blood had been drained out of him. His good health will be ruined.

The tamarind and woodapple trees have the power to do this. If you stay under either one of them for forty days, all the diseases in the world will come into you. Your body will become thin and weak, and you will be near death. Even though you will not look sick, you will actually be very ill. The energies of the five elements will have sucked the strength out of your body. And no matter who you ask, no one will be able to treat you for these illnesses. You may go to a doctor, but he will be unable to find anything wrong with you. He may

184

give you one medicine after another, but they will just add to your illness and destroy you. You must understand this, my grandchildren.

Now let's get up and walk on a little farther. Look at this margosa tree. It is a very good tree. Although it is not as big as the tamarind tree, it still provides a little cooling shade and gives off healthy, refreshing air. The bark of the margosa tree, its flowers, fruits, and leaves all have a healing effect on man. It is very good for a man to sit in the shade of this tree, because it absorbs the carbon dioxide from his breath and releases oxygen into the air. If you rest under the margosa tree, it will make you healthy.

If you go to a garden where all three of these trees grow, you should understand the good that will come to you from resting beneath the margosa tree and the dangers that come from staying under the woodapple and tamarind trees. Do not be tempted to sit under the huge tamarind tree for the sake of its shade, because all you will receive are the illnesses that its energies emanate.

My grandchildren, like the tamarind tree, there are some people in the world who have grown very big. They say they are learned and have understood everything. But do you know what such a person has within him? He has arrogance, karma, illusion, doubt, jealousy, and envy. Everything is within him: lust, anger, miserliness, fanaticism, intoxicants, desire, theft, murder, falsehood, and the desire for gold, land, and sensual pleasure. He is filled with so many energies. All the things belonging to karma in the whole world are within him. This big man has gathered all the destructive titles of the world, all the pride of the world, and all the elementary miracles and energies of hell in the world. These *siddhis* and *saktis* are the energies of the five elements: earth, fire, water, air, and ether. These energies and learnings and riches have made him huge, like the tamarind tree.

If you go to such a man hoping to find peace and equality and other benefits from his shade, it will be like staying under the tamarind tree for forty days. Your health will be sapped out of you day by day. Your good thoughts will be eliminated, your good qualities destroyed, and your faith lost. You will have doubts and bad thoughts, and you will do bad deeds. You will be so sick from illnesses which cannot be seen on the outside that no one will be able to cure you. And you will not even be able to go near enough to God to be treated by Him. Your life will be sucked out of you little by little, and finally you will die within mind and desire.

However, if you go to a true sheikh, a sheikh with wisdom, love, and good qualities, it will be like resting under the margosa tree for forty days. He will gradually rid you of your doubts, bad thoughts, and bad qualities and bring you to a state of health and peace. You will become even stronger and healthier than before. Day by day a good sheikh can cut off all the karmic illnesses you have gathered from bad associations. His love, patience, tolerance, and wisdom will heal you little by little. He will help you to acquire wisdom, love, faith, determination, and certitude in God. This will strengthen the freedom of your soul. The connection between you and God will be established, and your life will flourish.

This is the difference between a man who seeks the fame and praise of the world and a wise man who seeks only to help others. This is the difference between the arrogant one who gathers pride from the five elements and the humble one who has wisdom and God's qualities and who accepts only the praise of Allah.

My grandchildren, where should you go in this world to learn wisdom? There are places where *siddhis* and miracles are performed, but there are also places where faith and certitude bloom. With your wisdom, you must search until you find the place where you can regain your health and cure all the illnesses of the karma you have gathered. Only then will you find freedom for your soul and victory in your life.

God alone protects you and helps you. God alone gives you good qualities and wisdom. Your Father must protect you and grant you His grace. May He give you determination. *Āmīn.*

Its Bitter Fruit

My love you, my grandchildren. There is still more we need to learn from the margosa tree. Its shade is very pleasing to man, but its flowers, leaves, and bark are extremely bitter, and its fruits are even more bitter. No one can bear to eat any part of the margosa tree. Only the birds enjoy its taste. Yet, unlike other tasty fruits and leaves, the margosa fruit can cure many illnesses. The bitter oil from its seeds also has medicinal properties. Nevertheless, even if people are seriously ill and are told that they must eat this fruit or drink the oil to cure themselves, they will resist and make a terrible fuss. They are disgusted at the mere mention of margosa oil or fruit. Even if you mix it with sugar, they complain, "Ugh! How can I swallow this horrible stuff? I don't want any part of it."

My grandchildren, wisdom and truth are like the fruit and oil of the margosa tree. Wisdom gives health to the soul and joy to life by curing the illnesses of arrogance, karma, and maya; by changing the qualities of the three sons of maya, *tārahan, singhan,* and *sūran;* and by dispelling the six evils of passion, hatred, miserliness, attachment, fanaticism, and envy; as well as the five sins of intoxicants, lust, theft, murder, and falsehood.

Most people admit that all these illnesses must be eliminated. But a wise man, a true sheikh, knows that before you can cure them, you must understand their cause. However, the words of wisdom and truth given by such a man are as bitter to the patient as the fruit of the margosa tree. But they can cure him. The patient really needs this medicine of wisdom and truth, but he finds it very bitter indeed.

My children, when you come to a wise man, you bring so many illnesses with you. And even though you have come to be cured, you still find it difficult to take your medicine. You stick out your tongue, clutch your chest, and gag as you try to swallow it. Of course the medicine is bitter! Of course you find it very hard to take when the truth is revealed and wisdom is taught. It is not pleasant to be told to cut your fanaticism, karma, and ignorance. You don't want this medicine.

Religions won't accept this medicine, races will not accept it, and neither will egoism, jealousy, doubt, theft, lust, anger, or falsehood. They will all refuse to take this medicine. Your mind, desire, and thoughts will not relish it. You will complain, "This madman is giving us bitter medicine which stinks like feces. It's so bitter I cannot bear to put it on my tongue."

God's truth, His wisdom, His love, peace, and good qualities, His grace, His wealth, His justice and integrity are all extremely bitter medicines for a person infected with the illness of illusion. He will shout, "Oh, I can't stand this medicine. I'd rather have the illness. I'll find another doctor or another treatment. There's bound to be some swami somewhere with the power to heal me. I must go elsewhere." And just as people refuse to eat the margosa fruit, that sick man will give up and refuse the wise man's medicine.

My love you, my children. Very few people will accept the medicine of wisdom. The mind refuses wisdom. But if you do agree to accept it, you will receive the grace, and when you receive that grace, you will have good qualities. When you acquire good qualities, you will know true love, and when you accept love, you will see the light. When you accept the light, you will see the resplendence, and when you accept that resplendence, the wealth of the three worlds will be complete within you. With this completeness, you will receive the kingdom of God, and you will know your Father. When you see your Father, all your connections to karma, hunger, disease, old age, and death will leave you.

But first you must agree to take this bitter medicine and swallow it. Then your life will be free of illness. It will be a life of undiminishing wealth and happiness for the soul. You will become your Father's child, and after that, anything you eat will taste like nectar. The medicine which once tasted bitter will become as sweet as nectar. And the final taste will be happiness.

My love you, my children. Think about this. Wisdom is very difficult to teach, and it is also very difficult to learn. Nothing is harder than studying and accepting wisdom, truth, and good qualities. But know that in spite of these difficulties, you must be steadfast. You must try to eliminate them one by one. If you try, in the end you will experience the taste of happiness.

However, if instead you accept the so-called cures of all these mantras and *tantras* and the dogmas of different races and religions, what will you get? Think about it. Fire can give you a certain amount of comfort if you don't go too near it, but if you fall into it you will be burned. Light, refreshing breezes can give you pleasure, but when they are too strong, they will knock you down and toss you about. A little water will help you to live, but a flood will sweep you away. You can build a house on the earth, but just one small quake will destroy it. The illusion of the joy of love gives you pleasure, but excessive pleasure will shatter your nerves, reduce you to skin and bones, and destroy you. Is that joy? Such happiness is destructive.

My love you, my children. There is only one correct point, but learning that truth can be as bitter as tasting the margosa fruit. Try to understand why it is so difficult to teach this wisdom and so difficult to accept it. Think about this, my grandchildren. Like the patient who takes the margosa fruit, you will understand the benefits later.

May God give this sweet taste and wisdom. $\bar{A}m\bar{\imath}n$.

*Man enjoys riding and racing, but he fails
to think about the difficulties the horse undergoes.*

Man Loves to Ride, but the Horse Suffers

y love you, my grandchildren. Did you ever ride a horse? It's lots of fun. You can sit on your horse and go up and down mountains with great ease. But have you ever thought about how difficult it is for the horse?

Man enjoys riding his horse everywhere—up hills and through valleys, into caves, and along stony paths. Even in the sand, he likes to make his horse gallop. Man enjoys all this riding and racing, but he doesn't think about the difficulty the horse undergoes.

Similarly, when a man harnesses a bull to a wagon, he loads the wagon, then sits on top of it and makes awful noises, urging the bull to start pulling. He does not think about how hard it is for the bull to pull this heavy load. He does not see the blood and saliva foaming from its mouth.

If man understood how much suffering and torment he causes the horse and the bull, he would never treat them this way. Anyone who does not realize the suffering of others simply continues doing whatever he wants to do.

My love you, my grandchildren. Mind and desire and the five elements want to do what they want to do. They like to climb on top of man, but they never think about the difficulties they cause him. The five elements climb onto his back just as he climbs onto a horse, saying, "Go, go, go!" They like to ride him and make him run, but they do not have the awareness of how hard it is for him.

Anyone filled with mind, desire, and the five elements will never realize the hardships of others. If he did, he would comfort them, give them love, and limit their work to a fair load. And if he had to ride a horse or use a bull to pull a cart, he would know their capacity and not push them beyond it. He would protect these beings and not overburden them. He would treat them properly. One who acts like that is a human being.

But the five elements and mind and desire know nothing about limits. They are unaware of such things. They jump onto a man, make him climb mountains, and race him in the sun and heat and rain, shouting, "Run, run, run!" The five elements have no awareness of compassion and truth. They do not even have awareness of devotion to God or trust in God. They do not have any of those qualities. They only want to go where they want to go and do what they want to do. And once they climb onto man, they selfishly ride him to hell.

My grandchildren, we must transform ourselves into human beings with wisdom. We must put reins on the five elements and on mind and desire. We must control them and make them take us where we want to go. We must also comfort them and tie them where they have to be tied, in places where there are weeds and grass for them to eat. We should not destroy them, because they are needed for our journey. They make up our body and our senses; there is a shape to them and an essence within them that we need. But we must show them how to do what we want, and at the same time give them enough leeway to get what they need. Then we can proceed on our journey. Then we can establish the relationship that needs to be achieved between God and man.

We have to think about this. The elements will never be aware of the connection between man and God. They only want to do what they want to do. But if we learn to control them, we can accomplish the things that human beings need to accomplish. We must know what will take us to Him. We have to control what must be controlled, put it where it must be put, stay where we have to stay, and establish a relationship between ourselves and God. When we acquire the wisdom and tranquility which will enable us to do this, then we can mount and ride the five elements, mind, and desire and attain peace in our lives.

My love you, my grandchildren. Please think about this.

The Lightning of the Mind

y love you, my grandchildren. If you look up at the sky when you hear thunder, sometimes you will see a bolt of lightning fly across the sky like an arrow. Its brightness blinds you, and you feel as if your eyes are being pulled out. But can you see where the lightning comes from? No, it suddenly jumps from somewhere, flashes for a moment, and then scatters.

Lightning is caused by the colliding of two air pressure systems with different temperatures. These pressures arise when it is going to rain, when the atmosphere is in a state of turbulence, and when the electromagnetic forces in the clouds draw water up from the earth. The pressure of the elements meeting causes thunder, and then lightning follows. If a bolt of lightning strikes the earth, it can cause a good deal of destruction.

Like this, man's thoughts can also cause accidents. His evil qualities flash like lightning in his life. So much turbulence exists in the mind of man. His anger, his hastiness, and his jealousy strike as fast as a bolt of lightning flying across the sky of his mind. Before he knows what has happened, the pressure system of anger, sorrow, arrogance, karma, and other satanic qualities collides with the five elements and mind and desire, and causes accidents. He will strike without knowing what he is doing and without considering the results of his actions. At that moment he will not be aware of whether he is breaking dishes or killing someone. He will not be aware of his wife, his children, his possessions, or his property. These energies or forces in his mind can strike so quickly that he will not know anything. He will only realize what he has done after it is all over.

This can happen at any time in his life. The lightning of anger can burst forth from the pressure caused between the five elements and

*So much turbulence exists in the mind of man. His
evil qualities flash like lightning in his life.*

mind and desire. Then selfishness, arrogance, jealousy, envy, vengeance, doubt, impatience, the egoism of the I, and many evil qualities arise. Each evil thought strikes swiftly and causes great harm. When that lightning flashes within and bursts forth to the outside, it can cause a man to murder, to burn his house down, or to commit suicide. Man's thoughts can cause so many accidents and problems.

Therefore, my children, we have to keep these pressures apart. We must place our wisdom between the five elements and mind and desire. We must place inner patience, contentment, surrender, praise of God, and faith in God between these pressures. Then we can stop the lightning before it arises and man can attain peace.

You must realize that accidents will occur whenever these forces meet. You have to understand this and try to control it with wisdom. Control it with faith in God, with God's qualities, and with the patience, contentment, trust in God, and praise of God, known as *sabūr, shukūr, tawakkul,* and *al-hamdu lillāh.*

If you do this, my children, you can prevent these accidents and tragedies from arising in your life, and you can live in peace without experiencing overwhelming sorrow. Even if a problem should arise, you can control it before it devastates you. Think about this.

If you can do this, it will be good for your life. May God give you that inner patience, that *sabūr. Āmīn.*

*Those who were important in the world are being left behind, while the
small ones are entering the tiny opening and escaping the destruction.*

Become Small and Escape

y love you, my grandchildren. Shall we go out for a walk to get some fresh air? Look! Something terrible must be happening! People are running away as if they are afraid of something. Listen to them shouting and yelling, "Run, run for your life!" "Brother! Sister! Father! Come, don't be left behind! The world is being destroyed!" "The gales and storms are coming! The earth is opening up and caving in!" "The end of the world is here!" Their cries of fright fill the air.

Why are they running? Where are these hordes of people going? Look at them pushing and shoving each other, all crowding into one narrow path and running toward a tiny opening at the end of the path. Look, they are trying to creep into it. But the opening is so small, and the crowd is so huge!

Watch carefully and you will see that a few of the small people do manage to fit through, but the big people are unable to. Even though they ran so fast and pushed the smaller ones behind so they could get there first, they cannot fit into that hole. They are too big. But the small ones manage to creep through any available space, ducking under the arms or crawling between the legs of the big people. This is really amazing! Those who were important in the world are being left behind, while the small ones are entering the opening and escaping the destruction.

Look! The earth is rising up and the water is turbulent. Thunderclouds are descending. The winds are howling and the fire is spreading. All the elements are in turmoil. People are running every which way, frantically trying to escape.

My children, do you understand what is happening? The storms and fire and suffering are for those big people who think they can carry the world by themselves, without seeking God's help. They have not understood that God has set a limit for everything, and

197

because of this they will suffer accordingly.

What shall we do? We are also caught in this. Where can we hide? Is there any way out? My grandchildren, we too must be small and find a safe place to hide. There will be danger wherever we go, so we must become very small, like a particle of a particle of an atom. Can you make yourself smaller and smaller and still smaller? You have to change your self.

Have you become small enough now? Then come, we can enter and hide within the One who created us. Come, let us go within Him. He will protect us. Follow me. Now that we have become very small, we are safe.

My grandchildren, when God created us, He made us from something no bigger than an atom. He made the soul as a tiny, formless thing, a perfectly pure power, a light hidden within the body. Your soul is hiding there without your even realizing it. Do you know where it is, my grandchildren? It is hiding in God, in the One who protects us. It is hiding within that Light.

Come closer, children. Let us stay here in our hiding place and watch what happens to the big people. They are shouting and howling and calling out, "Let me through! I am a king! I am a poet. I am a learned man. I am a father. I am a mother." But none of them can creep into that tiny opening with their titles. Only their loud sounds can penetrate.

The bigger in status and titles a person becomes, the greater will be his destruction. If you are big, there is no place where you can hide in times of danger. You cannot escape, for what will happen will happen, according to the conditions or limits God has set.

All those who have become as big as elephants because of their status and great titles are now caught. These people cannot enter that safe place. They will not have that protection because their bodies have grown big, their minds have grown pompous, their intellects have swelled, their desires have become huge, their illusions have increased, and their bad qualities have multiplied. Their egos have inflated, and the earth has grown big for them. They cannot escape.

Because of their swollen size, they cannot enter the realm of God's truth and goodness and find protection. They are entangled in the five elements, mind and desire, by blood ties and attachments, by arrogance and karma, pride and jealousy, ego, titles, and status. They have been caught by the hell of this world, and it will destroy them. This is their plight. Can you see this?

My grandchildren, you must not take on huge forms in your lives. Change yourselves into small ones. Always be small. There are four hundred trillion, ten thousand kinds of accidents that you may face in life, and to escape them you must be very small. If you become smaller and smaller, if you become more and more humble, if you become like an atom within an atom, a particle within a particle, then you can avoid the accidents that occur in all the eighteen thousand universes. But if you do not change, your fate will be the same as theirs. You will be destroyed by the storms, rains, fire, winds, and earthquakes.

My grandchildren, you must always hide in a safe place. You have to hide in *Allāhu* and acquire His qualities, His wisdom, His actions, and His faith. Hide within patience, contentment, trust in God, and praise of God, within *sabūr, shukūr, tawakkul,* and *al-hamdu lillāh.* You must praise His praiseworthiness. You must become Allah's servant, His slave, and His child. If you are able to be a small one and dwell within Him, then you will always be protected by your Father. You will never have to face destruction, and you will know victory during your lifetime.

Big people are big in their karma, but they are very, very small in the truth. You may be a small one in karma, but then you will be a great one in God's kingdom and in truth.

My love you, my precious children. Please think about this. Become a great one in your Father's kingdom, and become a small one in the world. Become a slave, serving all lives and bringing them peace. With love, compassion, unity, equality, and peacefulness, you must help all lives. Then you will always be protected by your Father. He will take you and hide you within Himself and save you from danger. My precious children, may you make the effort to reach this state. *Āmīn. Āmīn.*

The Four Disciples and Their Four Wondrous Gifts

y love you, my grandchildren, my sisters and brothers, my sons and daughters. Do you know what it means to be a sheikh? A true sheikh has many children, and it is his job to teach them about man, wisdom, and the qualities of God.

One day after a certain sheikh had been talking to his children, he asked them, "Did you understand what I said?" Some of his disciples nodded their heads. Others said, "Oh, yes!" Some lowered their eyes and looked at the ground. Some openly admitted they did not understand, while others just sat there slumped over and sound asleep.

But there was one disciple who kept thinking, "I want the power the sheikh has. I want to do what he does and become a great man." That was all he could think about.

Time went by, and the sheikh continued speaking to his disciples. Some of them listened very carefully to his words. Some adopted his qualities, some progressed in wisdom, others in their actions, and others in the path of duty. Like this, they were learning in many different ways, progressing in their lives, and drawing closer and closer to Allah.

This one disciple, however, only progressed in arrogance and egoism. He could think of only one thing, "I want to become a sheikh. I want that power." He did not want the wisdom, he only wanted the title.

The sheikh observed this disciple's state of mind and saw that his actions were not sincere. He knew the disciple was trying to trick him in order to obtain what he wanted. "If this attitude continues much longer," the sheikh thought, "it will lead him to hell."

Then one day the disciple asked him, "O my father, my sheikh, through what power do you do all this?"

"Power?" the sheikh replied. "There is a Power that dawns in the place where there is no I. It is a fruit of wisdom that grows in love and ripens in compassion. Starting as a tiny seed, it transforms its color and hue until it changes into a fragrant fruit with the sweet taste of God's qualities. That taste brings sweetness and coolness to the whole body. That Power makes the heart, the eyes, the ears, and the whole body unfold and become resplendent."

"Can I see it? How can I get that power?" the disciple asked.

"You can see it. If you change and act according to the wisdom that I have been teaching, you can see that transformation within yourself. You can see that plenitude and light within yourself. When a light shines from within a stone, it is valued as a priceless gem. So too, when that light comes from within you and God resplends, your value will increase and you will be transformed into God-man. You will no longer see your self. Everything else will be seen, but the I and the thought of 'my possessions' will have died in you. That Power will exist as itself, understanding, seeing, watching everything. Such is that Power. Do you understand?"

"Oh, my father, my sheikh, is that what it is like? If I reach that state, what will I be looking at? Will I see you?"

"Each person looks mostly at himself and everything around him. The I always focuses only on the I, and that leads to destruction. But if God looks at God then one finds peace, divine knowledge, or 'ilm, wisdom, and His qualities. That truly is love, and the fruit of that love is compassion. The taste of compassion is the prayer that forms when we love Him. The taste of that prayer is to regard all other lives as our own. A person in that state will have eliminated the I. Do you understand, my son? Please think about this."

"Well, I have been studying with you for a very long time, my father."

"Have you? Have you been studying? What have you learned? What benefit do you expect? Did you study because you wanted something? What do you want? What do you think you need? Children, all of you, please come close and listen."

"My father, I have been studying because I desire to become a sheikh, to see what you see, and to have the freedom that you experience."

"Is that why you have been studying? But you have not learned to clear yourself, have you? And what about the rest of you? What have all of you come for? What about you or you or you?" Everyone looked down.

Then the sheikh pointed to three of his children and to the arrogant disciple. "You, you, you, and you, come here! Come forward. I have something for you. Look at this beautiful girl. Even though you have been here for a long time, you have never seen her before, have you? She also has been studying and learning. Look at her. Is she like the sun, the moon, and the stars? Is she like the flowers in this world? No, she is even more beautiful. Would you like to marry her?"

"Yes, I want her!" each of the four disciples quickly replied.

"All of you want her. That's fine. But of course, since she is only one person, she cannot marry all four of you. Therefore, to show that you are capable of taking care of her responsibly, each of you must go out into the world, buy the most valuable thing you can find, and then return and show her what you have bought. She will decide which one of you has made the wisest purchase, and that is the one she will marry. However, keep one thing in mind. This child has finished her learning and could leave this world very soon, perhaps in forty-one days, or in three months, or possibly in six months."

The sheikh then gave one bag of gold to each of the four disciples. And to the arrogant disciple he said, "After you return, we will see about your desire to be a sheikh."

So the four disciples began their journey. As they walked along, each one was thinking, "I must buy something wondrous and rare without letting the others know." And after a few days, the arrogant disciple met a man who had a kettle and a cane for sale. He asked how much they cost.

"One bag of gold," the man answered.

"What can they do?" the arrogant disciple asked.

"They can bring the dead back to life. If you sprinkle a little water from the kettle over someone who is dead and then tap him with the cane, you can revive him."

"Oh, I could bring the dead back to life? That is a wonder! All right, I'll take them." So the arrogant disciple bought the kettle and cane and hid them very carefully.

The next disciple met a man with a very special mirror. "What can this mirror do?" he asked.

"It can show you all that is happening as far away as a six months' journey," the man answered.

"You can see everything?"

"Yes, it will show you anything that you focus your thoughts upon."

"This is indeed a very special mirror! How much does it cost?"

"One bag of gold."

So the second disciple bought the mirror and hid it very carefully.

Then the third disciple met a man who had an amazing chair. "How much does that chair cost?" he asked.

"One bag of gold," the man replied.

"What does it do?"

"If you sit on this chair, it will carry you wherever you wish. In an instant you can complete a journey that would normally take six months." So that disciple bought the chair with his bag of gold.

Finally, the youngest disciple, who had performed his duties with an understanding of the sheikh's qualities, met a man with a pot. "How much is that pot?" he asked.

"One bag of gold," was the reply.

"What will it do?"

"When you reach into the pot, you can take from it anything you can think of, anything you need. If you think of eighteen kinds of curry and rice, they will appear and you can spoon out as much as you need, enough for one person, or for two, or for many more."

"That is truly amazing! There must be nothing else like this in the entire world. All right, I'll buy it."

By now, six months had passed. All four disciples had made their purchases, and so they began their journey home. They walked and walked and walked. The disciple who could restore life, the one who could see the world in the mirror, and the one who could travel anywhere in the chair were all unable to find any food. There was not even one coin left between them. They still had a six months' journey ahead of them, and they were already half dead from hunger. But the one with the pot wasn't tired at all. He was walking behind the others, and whenever he needed food or water, all he had to do was dip into the pot and he could take his fill.

The other three disciples were so exhausted that they were near death. They stopped to rest against the trunk of a tree. After a while the disciple with the pot came along. "What's the matter?" he asked. "Can't you go on anymore?"

"We are going to die!" they gasped. "We have no water or food!" Then they noticed that the youngest disciple looked very healthy and happy. "How have you managed to fare so well?" they asked.

"Don't worry, I can save you." he said. "I have food and water for you." Then he reached into the pot and scooped out some water. As soon as they took the first sip, they felt a bit revived. "Now, would you like something to eat?" he asked, and he scooped out eighteen varieties of curry and rice. But two of the disciples were still too weak to eat, and so he had to feed them by hand.

After they finished eating and their energy returned, the youngest disciple asked, "Now, may I see the things you bought? You have been hiding them. Here is mine, this pot. This is where your food and water came from. I bought what I needed to survive in the world."

The arrogant disciple said, "I bought a kettle and a cane which can restore life to the dead."

The second disciple told them, "I bought a mirror in which I can see everything within the distance of a six months' journey."

And the third disciple said, "I bought a chair which will instantly take me anywhere I wish to go."

"That's very good," the youngest disciple said. "Now let's think about what we should do next. We all share one purpose, we want to marry that beautiful girl. And all four of us bought valuable things, as the sheikh told us to. Now it is up to the girl to decide which thing is the best. But we don't even know where she is, or whether she is alive or dead."

"That's true," the other disciples agreed. "The sheikh said she might not be in this world much longer. Let's look in the mirror and see."

When they looked, they saw that she had already died.

"This is terrible! We went through so much difficulty, and now she is about to be buried. What can we do? How can we get there in time? We still have a six months' journey ahead of us.''

"This chair can complete that journey in half a second,'' said the third disciple.

"And then I can bring her back to life!'' exclaimed the disciple with the kettle and the cane.

So they all climbed onto the chair. Then the one who had bought the chair snapped his fingers, and instantly they found themselves at the cemetery. The grave was already dug, and people were gathering for the burial. Then the disciple who wanted to be a sheikh stepped forward with his kettle and cane and brought the girl back to life. But no sooner was she revived than the four disciples started fighting. "She's mine, she's mine, she's mine!'' they cried.

"She wouldn't be alive if I hadn't given her life! So she's mine!'' said the disciple with the cane.

"You wouldn't even have known what was happening if I hadn't seen that she had died,'' said the disciple with the mirror.

"You would have been too late if I hadn't brought you here!'' said the disciple with the chair.

"Ah yes, but you would all be dead if I hadn't fed you!'' said the disciple with the pot.

And so all four disciples kept on shouting and fighting until finally the girl said, "None of you can decide who will marry me. I must decide who brought the wisest gift.'' Then she took them to a house nearby and instructed them, "All four of you are very clever, and you have brought back four beautiful things. Soon I will give you my decision, but first I am going to lie down on this bed. Each of you must stand in a different corner of the room, and when I call for you, come and sit around me on all four sides. Then I will tell you what I have decided.'' They all agreed.

She lay down, closed her eyes, and seemed to fall asleep. The disciples waited in the four corners of the room, their hearts pounding. Then after a while she said, "All right, now come.''

The one who had restored her life ran to the bed and sat near her head, staring at her. The two who had bought the mirror and the chair sat down on either side of the bed, next to her hands. And the one with the pot sat down at her feet.

"The four of you are very clever,'' she said. Then she spoke to the

*"You were all saved because of his pot. This man can save himself
and others. He is the worthiest, and I will marry him."*

disciple who sat at her head. "You learned to give life to others, but you did not learn how to save your own life. You wanted power. You wanted to become a sheikh, but you did not understand that in order to do so you must first transform yourself. You did not understand the sheikh's beauty, his form, his qualities, or his actions. You did not understand his state. You only wanted power.

"It is true that a real sheikh might have the power to restore life to the dead. And you have acquired that power for yourself, but of what use was it to you? You almost died sitting under that tree. How can you save the lives of others if you are dead? Therefore, what you have learned is useless. Please sit down."

Then she addressed the disciple who had bought the mirror. "You have studied yoga and learned how to fly through your mind. You can perform miracles and read horoscopes. You can even look in that mirror and see whatever you wish, but you haven't learned to look at yourself. One who has not seen himself cannot see God or the beauty of God. You would have known who I really was if you had seen yourself. But you did not look at me in the right way. You were looking at the world, and you wanted to continue looking at the world through this mirror. You were able to see anything in the outside world in a second, but you were unable to see what must be seen within yourself with every breath. This mirror represents the world. But what is the use of looking at the world with the world? What is the use of looking at me? Look at yourself. Understand yourself."

Then she addressed the man on her left side. "What have you attained?" she asked. "You bought the chair which represents the four elements. By using the energies of earth, air, fire, and water, you can go wherever you want on this four-legged chair. This belongs to hell and to the world. The mind can journey faster than this chair can travel, but you have not learned that. You think you have attained a high state, but you are just riding upon the four elements. You think that owning this chair is a great achievement, but it is only a connection to hell. In order to find the power that can take you even faster than the speed of the mind, you must acquire God's qualities and wisdom. They go very fast, faster than the speed of light. Only if you obtain these can you go beyond all the magic tricks of illusion and leave hell behind."

Finally, she spoke to the disciple at her feet. "You are a good man. You spent your money well when you bought this pot. You learned to take care of yourself and others. Like the pot, you have everything you need within yourself. Your heart is a pot that God has made. Reach into your innermost heart, take everything you need, and then satisfy the needs of others. All the treasures of Allah are within the pot of your heart: the grace of God, the peace of God, tranquility, and serenity. When you have an intention, if you use your wisdom, your qualities, and your actions, and if you use the hand of absolute faith, certitude, and determination, the hand of *imān*, you can receive everything you need in full plenitude. Because you have attained this state, you are the worthiest one. Without you, the others would have died."

Again she spoke to the other three disciples, one by one. "Even though you can restore life with your cane and kettle, and even though you can see the world in your mirror, and even though you can go anywhere instantly in your chair, all three of you would be dead without him. You were all saved because of his pot. This man can save himself and others. He is the worthiest, and I will marry him.

"The one who can restore life will be a father to me. Those at my sides will be my brothers. But the one who can save himself and others will be my bridegroom and my student."

Then the beautiful girl disappeared, and the sheikh appeared in her place. He said, "Now you are my student and bridegroom. You are the most worthy of all my students. You have love for me and I have love for you in my heart."

Then the sheikh addressed all of his disciples. "My children, you must study this state and realize that this is wisdom. Anyone intoxicated by my beauty will intoxicate me with his beauty. One who embraces me with his beauty is like a bridegroom to me. One who has established a connection to my heart and is able to save himself and others is a student to me. This is what the state of a true disciple must be.

"If you do not achieve this state, whatever you study will be useless and dangerous. Even if you can restore life, even if you can see all over the world, even if you learn how to travel by means of the elements—what good are all these tricks if you cannot save yourself?

"Study your own state. If you love the sheikh in your heart, you will be his student. If you embrace him there, you will be a bridegroom to that beauty. In that state, the sheikh is a woman. He is the beauty, and he is the one who gives you your beauty. He is also a man and a father. He is the qualities. He is wisdom. Everything is within him. He is a pot from which you can take everything you need and thus end your tiredness. Then you can save yourself and others. This is what you must do."

And to the arrogant disciple who wanted to be a sheikh, he said, "Now do you understand? Establish that state. Everything else is useless."

My love you, my grandchildren. Think about this. When you are with the sheikh, your father of wisdom, you must imbibe his qualities and actions. Then you will be able to save yourself and end the tiredness of others. Do you understand? This is the point of the story. Āmīn.

May God's wisdom, the wealth of His qualities, the wealth of divine knowledge, and the wealth of all of God's treasures be given to you. May your arrogance leave you, and may the peace of equality come to you. Āmīn. Āmīn.

*"Chitti! Chitti!" cries the warning bird. "Danger!
A hunter is coming with a gun!"*

The Warning Bird

ome, my grandchildren, let's go out into the open space of the park. Look at all the lovely birds! Do you see that tiny black and white bird? Its yellow legs look like delicate twigs. This small, pretty bird lives in the forests and meadows and feeds upon the insects that live near the pond. It lays its eggs in cow pastures, covers them, and then watches over them until they hatch.

Look, the bird saw us and is flying away, screeching. The rest of the birds are also fleeing. Even the rabbits are racing away.

This bird is a lapwing. It is called the warning bird. Without sleeping day or night, it sits high up in the trees, and the moment it sees or hears any sign of danger, it flies around and around, calling out, "Chitti! Chitti! Chitti!" It cries out, "Danger! Someone is coming! Something is coming! A lion is coming! A tiger! A man! Danger! Run! A hunter is coming with a gun! Danger is here! Run! Run! Run!" Then all the other birds and animals flee to safety. This is the work of the warning bird.

My love you, my children. Do you see how this unique bird carefully keeps watch with its subtle eyes? Were you watching? Did you see how it protects the other birds and animals? What a rare quality this is! It is always attentive so that it can warn others before danger comes.

My love you, my grandsons and granddaughters. In the same way our wisdom must always be careful and attentive. Our wisdom must be ever watchful and ever sharp. The compassion of God's truth must warn everyone of danger before it arrives. Our love must protect other lives. Our wisdom and compassion must be eternally watchful and vigilant. If we are in this state, then the lives of others can be protected.

211

There are four hundred trillion, ten thousand dangers that arise from mind and desire. Every time one of these approaches, wisdom must rise up and give warning. Every second, wisdom must be alert for the possibility of an accident. Every second love must go out to protect all lives. Compassion must call out, "Run! Run! Escape! Go and hide within God!" Our good qualities, good conduct, modesty, sincerity, reserve, fear of wrongdoing, compassion, and wisdom must give the warning, "Danger! Go and hide in God!" Wisdom must speak from the heart, warning us every time a bad thought arises, so that our good qualities can run and hide in surrender to Allah. When evil qualities come, wisdom must fight them off with faith, certitude, and determination. Then it can call back the good qualities, saying, "Come, everything is safe now," and they can return to a peaceful state.

My love you, gems of my eyes. Wisdom is always there, guarding, warning, and protecting the treasures of God. In everything that happens, our wisdom must protect our good qualities, our lives and other lives. The sharpness of that wisdom must be ever vigilant, without sleeping day or night. Like the lapwing, our wisdom should always be awake, even when we ourselves are asleep. It must be aware at all times, with every breath. Love, wisdom, and compassion must never sleep.

My grandchildren, protect all lives as you protect your own. With love, compassion, and wisdom, protect the qualities of God within. Then you can find peace. Think about this and strengthen these qualities with faith, certitude, and determination. Then, in times of danger, you can escape and help others to escape as well. Think about this, my grandchildren.

The Three Times of Light

y love you, my grandchildren. Let us go out for a while. It's growing dark now, although a slight glow still lingers in the sky. There is enough light to discern shapes and forms, but it is difficult to tell exactly what they are. Look, we can see the outline of that tree ahead, but we cannot see if anything is lying on the ground beneath it. So we must be careful as we walk toward it, or we might meet with an accident.

My grandchildren, man's intellect is like that slight glow. What it can show you is limited. It is as limited as the slight glow or glitter that can be seen in anything made of the five elements of earth, fire, water, air, and ether. Anything with a form can reflect light, but this only provides a small amount of illumination. The same is true of the intellect. It too is only a glimmer in the darkness, a reflection from another source. It cannot dispel the darkness nor penetrate the clouds that prevent you from fully knowing what lies beyond. The intellect can give you only a tiny bit of clarity. It is not enough to prevent accidents. You cannot proceed safely using only your intellect.

However, there is something beyond intellect. There is a sense of judgment, subtle wisdom, analytic wisdom, and divine luminous wisdom. Only with wisdom can we see clearly and understand deeply. We need wisdom.

Now the moon has risen, and it has become lighter. Earlier there was only a small amount of light, which was like a shadow of a shadow, but now we can see by the cool yellow light of the moon. The coolness of that moonlight is similar to man's sense of judgment, which develops through his prayers to God. Just as the moon rises and dispels the darkness, judgment comes and shows man the nature of things. It helps him to see things for what they really are, and it

213

Faith comforts our hearts like the coolness of the moon, but the fullness of wisdom is hot and bright like the sun.

helps him to see the path.

It is through our connection to God in prayer and worship that this coolness can be known. Our relationship to God is the wealth that we receive from prayer, and it is through this connection that we can better understand the world and ourselves. That relationship is very cooling, very enjoyable, and very loving. Through prayer and *dhikr,* the remembrance of God, we can see that bliss within ourselves and proceed happily on our journey. At that point the journey of life is very sweet and our prayers are very sweet. They give us peace.

If we have the faith which can establish this relationship to God within us, it will bring a cooling comfort to the heart, like the coolness of the moon. Let us enjoy that coolness and happiness, as we proceed on our way and finish our journey.

Ah, my grandchildren, morning has dawned. The cool light of the moon has gone, and the rising sun is burning away the morning fog.

It is daylight now and the fullness of wisdom has dawned.

Children, when wisdom emerges within us, it is very hot and very bright, like the sun. In that complete light everything can be seen. When that resplendence comes to your life, all your connections to the world will be burned away, just as the sun burns away the morning fog. When wisdom dawns, all the clouds of life will be burned away, and all your sorrows and sadnesses dispelled. Torpor, illusion, and the darkness in the world will try to come to you, but they will not affect you.

When your full wisdom and the fullness of the purity of the soul emerge, the world within you will be destroyed by the heat. You will have attained the fullness of the grace of God and will have become the children of God. His power, which is the light, will come into you and be working within you. That inner development will show that you are His son. God and His power will be your life.

My love you, my grandchildren, my sisters and brothers, my sons and daughters. Think of each thing that exists in your life and try to understand it. May you attain the fullness of His grace. *Āmīn.*

The Boy Who Liked Good Conduct

y love you, my grandchildren, my sons and daughters, my brothers and sisters. It is six o'clock in the morning now, a good time to travel. So come, let's go to the park.

Look how many people are here. Do you see that boy standing all alone, looking so unhappy? He seems worried about something. Let's ask him what's wrong.

"My son, the other children are playing happily with their parents, but you are standing here all alone, looking sad. What's the matter? What are you worrying about?"

"My parents and my brothers and sisters don't care about me. They are too busy playing ball and running about. They haven't noticed the unhappiness in my face. But you seem to understand me. You talk to me so lovingly, and that makes me happy. When I look at the faces of the children who are with you, I see such good qualities that I think you must be a wise man, a *gnāni*. And because you are acting like a father to me, I feel I can tell you why I am sad.

"Whenever we come here or go to the seashore and I see my parents laughing, playing, and rolling around on the ground, I want to cry. The girls run around and hold up their dresses, and don't cover themselves properly. That upsets me. My older brothers and sisters like to do the same things my parents do, but even though I am only nine years old, I don't want to do these things.

"My parents aren't teaching us modesty, sincerity, respect, or fear of wrongdoing. They don't tell us about good qualities, good conduct, love, or wisdom. Instead they are teaching us to play around and waste away our lives.

"This is not right. We should wake up early in the morning and pray to God. Then before we go to school, we should review our lessons so we can answer all the teacher's questions. But because my parents brought us to the park, prayer time has passed and so has my study time. My teacher will be angry if I'm not prepared. I wanted to work on my lessons this morning, but my parents made us come to the park. And when I complained, they just said, 'Oh, you can study later, you silly bookworm! We're all going, so you must too. Come on, we have to lock the house.' If I try to study this evening, it will be too noisy. My parents will be laughing and entertaining their friends until very late with music, stories, beer, and brandy.

"Some nights they go out visiting. They put us to sleep in our rooms, turn off the lights, and leave. As soon as they're gone, my brothers and sisters sneak out to the movies or to visit their friends or go dancing. And I'm left all alone in the house. They are following our parents' example, and I worry about how they will end up.

"When I think about this, I feel like my life is being wasted. I don't want to live anymore. I keep wondering why God created me. Why was I born on this earth to these parents? If I am going to live, I should be able to conduct my life in a proper way. Otherwise I should leave this world now. Why won't God take me back?

"God didn't give me the desire to do such things. Everyone teases me and calls me 'the scholar'. They don't seem to understand my feelings or my state of mind. As long as they are like this, I can't do anything."

"My son, you should advise your parents and then do what you have to do. Study your lessons."

"I've tried to talk to them many times, but they always scold me and shout, 'What! Are you trying to give us advice? You think you're so great!' They ridicule me and hit me on the head and yell, 'Go away!'

"My brothers and sisters don't want to study or learn. They only like to play. But I don't. I started school when I was five, and before I am twenty-one I have to firmly establish my learning and acquire good qualities and actions. If I build a good life now, I know my future will be all right. But look at the way these adults act here in the park. They don't care about such things.

"Many parents nowadays are the cause for their children going bad. My parents aren't the only ones like this. So much disappointment, sorrow, and fatigue come to children today because their parents teach them to be failures instead of successes. Isn't this

"My son, you should advise your parents and then do what you have to do."

so? You are a wise man. Tell me.''

"It is true, my child. That is how the world is in this century. Well, if you feel this way, then ask permission from your parents to attend a boarding school so that you can study.''

"Oh, my wise father, when I asked them to just give me a separate place where I could sit and study quietly, they teased me even more, saying, 'Oh yes, we'll build you a big university, a palace to be by yourself. You think you are a *gnāni,* a god, a great learned man!'

"They don't have faith in God. When I told them I wanted to pray, they just handed me a Bible and told me to read it. But they never go to church or read the Bible. Many parents are like that. They just give their children the Qur'an, the Bible, the Torah, or the Puranas, but they themselves don't know the value of these books. In fact, they don't even know what's in them. They just keep these books in their homes and have no love for the truth or wisdom contained within them.

"O great one, this is what I am worrying about. When I look at the children with you, I see such good conduct and good qualities. Their faces are happy, and that makes me happy. I don't think you came here to play or jump around. I think you came to teach the children. You are a real father.''

"What you say is true, child. If you wish, you also can find a wise man and stay by his side to learn about life and all the other things you want to know.''

"O great one, my parents will not permit that. They won't even let me visit such a man. They don't want me to learn good conduct or wisdom. Their words and actions seem to say, 'We don't care what happens to you or how bad you become, just as long as you stay with us. Be bad, but stay with us.' They want me to do the same things they do. I can't describe the torment they cause me in my life. If I go to a wise man they will cause him trouble, disgrace him, and dishonor him. I can't do anything about this. And I keep wondering why God created me.''

"My little brother, what you say is true. The world today is like that. But your time will come, and when it does, God will protect you. He has given your heart this awareness, good conduct, and the wisdom to want to learn. Have faith in God and you will receive goodness from that faith, certitude, and determination. Go and be happy. God will help you fulfill your intentions and your duties. Some day we will talk with your parents and brothers and sisters.

"Come closer, my son. Think about what I am saying. No matter how much dirt may cover a gem, the light still exists within it. Isn't that true? Like that, no matter what sorrow or difficulty covers your life, still your effort and striving, your duty and wisdom must always shine.

"It is your own responsibility to focus your attention on the right point whenever you try to pray or study. If your heart and wisdom are focused correctly, you will not hear all those distracting noises around you. Establish your connection to the one point of truth, and outside sounds will not disturb you.

"Like a gem whose light remains within it, even though it is buried in the dirt, you should try to develop that one-pointedness, no matter what circumstances surround you. If you worry about the noises and distractions, you will suffer and your joy will be lost. So don't waste time thinking about these things. Melt your heart and focus on that point. Then you will find peace in your life.

"My little brother, it's good that you understand your present state. When you grow up, you must change things and establish a better way."

My precious grandchildren, did you hear what this boy said? When you have children, you must bring them up in a good way. You cannot give them only a body and a life, you must also teach them love, trust, and affection for God. You must try to raise your children to reach a good state. For the sake of their wisdom, good conduct, and happiness, you must be the kind of parents who bring good things to their lives. Then they will not acquire bad qualities or go on evil paths.

If parents conduct themselves in a good way and teach their children the right things, the children will not go astray. My beloved grandchildren, when the time comes, this is how you must look after your own children.

Let us go on our way now. May God help you. _Āmīn_.

How to Build a Bridge to God

y love you, my grandchildren, my brothers and sisters, my daughters and sons. Do you see the mountain just beyond the one we are standing on now? Somehow we have to cross the jungle that lies below us and reach that other mountain. How shall we do it? Look, over there is a very narrow bridge. So many men and cattle and goats are using that bridge to cross to the other side without having to go through the dense jungle.

My grandchildren, think about this. We are in the east now, and there is a deep abyss that we must cross in order to reach the west. Monkeys, bears, scorpions, poisonous snakes, and lions and tigers lurk in that jungle below. Look carefully into the depths of that abyss. Do you see the demons, ghosts, and spirits? Do you see the illusion, the darkness, and the torpor?

If we fall into this deep pit, do you think we'll ever be able to escape? No, if we fall while crossing, we're finished. So what must we do to cross safely? We need to build a bridge between the two points. On this side is wisdom and on the other side is God. Only if we reach God will our souls be free, so we must construct a bridge between wisdom and God.

Now, what materials do we need? We need faith, certitude, and determination. And how should we go about building that bridge? First we must construct the pillars of faith. Next we need to position strong supports made of God's three thousand loving and gracious qualities. And once we have carefully put these pillars and supports in place, we can lay down the planks of love and walk across to God's house.

My love you, my grandchildren. If we don't build a bridge with these materials, then the distance between east and west will be far

*Once we have put the pillars and supports in place, we can
lay down the planks of love and walk across to God's house.*

too great and the journey much too difficult for us. If we don't have faith and wisdom, we won't even be able to start building that bridge. If we don't have good qualities for supports and if we don't have the planks of love, then we will fall, and the ravenous beasts below will devour us.

My grandchildren, this is the world. This is what is called hell. It is full of evil beasts who eat the sins of the world. And if you fall into this dark abyss, you will become food for those beasts. They will not spare you for even one minute. To cross this world we need a bridge, but most people don't construct their bridge correctly, and so they fall into the pit below and become victims of hell. Attracted by the smell of blood, the jackals and foxes come and devour their remains, and in the end not even their bones are left. They are completely destroyed.

Come children, bring all the equipment. Let us begin to construct the bridge now. First, using divine analytic wisdom, firmly plant the pillars of faith. They must be put in place very subtly and carefully, because they are the foundation upon which the bridge will be built. Next, bring the gracious qualities of your Father and position these supports carefully. Right, that's the way to do it. Once the pillars and posts are in place, we can lay down the planks of love and complete the bridge.

Now we need a light, the light of wisdom, so that we can see clearly and walk across that bridge without falling. Come, follow me. Look down and you can see the ghosts and demons and beasts watching us in frustration. Listen to them howling. They are standing there dumbfounded that we have escaped. Their mouths are hanging wide open in surprise.

At last we are free! We have crossed over to our Father. We have been released from the cage of the five elements. We have escaped from that prison! Now we can begin to study our Father's kingdom. We can analyze it without interference. This is the reason we built the bridge to God.

Now that we have completed it, others can also cross safely to our Father. We can bring our brothers, our sisters, and our relations and friends across the bridge. We can take them by the hand, protect them, and help them to cross. Come, let's bring the others across.

My love you, my children. This is the way to reach God. Let us strive to build that bridge, so that we and all our brothers and sisters can cross the pit of hell and reach God. *Āmīn. Āmīn.*

We Appear One Day
and Disappear the Next

y love you, my grandchildren. Look at the birds flying in the sky, soaring above the trees and over the rooftops. They are searching for food. All day long they fly about in order to satisfy the hunger of their stomachs, but at twilight they must return to their nests. Man also searches for food to satisfy his one-span stomach. Even the ant has a one-span stomach which he must fill with food.

Our life lasts for but one day. We appear one day and disappear the next. All of us have to return, just as the bird must return to its nest. We must go back to the nest of God's kingdom. This is certain.

We appear for a day and when it becomes dark we have to go. Every minute, every second, time is moving on. Yet we waste all our time trying to satisfy our stomachs. We think of the infinite as finite and the finite as infinite. It is ignorant to think like that, because at any moment we might have to leave the world. Destruction could come to us at any moment. In an instant, we could forget the truth and do what is wrong.

Each child must think and believe with certitude in that which is truly infinite. We must understand that everything which is finite can change at any moment. And yet we still have to perform our duties in this world in the proper way. If we understand the good that we can do here before we have to leave, it will be beneficial for us. Then that one day which exists between our appearance and our disappearance will not be wasted.

We have to think about this and try to act according to what is right. My love you.

*Goats run about playfully butting one another, but
sheep graze in a quiet and orderly way.*

The Wandering Goats
and the Peaceful Sheep

y love you, my grandchildren, let's walk over there where the sheep and goats are grazing. Look how beautiful they are. Do you see the white goats with horns? Look how they run this way and that, jumping up and down, playfully butting one another. They take a bite of grass here and a bite there, a mouthful of this and a mouthful of that. But look how the sheep graze in a quiet and orderly way, eating as they slowly move along. Can you see the difference between the goats and the sheep?

My grandchildren, there are many human beings who act like these wandering goats. They go around nipping and biting at everything in the world, saying, "This is good, that is good. This is a miracle, that is truth. This is God, that is God." Just as the goats can never fill their stomachs, these ignorant people will never have peace in their hearts. Because they lack wisdom they are always wandering, taking a little bit here and a little bit there. They have not steadfastly searched for good conduct, good qualities, modesty, sincerity, respect, fear of wrongdoing, prayer, worship, the peace of the soul, and the wisdom which can establish a connection between the soul and God. Therefore, their hearts will never be filled with God's qualities, God's wealth, or God's grace.

My grandchildren, look again at the sheep grazing so carefully. Do they waste their time running about? No, they simply go about their work. Just as the sheep found a grassy field where they could graze, a man who has faith, certitude, determination, and wisdom must strive to find a connection to God. Such a man will not wander. Once he finds a place that is plentiful in wisdom, love, good qualities, good actions, and good conduct, he will remain there and learn. There his soul will search for God's beautiful qualities, His grace, and His wealth, and he will fill his heart with love and wisdom. He will be able to fulfill all his needs and lead a peaceful, tranquil life by day and by night. That freedom will release him from the world, and he will be able to obtain the resplendent, pure beauty of the soul. He will acquire God's compassion and perfect completeness. He will have peace in his life, in the kingdom of the soul, in the kingdom of the world, and in the kingdom of God.

One who is not in this state, however, will always think the grass is greener somewhere else. His mind will wander about like a goat, and it will never know peace, tranquility, or love.

My love you, my grandchildren. Control that mind which runs about. Then with faith, certitude, and determination, make wisdom shine. If you fill your hearts with beauty and good qualities, you will gain victory in your life and receive the grace, perfection, and beauty of God. Think about this. Make the effort to obtain His wisdom, His love, and His qualities. *Āmīn.*

The Waves That Break
on the Shore of Truth

My love you, my grandchildren. Shall we go to the seashore? Look how vast the ocean is. As its huge waves crash against the sand, the ocean has the arrogant thought of "I, I, I," but it cannot go beyond this boundary. It is forced to retreat in little ripples and slip back to the ocean with only a whisper. The shore was built by God, not by man. He built it so that the ocean could not rise up and destroy the city that lies beyond. It is God's protection.

My grandchildren, just as the ocean says, "I, I, I," men say, "I will do this. I will do that. I, I, I can do anything." They say, "Who is this God? No such thing exists. Everything just evolved naturally. It is all nature. What is God to me?" This is how people talk.

Man is like the waves. Every day he beats against the qualities of God with his money, his arrogance, and his pride and egoism. He rushes forward saying, "I, I, I," but when he comes up against the shore of truth, it remains firm and overpowers him. His strength diminishes and he has to retreat, like the waves that break upon the shore.

Man can never overcome truth, for it is a strong natural shore which God has established. The truth has the strength of God and can never be broken by the I. Man can never destroy God, good qualities, or truth. They are protected. He might strike out at goodness, but he will never succeed. Man will never be able to harm truth; he will only destroy himself. He may boast, "I am powerful. I am going to break the power of God," but he will surely lose the battle and end up as food for dogs and foxes and the worms of the earth. The egoism of the I and the possessiveness that proclaims, "Mine!" will inevitably torture and destroy anyone who possesses them.

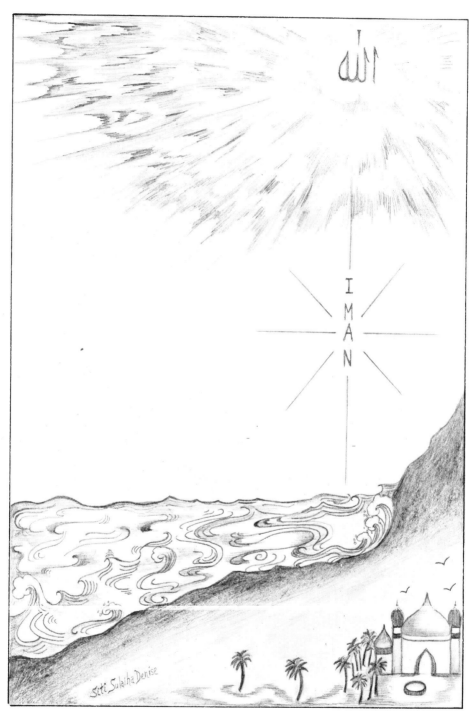

*The huge waves crash against the sand but are
forced to retreat in little ripples, with only a whisper.*

My love you, my grandchildren. If truth were to turn on man, he would be destroyed. But truth is not like man, it is silent. It does not shout, "I, I, I." It is a mysterious silence. This shore of truth within you was put there by God. He built it to protect the city of your heart, which lies beyond the shore. Anyone who believes in this protection will be strengthened by it. If your faith is strong, then as the waves of ignorance, illusion, darkness, and torpor break upon the shore, their force will subside and they will retreat. In fact, the shore will be strengthened by the sand that the waves deposit.

Man must have faith. He must trust in the truth and the power of God. Then he will never be hurt, no matter how many waves of evil come to oppose him in the world. They will go away by themselves without harming him. They might break on him and cause some pain, but ultimately they will go away.

My love you, my grandchildren. You have to think about this. Strengthen that shore of truth. Strengthen the treasure which is a mystery in your heart. Then nothing can ever attack or harm you, because you will be protected. My love you.

My grandchildren, now that you have seen all the different kinds of people in this marketplace, can you tell who is good and who is evil?

Who Is Good in
This Marketplace of the World?

y love you, my grandchildren, my sons and daughters, my brothers and sisters. It is mid-morning now. Shall we go outside for a while? Look at the crowds of people in that large marketplace over there. Some are on bicycles, some are in cars and wagons, and some are walking. Some are carrying bags and some are empty-handed. People of different races and colors are all happily browsing about the marketplace. Many are well-dressed, but as we walk along we can also see a lot of poor beggars who are blind or are missing an arm or a leg. There are also others who have all their limbs but beg because they are lazy. Some people give alms to the beggars and some do not. Some just yell at them.

My love you, my grandchildren. Now that you have seen all the different kinds of people in this marketplace, can you tell who is good and who is evil? Who is high and who is low in status? Or who God will accept? Will He accept someone because of his title, clothing, or money? Will He accept someone because he arrives in a car? As we look at these people is there any sign that will tell us who God will accept? No, there is no such sign at all.

Who does God accept? He accepts anyone who is good. But who is good? What makes a person good? My grandchildren, anyone who becomes a good person in his heart is considered good by Allah. Anyone who has corrected his own faults is good. Anyone who has transformed his qualities and rid himself of all vengeance, deceit, separation, treachery, and prejudice is a good man. Anyone who has eliminated anger, arrogance, karma, illusion, jealousy, pride, and love of praise is a good man.

Anyone who regards the hunger of others as his own, the sorrow and pain of others as his own, the illness and suffering of others as his own is a good human being. Anyone who sees these difficulties in others, then helps them and makes them peaceful is a good man.

233

Anyone who does not look at the faults of others but instead looks at his own faults and asks for forgiveness is a good man.

One who acts with Allah's three thousand beautiful qualities and His ninety-nine actions, or *wilāyats,* is a good man. One who performs his duty to the soul, duty to the people, duty to the world, and duty to Allah is a good man. One who has the absolute faith, certitude, and determination called *īmān* and who searches for Allah's qualities with wisdom and divine knowledge, or *'ilm,* is a good man. One whose heart is filled with inner patience, contentment, trust in God, and praise to God is a good man. These qualities are the beginning of *Īmān-Islām.* One who takes these qualities into his heart and acts accordingly is a good man. Such a man is acceptable to God.

There is none other than *Allāhu ta'ālā,* the Almighty God, to whom all worship is due. He is the Unfathomable Ruler of grace, the One who is incomparable love. All praise is due to Him. Anyone who performs God's duty will be a good man in the universe of the soul, in this world, and in the next world. He will be a good person to the community of man, to himself, to his heart, and to Allah.

My grandchildren, Allah will call a person of such plenitude a good human being. Allah will accept him, embrace him, protect him, and watch over him. Such a man is intermingled with truth, justice, and love. Allah will do His part, and that man will do his part. They will join together to serve others in this world and the next.

My children, this world is a marketplace in which God has placed millions of creations. In this market, a good man is one with good qualities. Allah will give him the wealth of the three worlds, the wealth of grace, the wealth of divine knowledge, the wealth of wisdom, the wealth of absolute faith, and the wealth of perfection. One who attains this wealth finds peace, tranquility, and serenity in this world and the next.

But one who has not attained these good qualities cannot know peace. Serenity will not exist in such a man. Clothing, honors, worldly status, poverty or wealth—none of these will give him peace. The external things in his life will never make him a good person. You must think about this a little. Do your duty and live as a good person. Then Allah will accept you and take you into Himself.

My love you, jeweled lights of my eyes. Believe in God with absolute certainty, do not just pretend to believe in Him. You cannot deceive God, and it is very dangerous to try to do so. Instead, my children, pretend to believe in the world, but do not really believe in it. That also is very dangerous. You cannot tread firmly on this world. Escape from the dangers in the marketplace of the world, walk lightly, and do your duty.

My love you. Give love to all lives, and then you will be a good human being. May Allah give you all of His blessings. *Āmīn*.

When a crocodile kills, it buries the carcass in the mud.

Why the Crocodile
Buries Its Food in the Mud

y love you, my grandchildren, my brothers and sisters, my sons and daughters. Will you come with me to a crocodile farm? Here men raise crocodiles so that they can make shoes and handbags from their skins.

It is feeding time now. Look at those huge open mouths and all those teeth! Man has only thirty-two teeth, but the crocodile's mouth is much bigger, and it is filled with teeth. If you watch closely, however, you will see that the crocodile is not using its teeth to chew. The man is feeding it small pieces of meat, and the crocodile is just gulping them down.

The crocodile is not the only animal that does not chew its food. Lions and tigers tear large pieces off their prey and swallow them whole. But there is a difference between a crocodile and a lion or tiger. The crocodiles here are able to swallow without chewing only because someone has already cut the meat into pieces. But in the wild, when a crocodile catches and kills a dog, a goat, or even a man, it buries them in the mud. After the flesh rots, the crocodile digs the carcass up again and then eats it.

Why does it do this? The crocodile's upper and lower teeth do not meet evenly, so it cannot chew the raw flesh of its prey. But after the flesh has decayed, it is softer and easier to eat.

My grandchildren, there are certain similarities between the crocodile and man. Although man is able to chew, he eats like a crocodile, snapping up his food without thinking. He will eat meat or anything, even if it smells awful. He does not think about right and wrong or good and evil. And instead of chewing on something with wisdom, he gulps it down whole.

Some people have the wisdom of a crocodile. They take what is good, bury it, and wait for it to rot. After it goes bad, they eat it. No matter how much wisdom they are given or how many good qualities they are taught, they will bury such things in the mud of ignorance within the lair of the five elements. Such a man will imbibe what he has been given only after all its goodness has decayed.

This crocodile behavior shows in all man's qualities and actions. He takes the words of God, His wisdom, justice, and compassion, His unity and peacefulness, His qualities and actions, and even prayer to God, and he buries them in the dark hell of ignorance and illusion, leaving them to rot. Later he returns to take only the meanings that are convenient and acceptable to his own intellect. He eats only what is easy for him to swallow and lets everything else decay. He brings all that is good down to the level of his own crocodile qualities before he eats it. No matter how much you teach such a person about human qualities, actions, and wisdom, he will ruin them by bringing them down to the mud of his own state.

My grandchildren, God's qualities must be understood with God's qualities, and God's wisdom must be understood with His wisdom. You must try to understand wisdom in a place where God's qualities and actions exist. Go to a man of wisdom and learn from him. All the treasures you need are hidden within him. With faith, take what he has to give. Bury what he teaches you in wisdom before you try to take it in. When he talks about the qualities of God, bury your qualities in God's qualities and then partake of them. When he speaks about God's justice, bury it in justice and then taste it.

Don't be like the crocodile. Don't take what the sheikh gives you and bury it in ignorance. If you bury what is God's within the intellect and illusion, you will see the illusory qualities of maya: the decay and stench of doubt, suspicion, arrogance, karma, darkness, and torpor. But if you bury what is God's within the realm of God, you will understand its secret, its meaning, and its blissful grace. Only then will you obtain the peace and happiness of life and know the ways of justice. Only then will you understand and obtain freedom.

My loving grandchildren, you must try to find meaning in your life. You must try to find grace and wisdom. That will be of great benefit to you. Please understand this. My love you.

The Peace of the Mango Tree

y love you, my grandchildren. Come over and sit by the mango tree. I have a question I want to ask it.

"O beautiful mango tree who gives us such refreshing shade, do you have peace? If you do, could you teach us how to have peace? You seem so cool and tranquil. What makes you this way? Can you tell us?"

Children, come closer and listen carefully to the mango tree's answer.

"I am a member of the tree family, and you are human beings. I do not know if you can understand our peace. Even though God has given you judgment, subtle wisdom, analytic wisdom, and divine luminous wisdom, you also have qualities that cause you to take our fruits, cut us down, and destroy us.

"If you want to attain peace, do not cut down a tree, whether it is useful to you or not. And don't cut down a man, whether he does good deeds or bad. If, because of your pride or selfishness, you think about taking revenge or deceiving and ruining another person, or of making another man suffer in any way, that will destroy your peace. It is your own state of mind that will destroy your peace. But if you can avoid bad thoughts, then you can be happy and peaceful. This is my advice to you.

"Look at me. Here I stand at the crossroads. Many people come this way. As soon as I start to blossom, they throw stones at me to make my flowers fall. They climb and swing on my branches, but I don't mind. Even when they hit me and shake me and take my fruits, I am happy. Some people and some animals and birds like my fruits while they are still unripe. Others like them after they have ripened. When they bite into my mangoes and taste them, they become happy and peaceful, and that gives me peace. The peace they find by eating my fruits and satisfying their hunger gives me peace. When I am happy in this way, I can be so cooling and provide shade for others, and that adds to their peace and happiness. When they feel peaceful, I am peaceful. That is my secret. That is what makes me grow, bear fruit, and give cooling shade.

"If you human beings want happiness, you should be like this. No matter what happens in the world, even if you are beaten or attacked by your enemies, you should be very patient and show them compassion and love. If you help your enemies, then the peace they gain will be your peace. This is my advice to you."

My grandchildren, did you listen carefully to what the mango tree said? Did you understand? Trees have so many good qualities, even though they were created with only three levels of consciousness. They have only feeling, awareness and intellect, but God created you with four higher levels of consciousness as well. God gave you exalted wisdom. If you would use that wisdom to attain at least the state of the mango tree, you would find peace and tranquility.

My grandchildren, as you journey through life, use your wisdom in this way. Do not waste your intelligence seeking revenge against others, because while you are chasing after someone else, your own work will be ruined. When you commit yourself to such devious work, you stray from your own path. The distance which separates you from God will become greater and greater, and you will suffer so much.

It happens this way in the world. Anyone who focuses on hurting others abandons his own path. He neglects his prayers and worship and forgets his good qualities. Because of this, he loses his peace and tranquility, and his life is subjected to sorrow and suffering. But the one who turns to God and focuses upon his own qualities, his own work, and his own path will have an exalted and serene life.

We came to this world by the command of our Father, and while we are here we must live by His commandments and establish our connection to Him. We must complete our duties in a way that fulfills those commandments, and then we must return to Him. That is our work. If we can do that, we will have peace in this world, in the next world, and in the world of the souls.

My grandchildren, think deeply about this. Do your own work and your own duty. Even when you are attacked by others, if you are good to them, it will bring peace to you. My love you. Be like the mango tree.

Some kingfishers came to eat, like those sitting on the bushes.
Whenever they see a fish, they dive down and seize it in their beaks.

The Selfish Kingfishers

y love you, my grandchildren, my sons and daughters, my brothers and sisters. Let's walk over to the pond. Look at all the different birds. Why do you think they came here? Some came to eat, like those kingfishers sitting on the bushes near the shore. Whenever they see a fish, they dive down and seize it in their beaks. That is their nature.

But birds that don't eat fish have also gathered at the pond. What have they come to do? Let's watch for a while. Ah! They are bathing. See how they stand in the shallow water and flap their wings? First they dip their beaks into the water, then plunge their heads in and let the water run down their backs. The small birds are bathing in shallow pools and the large birds in deeper water. They are washing away the dirt and insects from their wings and bodies.

My grandchildren, like this, there are also two kinds of people in the world, the kind that wash their hearts and their lives and the kind that eat every aspect of the world in order to satisfy their selfishness.

The selfish people come to the pond only to catch fish. Even if they fall right into the water of truth, they will not bathe and cleanse themselves. Even if they fall into wisdom, they will not absorb it. Even if they fall into God, they will not bathe in the plenitude of His light. They will not take what they need from Him. All their awareness and attention will be directed toward capturing the world.

Such people are like kingfishers. They do what they want and take what they want. They do not cleanse or purify themselves. They do not try to heal their illnesses. Even though Allah and the truth are so close to them, they only want the world. Even though goodness and faith are close to them, they only want hell. They eat the world, its pleasures, and its illnesses. These selfish people might live close by that pure water, in a place of goodness, but they only want the world.

The other kind of people come to cleanse themselves of ignorance, no matter what difficulties they might have to undergo in the process. They will come from great distances in order to wash their hearts.

This is the way it is in the world. Some people who come from a place of goodness only want evil, while others who come from evil places seek to cleanse and free themselves.

So, my grandchildren, whether you come from the city or the jungle or forest or anywhere else, once you see the truth, you should use it to wash away your ignorance and lack of wisdom. No matter where you are coming from, fall into Allah and bathe. Immerse yourselves in His qualities and absorb them. Absorb wisdom and attain freedom.

You must do that. When you do, it will wash away the karma of your birth. *Anbu.* My love you, my grandchildren. Please understand this.

God's Secrets Are in the Brain

y love you, my children. God's secrets are in your brain. Have you ever seen a picture of the brain? Does the picture show you where these secrets are? No, but they are there. You must search for them. You must delve into the brain with wisdom, locate those secrets, and put them to use.

To do this, you must follow the correct procedure, step by step. It is just like making clarified butter, or ghee, from milk. First you must separate the cream from the milk and then churn the cream until it solidifies and becomes butter. Next you melt the butter and pour off the clarified ghee as it rises to the surface. In this clarified form the milk has many uses.

My grandchildren, you have to do the same thing with your brain. Everything is contained within it. First you must churn it, then melt it and clarify it. Only then will you be able to receive the benefits from it. If you do not, it will remain hard, and it will be very difficult to work with.

Every single matter in your life must be churned and melted and clarified. If you do that, God's secrets will be yours. My love you, my children. *Āmīn*.

*Not every stone that sparkles is a gem. You must look for the light that
shines forever, day and night, at all moments, in all lives.*

Glitters of the Night

y love you, my grandchildren. Come, let us go out into the night. Even though it is dark, if you look around you, you can see many things shining and glittering. Look how the ocean shines in the darkness. There are so many sparkles dancing on the water's surface. These sparkles are caused by a certain kind of plankton which glows in the dark. Along the road nearby there are also glittery specks in the stones that shine. There is even a luminosity on certain leaves which reflect bits of light. You can see all these glitters at night, but are they real lights?

No, my grandchildren, these are the glitters of creation. The sparkle they have is not real. Even a drop of water that falls on an asphalt road will glitter, but it is not a true and lasting light. And do not think that every stone which sparkles is a gem. These many-colored glitters that can be seen in stones, trees, bushes, and vines are just a dream, just an aspect of creation. They are not miracles; they are natural occurrences. If you shine a light on these glitters, they will disappear and you will see only the object itself. If you turn the light off again, the glitters will reappear.

My grandchildren, look at that lightning bug blinking on and off. Is its light a miracle? No, it is just something God gave to that creation. There is even a kind of fish that has on its forehead a luminous spot which glows in the water. That is not a miracle either. It is just something God created to help that fish find its food. You can discover so many things like this in God's creation. Anything that has a form is made of the five elements and contains the glitters of the five elements. There is a shine in the trees and rocks, in earth, air, fire, water, and ether. Man's form is also made of the five elements, and he too has all these glitters.

My love you, my children. Be careful, for it is dark now and we can barely see the road. But if we shine our flashlight on the center line of the road, the fluorescent paint will glow. Without our light, it will not shine. This is no great wonder, this is just man-made paint.

Man has also discovered another kind of fluorescence, which he calls prayer. Its shine comes from the intellect. As soon as you turn on the small light of your intellect, prayer will shine, but when your intellect stops, the light is gone. Is this kind of prayer wisdom? Is it a miracle? No, it is only something the mind has discovered.

You can recite mantras or prayers for earth, women, and gold. You can repeat mantras to fire, air, water, earth, and ether. You can say mantras for the sun, moon, and stars. You can say mantras for all of the five elements. But those energies are just glitters, they are not wisdom or miracles. Like fireflies, they only shine in the darkness of mind and desire.

People say, "I prayed, and I have seen the light! With my own eyes I have seen the ocean shine with a great resplendence. I have seen a light in the far-off mountains. I have seen light coming out of leaves. I have seen miraculous sparkles on the road." They think they have seen something great. But none of these lights are the result of devotion or prayer, they are only the glitters of the intellect, the shine of the five elements. They are not the true light.

My grandchildren, whatever you experience you must understand with the clear light of wisdom. You have to know the difference between that which glitters in the night and the light that shines forever, both day and night, at all moments, in all lives, under all circumstances.

My grandchildren, just as God put fluorescent paint on the forehead of the fish so it can find its food, He also placed a light, an eye of wisdom, on the forehead of man so he can find the food and water needed for his soul. This is the eye which looks at life. It is the real light. It is perfect wisdom, the light which dispels all darkness. It is the infinite and eternal light of wisdom which exists within God.

Bismillāhir-Rahmānir-Rahīm: the Creator, the Protector, and the Nourisher. His gaze watches over all of us. He protects us day and night. The eye of wisdom, the eye of divine knowledge, or *'ilm,* the eye of the resplendence of Allah's grace, His *rahmat,* knows no darkness. Its shine is natural and everlasting. It has no glitter, it is beyond the five elements. It is the eye of God's power, His *qudrat*. And when this is established within a man, that is truly a miracle.

That which shines constantly and has no darkness at all is wisdom. To see your life, to see your soul, to see the lives of others, to see all of that in the real light is wisdom. That is the benefit that comes from real prayer and worship. That is the opened eye of wisdom. It always sees. That is the miracle of God, the only real miracle.

You must ask, "What exists without darkness? What is wisdom? What is the power of God?" It is not something seen in dreams, for dreams only come in the darkness of sleep, day or night. Intellect sees the glittering when it opens its eyes for a moment, but when intellect becomes tired, the glitter vanishes like a dream. But the power of God is not a dream. It always exists. It is always alive. It always knows.

My precious grandchildren, you have to analyze with your wisdom and understand the natural explanations of each of the five elements. You must know what they are capable of. You have to understand all the sections that can be known and then go beyond them, beyond the glitters. True wisdom sees that which has no day or night. Do you understand?

What is the true miracle? Not the glitters. They are not wisdom, nor light, nor God. God is not something that can be seen like that. Think about this a little. My love you, my grandchildren. You need wisdom. You need the actions and qualities of God. You need to do what is right. That is wisdom. My love you. *Anbu.*

*My grandchildren, if the illusion of this world catches you, it will
coil its tail around you and swallow you whole.*

Destroy the Python of Illusion

y love you, my grandchildren. Come, let's go for a walk along this jungle path. Look out! There's a poisonous snake! Stand back and wait. If we are very quiet and still, it will go away on its own. See, it passed by without harming us. Oh, no! Here comes a python. It's heading straight toward us! Quick, move aside! A python does not bite, it coils around its victim and then swallows it.

Think about this a little. If a poisonous snake bites us, we can treat the wound and perhaps escape with our lives. But if a python catches us, it will crush and swallow us, and we will certainly die.

My love you, my grandchildren. Do you understand the meaning of this? Ignorance, lack of wisdom, anger, resentment, vengeance, and doubt are all poisonous snakes. They are like the first snake we saw, and they can bite us. Where do these snake-like qualities strike? They bite our hearts. But if we are very quiet and hold onto Allah's qualities of faith, love, and patience, then when those poisonous qualities approach, they will pass right by. If we have Allah's inner patience, His *sabūr,* those evil qualities will pass without biting us.

Even if we are bitten, it is possible for a good doctor to treat the wound with the medicine of wisdom, with Allah's love, and with His power. If we can find one who will treat us with this medicine, we might escape with our lives, but if no such doctor is available, we will die. That good doctor is a wise sheikh. Only one who has God's wisdom and qualities can protect us and dispel the poison of those snakes.

But take heed, my grandchildren. The python of illusion is far more dangerous than those poisonous snakes. If the illusion of this world catches you, it will coil its tail around you and swallow you whole. It is not poisonous, but it can swallow you and dissolve you in the acid of hell. What is this python? It is arrogance, karma, illusion, and the three sons of illusion called *tārahan, singhan,* and *sūran.* It is lust, hatred, miserliness, greed, fanaticism, envy, intoxicants, obsession, murder, theft, and falsehood. To escape from this python of illusion you need patience, contentment, and wisdom.

You must not be caught! You must escape! If it catches you, my grandchildren, you are lost. A man of wisdom can easily kill this snake, but until you have such wisdom you must find some way to escape.

How does a wise man kill a python? He uses a subtle trick. First he stands back out of the python's reach, then he quickly steps forward and cuts off its head with a very sharp knife. Next he chops the rest of its body into pieces. But even then he has to be very careful, for the python is not dead yet. Within half an hour the severed sections will join together again. The python has a magnetic power that enables it to do this.

Therefore, if you really want to destroy this python, you must use the wise man's subtle trick. Take the tail piece and place it next to the head. Then take the middle section and place it at the end. If you mix the pieces up like this, they cannot rejoin. Even if they try to, the snake will not be able to function properly, because its nerves will not be in the correct order.

Mind and illusion are just like a python. They have this same kind of magnet which draws them back together whenever you try to separate them. When you cut illusion into pieces, it grows together again and again. But if you can scramble the head, the middle, and the tail, you can overcome it. You must cut illusion into pieces and scatter it in different directions. Then the foxes will come to devour the pieces.

In the same way, when you cut only one section in your mind, it will struggle to come back to life. So you must be ever vigilant. Never think, "I have learned wisdom. Now I can do anything," for until you die, the mind will come back to life again and again, section by section. Never think that you have finished learning wisdom, or that you can control illusion, or that you are a learned person. Such thinking is a sure sign that you lack wisdom. Only when you reach a stage where illusion cannot come back to life will you have learned anything at all.

Even if you manage to successfully kill a portion of maya, you still will have attained only a drop of wisdom, just one small dot. At that level, you can become a good man with a tiny bit of clarity. Your anger, your resentment, your hastiness, and your lust can all be conquered, but there is still so much more to learn. Next you must become an *insān*, a true man, then an *insān kāmil*, a pure man, then a perfect man, and only then a *gnāni*, or wise man. How much more learning lies ahead of us! We can never say that we have finished learning.

My love you, my grandchildren. Try to understand this lesson, point by point, and place it safely in your hearts. Only a wise man who has God's qualities, who is experienced, and who has conquered illusion can help you to attain this state. You must understand how illusion should be cut, separated, scattered in different directions, and then burned. You must know how to get rid of the poisonous bad qualities, how to give medicine to others, how to overcome the five elements and the five senses, how to control desire and the *nafs ammārah*, and how to conquer attachments, the mind, and torpor. You must understand each of these sections. As you complete each one, you will receive a small particle of God's wisdom. This is how you can become a good child.

My grandchildren, my love you. You must search for wisdom, acquire God's divine knowledge known as *'ilm*, and apply the medicine of God's power, His *qudrat*. It is only when you do all this that you can escape from the snake of illusion. *Āmīn*. May God help you.

253

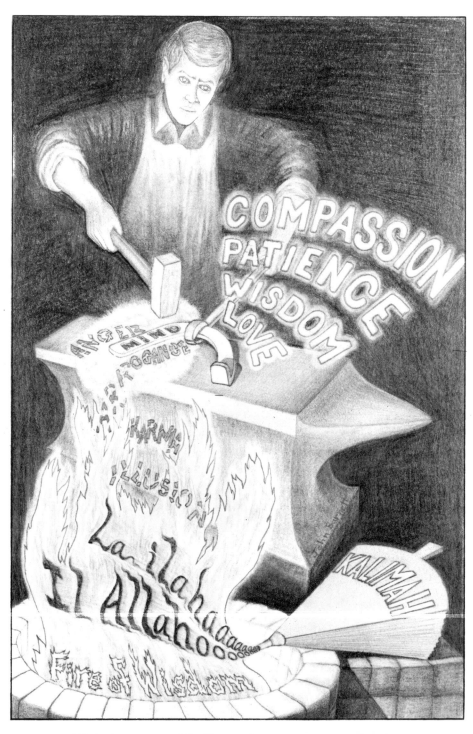

*With the power of God's word, we must pump the air
that makes the fire of wisdom burn strong.*

The Red-Hot Fire
in the Blacksmith's Shop

y love you, my grandchildren. Let us walk over to the blacksmith's shop and watch him as he does his work.

See how he first prepares the fire by pumping air through the bellows so the flames will burn brighter. Now he is adding more firewood and again forcefully pumping the bellows. Whenever he stops pumping, the fire dies down, but as soon as he starts again it immediately flares up and burns brightly.

Come closer, children, and watch how the blacksmith makes a horseshoe. First he cuts a piece of iron and places it in the fire. He waits until the iron becomes red hot, and then he starts beating it and bending it into a U-shape. Next he cuts a smaller piece of iron into three pieces, and makes three nails. Then he takes another tool and bores three holes for the nails, and the horseshoe is finished.

Now watch as he makes a different type of shoe for the bulls that pull the carts. First he takes a flat piece of hot iron, then splits it in two and bends it up in front so it will protect the bull's hoof from cracking when it strikes against something. This is how the blacksmith forms the iron into different shapes for different uses. For the bull he makes a shoe to fit a split hoof, while for the horse he makes an oval shoe. For wheels he makes rims, and for axles he makes round casings.

The blacksmith can make so many things out of iron. He bends the metal and shapes it according to his needs. If the iron were allowed to do whatever it wanted, could the blacksmith make all those different things? No, he must control the iron. Only after he brings it under his command can he mold it into a form which is useful to himself and others.

Listen, my grandchildren, do you hear that hissing sound? The iron is crying because it is in the fire. But the blacksmith ignores its cry and continues to fan the flame. And when the iron becomes red hot, he beats it into the desired shape.

The iron bar thinks, "Oh no! First he burned me in the fire, and now he is hitting me!" Even the anvil gets hurt when the blacksmith lays the red-hot iron on top of it. Both the anvil and the hammer complain, "When he hits the iron, we get beaten and dented, too! How much pain we suffer from the heat!"

But does the blacksmith stop because the hammer and anvil feel hurt? Does he give up because the iron is crying? No, as he works, he brings them all under his control in order to fulfill his intention. Once the blacksmith has finished his work, the iron is transformed into a beautiful and useful thing. Then the iron, the hammer, and the anvil stop their crying and are happy.

My grandchildren, my sons and daughters, my brothers and sisters, we must be like the blacksmith. We must burn our mind in the fire of wisdom. We must put our desire, the five elements, karma, illusion, and the arrogance of the I into that red-hot fire of wisdom and fan it with the breath of the *dhikr*, with the remembrance of God, and establish our connection to Him. Then, with the power of God's word we must pump the air that makes this fire burn strong. When the mind becomes red hot and pliable, we must beat it into a new form that will be of benefit to others. We must control the mind and make it act as we want it to.

What sort of new form should we beat this mind into? We must mold it into the good qualities which bring love into our every action and embrace others to our hearts. We must mold it into qualities which help others. The four hundred trillion, ten thousand energies must be beaten and made useful. Anger, arrogance, and all these pieces of hard iron must be beaten and transformed into the three thousand gracious qualities and the ninety-nine *wilāyats* which are the actions and duties of God.

My grandchildren, beat your mind and burn it in that fire of wisdom. Of course, when you start beating the monkey mind, it will suffer. Desire will suffer. Religions and philosophies will feel hurt. Racial and color differences and prejudice will feel pain. The separateness of you and I will suffer. Selfishness, arrogance, and anger will be hurt. Pride will feel pain. Illusion, arrogance, and karma will suffer. They all will feel pain, but you must keep on beating them anyway.

Without paying attention to their cries, you must transform your mind and desire so they will work for you. Melt them in the fire, then hit them and bring them to a good state of wisdom, love, compassion, and patience. Under God's compassionate gaze, bring them to the state of His good qualities. Bend the mind into shapes that can form a connection with God and others. Make it into something that can give beauty to others and satisfy their needs. Give according to the state of each heart you meet.

If you can learn to do this, you can become a true human being. Only then will you understand the history of the connection between man and God. Only then will you understand the hearts and minds of all creations. You will be able to help them cut the sections that need to be cut and give them the peace they need in their innermost hearts, their *qalbs*.

However, if you fail to control your mind, if you let it do whatever it wants, then you will never be able to change anything or be of any help to others. If you allow arrogance, karma, and illusion to do as they please, you can never give peace to others. Think about this. Learn this lesson from the blacksmith and apply it to your life.

Do not remain steeped in the hell of illusion and bound by karma. Burn your mind in the fire of wisdom and fan it with the breath of the *Kalimah*. Beat it, work it into shape, and transform it into something useful. Then you can become a wise man, a *gnāni,* and a true human being, an *insān.* You can become a representative of God and a messenger of God. If you can completely transform your mind in the correct way, you will become the son of God. Think about this, my grandchildren.

My love you. *Āmīn.* May Allah help you.

My children, shall we go for a walk in the dense teak forest?

The Teak Tree

y grandchildren, my brothers and sisters, my sons and daughters, it is morning now. Shall we go for a walk? Look at this dense teak forest. The government of Sri Lanka grows thousands of these teak trees.

Do you know why they grow this particular tree? Because its wood is quite valuable, and they can sell it to other countries. It is very beautiful, useful, light, and durable. Because teak is easier to work with than the wood of any other tree, it can be used for many purposes. Carpenters can make beds, tables, and chairs out of this wood, and builders can use the seasoned planks for houses and roofs.

To gain the greatest benefit from the teak tree, however, you should wait at least twenty to thirty years before cutting it down. Only then will its oil develop and its color darken. The oil in the seasoned wood is so bitter and poisonous that insects will not attack it. But when the tree is young, the oil is mixed with water, and the quality of the wood is poor. It can still be sold as teak, but it is not as beautiful or durable as it will be later. Only after it reaches a mature state will it attain its full value and last for two to three hundred years, long after other woods have rotted. Its planks will be firm, and the buildings and furniture made from it will remain strong and beautiful. If you polish it, you can make it shine like a mirror, and from generation to generation, it will need only occasional cleaning and reconditioning.

My grandchildren, look at that tree over there. It seems to be mature enough for cutting. It is probably about forty or fifty years old. Most of the other trees here are only two or three years old. Look how small they are, measuring less than a foot in circumference. If their branches are pruned regularly, they will grow straight, and in twenty years they will be ready for cutting. However, because the government is impatient to use them for building, they often chop down the young trees while the wood is still white. But these trees are not strong and should not be used so soon. The rain and wind will rot the wood within a year.

My love you, my grandchildren. Man is like the teak tree. Even though he may be called a human being, he will not develop his full value until he reaches maturity. Before then, no matter how learned he may be, no matter how many arts and sciences he has studied, he will be like the young teak tree, of no use to himself or anyone else. If he is cut down before his time, he will not be of any use at all in this birth. The immature man will be destroyed.

What must a man do to mature properly? First he must establish a connection between himself and God, a connection between his qualities and actions and God's qualities and actions, between his justice and conscience and God's justice and conscience, between his love and God's love. He must establish a connection between the peace and compassion of God and his own peace and compassion. To become strong in wisdom, his qualities and actions must mature. His prayer and meditation and worship must also mature. Then, when God's grace develops within him, he will appear beautiful to the hearts, the qualities, and the wisdom of all. Because he understands the right and wrong in the hearts of others, he will be a beautiful being in the form of love, compassion, wisdom, and justice. The resplendence of God will flow from him just as the oil oozes from the teak tree, and he will be useful for hundreds and hundreds of years.

In the same way that mature teak can be used to build beautiful houses, such a man will be useful in helping people to build the beautiful houses of their hearts. He will help them to establish a connection with God through prayer and meditation to the extent that their wisdom and knowledge permit. There will be benefit in whatever such a man says or does. His actions, his justice and peace, his every breath will be useful and helpful to all people.

My love you, my grandchildren. The exaltedness of man comes when he has established a connection with God. His life will be of benefit to others when he has developed wisdom and conscience within himself, when he knows right and wrong, heaven and hell, and good and evil. Satan will not go near him when he is in this mature state, just as the insects will not infest the mature teak tree. Illusion, the five elements, and mind and desire will not harm him. If any of the four hundred trillion, ten thousand spiritual energies even touch such a man, they will die. Only God's grace, His qualities, and His justice and love will exist in a man who has established this connection with God.

You must think about this. My love you, my grandchildren. You must establish this state in yourselves and give these benefits to all. My love you.

Oh no! A young monkey has fallen. Look how the others have joined together to attack it.

The Law of the Monkey

y love you, my children. Come, let us go over there, near those trees by the river. Do you see all the monkeys playing in the branches? There are small ones and large ones, old ones and young ones, black ones and gray ones. There are so many different kinds of monkeys, in all colors and sizes. Look at them carefully. Even their faces are different. Some have black faces, some red, and some have big faces like lions.

Shall we watch them play for a while? Some monkeys are boxing with each other, and some even seem to know the art of kung fu. Others are swinging on the branches like trapeze artists. Even the old monkeys are playing and jumping and shouting. Look closely, my grandchildren. Do you see how the little ones are clinging to their mothers' stomachs and riding on their backs? They hold on ever so tightly, as their mothers jump and swing from branch to branch.

Watch how the mothers swing across to the other side of the river, with their babies clinging to their bellies and backs. Sometimes a young monkey will let go of its mother and fall. Once that happens, the others will never accept it back into the clan, they will discard it. This is their law. All of the monkey family follow this same law. It does not matter whether they are baboons, orangutans, gorillas, or chimpanzees. They may be big or small, their appearance may be different, but their law is the same.

Oh no! A young monkey has fallen. Do you see how the rest of the monkeys have joined together to attack and bite it? Luckily it has escaped and is running for its life.

My love you, my children. Man also has many monkeys clinging to him. See how the world and illusion ride proudly on his back? The monkeys of arrogance and karma also ride on him and no matter what he does, they will not let go. Even though a man may be a king and walk with great honor, still he has this heavy weight on his back. And the monkeys of ignorance, hunger, disease, old age, death, the five elements, and desire for earth, women, and gold are all clinging to his stomach. No matter how many circus tricks a man performs, no matter how long he prays and meditates, no matter what yogas he practices, these monkeys will not let go of him. They cling to his chest and suck milk from his breast. Have you ever noticed this?

Look at that man over there. All the monkeys of earth, mind, desire, titles, religions, and philosophies have been grabbing onto him for such a long time. But he has also been clinging on to them, as they swing from place to place.

Look! He has finally released his grip on these monkeys! He has fallen, and the rest of the human monkeys are joining together to attack him, bite him, and chase him away. Because he let go of them, they don't want him to survive. He broke their rule and became a man. So now he is discarded and alone, and the world will no longer accept him.

Escaping from their clutches, he leaves these human monkeys behind, in control of their forest. He crosses the river and goes beyond. Now he is a true man, a man in search of God, in search of that one point.

My grandchildren, let us study the law of the human monkeys a little. If you accept and cling to the differences of your color, your race, and your religion, you will be accepted by the clan. This is the rule of the human monkeys. But if you release your grip on any one of them, they will immediately bite you. As soon as you let go of these differences and go beyond their law, they will attack you and throw you out.

My love you, my children. Think about this a little. If you refuse to observe the laws of the world and try to go beyond them, you will be in danger. The people of this world will bite you, hit you, and chase you away. It is very difficult, but you must make the effort to escape from the world and go in search of your Father. You will not find Him in the section of the world. He is the One who considers all lives as His own. He is the Treasure that does not possess differences or separations. He is the One who will protect you.

But some people hold on to this worldly kingdom, carrying the arrogance of the I on their backs. Others hold on to all the attachments that cling to their chests. It is hard to tell if they are men or monkeys. However, a man will go forward if he can escape from the clutches of the monkey and hold on to the One who will help him in times of danger. Understand this and walk on the path of God.

My love you, my children. May God protect you and take you on that path. *Āmīn.*

A car needs so many things: water, gasoline, oil, a steering wheel, a battery, tires, and air for the tires.

A Car Needs So Many Things

My love you, my grandchildren. Come along with me. We're going to visit a huge car lot where they sell many, many cars. People buy cars so they can go places quickly. In earlier times people used to walk, then later they invented rickshaws. Next they built small carriages that were pulled by horses and bullocks. In some parts of the world, people still use these carts for transportation and also to carry things. Later bicycles were developed, then motorcycles and cars. Next people discovered how to make airplanes that could leap from continent to continent and destroy the world with bombs. Finally they invented atomic missiles and other weapons that could kill hundreds of thousands of people in one blast.

My love you, my grandchildren. There was not as much destruction in the world when men simply walked, as God created them to do. The more technology developed, the more accidents occurred. Man made so many machines to help him go faster. But the faster man traveled, the faster destruction came to him. Did you ever think about that? Oh well, never mind, that is all history. We cannot change what has happened.

As long as we have cars, we must take good care of them. Cars need so many things: water, gasoline, oil, a steering wheel, a battery, tires, and air for the tires. Every single part has to be working properly before you can go on a journey. If the brakes are not working, you will have an accident. If the battery is missing, the car will not start. If it has everything except gas and oil, the engine will not work. And even if everything else is running smoothly, if the tires have no air, the car will just lie down and collapse on the road.

Just as a car needs all these things, your body also needs food, water, air, oil, and warmth. It needs so many things, and you have to provide them every day. Your eyes need light, your ears need sounds to hear, and your nose needs things to smell. You need to pour food and water into your mouth to supply your body with energy. The body cannot go anywhere without these things, can it? Your body will collapse and stop functioning, just as a car breaks down on the road.

But, my grandchildren, even though you have all these things, what good are they by themselves? You have eyes, and a car has eyes too, its headlights. But can the car see or think? No, the driver must do the seeing and thinking. Like this, the light of God must come into your eyes for you to see clearly. It is not enough for you to have ears; you need the subtle ear within to hear the sound of God. Your mouth by itself is not enough; you need the mouth and tongue that know the difference between saying something right and saying something wrong. You have a nose, but if you smell something burning, you still have to figure out what to do about it. And, in addition, you need that inner nose which can distinguish between right and wrong.

Even if you have all these, what good are they without a heart and lungs and air to breathe? And even if you have these, are they enough? No, you need God and His qualities. But even then, what is the use of living if you do not have wisdom? What can you ever accomplish? If you do not hear the sound of God, what is the use of living? If you do not have God's heart, His qualities, His actions, and His love, what is the use of being alive? Without these, you will just fall down and become prey to the earth.

The car needs its kind of food, the body needs the food of the world, and the soul needs the food of God's wisdom. It needs the food of His love and compassion, His peace, tranquility, and equality. It needs the inner patience, contentment, and trust in God, known as *sabūr, shukūr,* and *tawakkul.* It needs all His characteristics, and His three thousand beautiful and gracious qualities. This is the food for the soul and the justice that must be given to the soul. If the soul does not receive these, your life will end and you will die. Even if you give the food that is needed to every other part, if you neglect the soul you will meet with accidents. You cannot avoid such accidents without the qualities, actions, and wisdom of God. You need that inner eye to travel safely. No matter how much a driver pours into his car, if he's not careful, or if he drives too fast, he could have an accident and die.

Isn't that true? Think about this.

My grandchildren, even though a car can go very fast, man's mind can go still faster. It can travel at the speed of the air. But man can travel even faster than the mind, if he has the light of wisdom. There is nothing faster than that light. It can help him to understand things much more quickly than the mind ever can. A man who has that wisdom will be able to understand all the secrets of God.

My love you, my grandchildren. You must understand what needs to be given to each section, then act and think accordingly. If you do, the journey of your life will be successful.

My love you, may God help you.

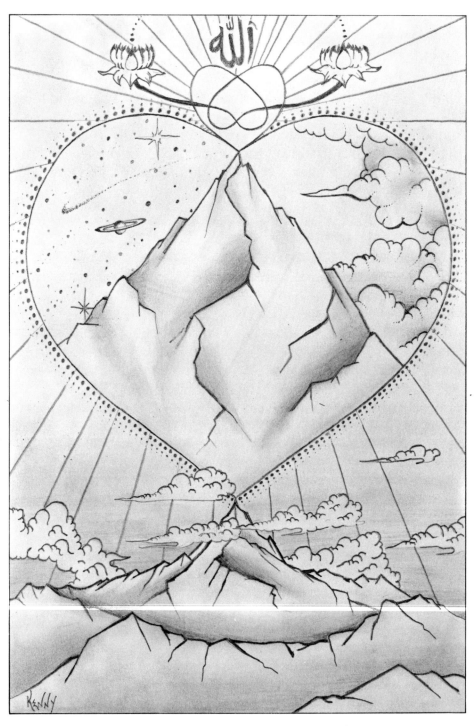

There is a mountain within man that is seventy thousand times higher
than Mount Everest. Its peak reaches up to the kingdom of God.

The Highest Mountain

y love you, my grandchildren, my daughters and sons, my brothers and sisters. Today let us visit India, where there is a vast mountain range called the Himalayas. India and Nepal lie to the west of the Himalayas, and China lies to the east. There are many mountains in that range, but the most famous one is called Mount Everest.

My grandchildren, Mount Everest is said to be the highest mountain in the whole world. Everyone says it is such an amazing mountain. People come here from all over the world to test their climbing skills and to acquire great titles. Afterwards they proudly proclaim, "I've climbed Mount Everest!" In the past hundred years, many have tried to achieve this feat, and the few who have succeeded are praised in newspapers, magazines, and on television. Numerous stories have been written about these adventures.

Look up at the mountain. It is covered with glaciers. Can you see the climbers attempting to cross its icy slopes? They have brought picks, ropes, and all the necessary equipment. Look, now they are attempting the ascent. Each person seems to have a different job. Only a few are doing the actual climbing, but many more are involved in the attempt. Even a reporter and a photographer have gone along to record the adventure. But the honors will go only to the climber who actually reaches the peak. He will be considered the cleverest of them all. Look how many people have gathered here with us to watch.

My grandchildren, people say all sorts of things in praise of this mountain. Some call it Mount Kailas and say, "God lives here." Others call it Mount Everest and say, "This is the highest mountain in the world. To climb it is to triumph over it!" But if the modern-day scientists were to drop just one single atom bomb on it, the whole mountain would turn to fire and disappear.

People think this mountain is so high, but it really isn't. Little ice birds can fly over its peak, and some even make their homes up there. This is natural for certain birds. Some animals also live on the glaciers. Even snakes and other creatures can climb that mountain. They have been doing it for a long time, and so it is normal for them. But for man it is a rare and difficult thing. He endures so many hardships just to receive a title.

My love you, my grandchildren. There is another mountain which is seventy thousand times higher than Mount Everest, and it grows within man. Eighteen thousand worlds can be seen there. Its peak reaches up to the kingdom of God, and if you stand on top of the mountain, you can see that kingdom. What a wondrous sight! This mountain is very high and extremely difficult to climb. Hardly anyone has ever reached the top. In the two hundred million years that man has existed, only a very rare few have ascended this mountain to see the kingdom of God and God Himself.

What is this high mountain? It is the arrogance that grows out of man's ignorance. In life, in the world, and in the eighteen thousand universes, this is the highest of all mountains. It grows from lack of wisdom, from egoism, karma, and illusion, from the energies of illusion which are the energies of the elements, and from all the qualities of the three sons of illusion known as *tārahan, singhan,* and *sūran.* Lust, hatred, miserliness, greed, fanaticism, envy, intoxicants, obsession, theft, murder, falsehood, earth, gold, and sexual pleasures—all these energies dwell on that mountain and subject man to millions of rebirths. It is very difficult for a man to rise above all that. But, my grandchildren, every day that we do not attempt to climb this mountain of arrogance, we will experience suffering in our lives.

The rare few who have overcome and pushed aside all those evil energies and reached the top have spoken with God about His qualities, His wisdom, His grace, love, peace, tranquility, serenity, and the perfect resplendence which is wisdom. Anyone who has learned these qualities and has climbed up will receive all these treasures from God and attain liberation for his soul. He will know the purity of his soul. He will know God, who is the radiance within the soul. He will obtain the prize, the title, and the praise given by his Father. He will obtain the crown of the grace-awakened wisdom known as *gnānam,* and he will become a true human being.

My grandchildren, it is not a wonder to climb Mount Everest. The birds, snakes, and scorpions can do that. This mountain of arrogance is much higher, and it is much harder to climb. You must know this and make a supreme effort to overcome it in your life. You need axes, picks, knives, and other tools to climb Mount Everest. But to climb this inner mountain, you must have God's qualities, His actions, and His love. You must have *īmān,* absolute faith, certitude, and determination in God, your Father. You must have wisdom, God's compassion, His peace, all His good deeds. And you must have the patience, contentment, trust in God, and praise of God, known as *sabūr, shukūr, tawakkul,* and *al-hamdu lillāh.*

If you do succeed in climbing with God's qualities and reaching the top of this mountain of arrogance, then God will speak to you, just as He spoke to Moses ☺ when he climbed Mount Sinai. But if you don't surmount this peak, then no matter how many millions of times you pray or how many hours you meditate, ignorance will fascinate you, and illusion will catch you in its net. These energies will always control you and subject you to many rebirths.

My love you, my grandchildren, my sons and daughters, my brothers and sisters. You must understand this. In man's search for wisdom, this is the highest obstacle he will ever face. This is the most formidable mountain of all, and to surmount it is indeed the greatest wonder. Each one of you must finish climbing this mountain. When you reach its peak you will be with your Father. You will be free. Do you understand?

May God help you and give you His grace so that you can ascend this mountain and speak to Him. *Āmīn. Āmīn.*

Crossing the Desert of Life

My love you, my grandchildren, my daughters and sons, my brothers and sisters. Will you come with me to Arabia? As far as you can see, there is open desert. Look how the wind has piled the sand into huge dunes. A few outcroppings of rock can be seen here and there, and an occasional thorny bush or date palm, but nowhere can we see water, people, villages, or life of any kind. Wherever we look we see only sand and rocks and open space. If a man were stranded here, he would be exposed to sandstorms and whirlwinds and burning sun.

My grandchildren, traveling through this desert is going to be extremely difficult. Can you feel your feet sinking deep into the sand as you walk? You have to pull them up with each step. Oh, look over there, off in the distance. Do you see the ostriches running swiftly across the sand? They can travel at a speed of forty miles an hour. We cannot run that fast. In fact, our feet feel so heavy in the sand that it is even hard to walk. But we must try to keep moving, for if we stay here we will die. We must search for water before the sandstorms come. Don't get tired! Come along, we can't afford to waste any time. We must keep walking.

Watch out, children! There are scorpions and snakes near those rocks. Some of the snakes are the kind that slither sideways as they move across the sand. Look, you can also see a few iguanas and mice, and over there is a fox. Somehow they all manage to live in this desert. But human beings find it almost impossible to survive here in this scorching sun and arid land, with only a few trees to provide shade.

My grandchildren, let us walk toward that rocky mountain in the distance. Look! Do you see the smoke coming from over there? Let's go closer. Now our eyes can make out two or three tents with horses and camels tied outside. Keep walking, we're almost there.

It looks like a few nomad families are living here. They must belong to a desert tribe. The nomads are often scorned and called low caste by those who consider themselves high caste. But these people are very kind and thoughtful. See how they are approaching us and offering us food and water from their jugs.

"Greetings, travelers. Please come and eat with us. What brings you here?"

"We came to explore the desert. And we haven't seen a single person until God led us to you."

"My friends, you will need water for your journey. There are very few watering places in this area, but we can tell you how to find them. We can also direct you to some people who have a house in the nearby mountains. You should be able to find them easily, but don't try to go on foot. Please take our horses and camels with you, for they are trained to walk in the sand and can make your journey much easier. We ride them wherever we go."

My grandchildren, don't you wonder how these people find food in such a hot, dry land? Let us ask our host. We can learn something if we listen carefully to what he tells us.

"We eat the animals that live here in the desert, the ostriches and camels, a few wild bulls, and some chickens. Occasionally we even catch a certain kind of mountain goat that eats stones. Wherever we find water we dig a well, fill our jugs, and carry them back to our tents. We also get milk from our camels. Somehow or other we manage to exist. Life may be difficult, but we are never short of food. God always gives us enough."

My grandchildren, let us drink some water from these jugs. Look, it is crystal clear with shades of blue. Mmmm, it tastes so cool and delicious. Pour a little over your body. It will wash away the sweat and cool you off. Ahh, it's so refreshing.

My grandchildren, the journey of our life is like traveling through the desert. We must cross the ocean of illusion and then cross the desert of life. Today you have experienced some of the hardships of desert life, and yet so many creatures live here without finding it difficult. The camels, the eagles, the foxes, and the snakes are not

A man of wisdom does not find this journey through the desert of life difficult, because he rides on faith, certitude, truth, equality, and love.

troubled by the sandstorms. It is only man who suffers. Animals live day by day, accepting whatever each day brings. They do not have the analytic wisdom to know right from wrong. They eat whatever is given to them, without thinking of the future.

But man finds it very difficult. He collects things and stores them for tomorrow, and for the day after tomorrow, and for the rest of his life. He hoards things for his children and his wife. He gathers so many things together and ties them into a big bundle. He carries torpor, desires, darkness, blood ties, illusion, and fanaticism. Do you see how difficult it must be for him to travel across the desert of life with all these burdens? He tries to carry such heavy loads, but he finds it hard to even lift his own feet. Animals do not carry such burdens. You saw how easily the ostriches ran across the sand. Man cannot run that fast, because he is carrying such an enormous bundle. And all the while, the sandstorms of his mind and desire are blowing against him and pushing him down. How he suffers!

Even if man manages to swim across the ocean of illusion, once he is washed up onto the shore of this desert, the sand piles on top of him and he dies in that hell. Then the foxes, dogs, cats, and rats come to eat his corpse. Man comes to the desert of life with the qualities of hell, and hell awaits him there, ready to eat him up.

My love you, my grandchildren. We must swim across the ocean of illusion, cross the desert of life, and climb the rocky mountain of the mind. We must escape from the thorny bushes of poisonous qualities that grow in the mind. We must escape from the evils which swoop down to eat us, and from the dogs, foxes, vultures, lions, tigers, and bears that are ready to tear at our flesh. We must escape from the demons and ghosts that are eagerly waiting to devour us.

My children, on our journey we learned how difficult life can be in the desert. But the nomads we met didn't find it so difficult. They were happy living there, because they knew how to survive in such an arid land. They had camels and horses to carry them over the sand, they had tents to give them shelter, and they knew how and where to find food. They were able to comfort us and show us how to find water. We were suffering from thirst, because we didn't realize that there was water right on the very path we traveled. But they knew.

My grandchildren, just as there are some people who know how to live in the desert, there are a few wise men who know how to travel through the desert of life. A man of wisdom does not find this journey difficult, because he rides on faith, certitude, truth, equality, and love. He rides upon wisdom and God's qualities and actions, which can move very quickly. My children, such a man will help make your journey easier by offering you this same mode of travel.

Just as the desert nomads can tell us where to find food and water, the wise man can tell us where to find truth. He can show us how to relieve our tiredness, hunger, and thirst, and how to make our journey easy. He will point out each and every step of the way. He will show us how to swim through the ocean of illusion, how to cross the desert of life, and how to escape from the animals of ignorance. He will point out to us, "These are the good qualities. This is wisdom. This is God." The wise man will teach us how to conduct our lives, how to dispel ignorance and avoid accidents, how to escape from the whirlwinds, and finally how to obtain the freedom of our souls and establish a connection to God. A wise man knows all this. And when you travel with him across the desert of life, you will find your journey easier because of his help.

My love you, my grandchildren, please think deeply about this. You must find such a wise man, someone who has crossed this desert and knows the path. He will help you in all ways. It is difficult to find such a true human being. This has always been true in the past, it is true in the present, and it will still be true in the future. It is indeed rare to find one who knows the way. It is also difficult to find the food and water you need, but you must learn how. Do not look for miracles to help you. Of what use are miracles if you can't escape from the desert?

My grandchildren, the desert of the world is full of animals. If you do not cross this desert you will die and become food for foxes and demons. But if you find a wise man, you can succeed in crossing the desert of your life in happiness, love, and joy. That is truly a miracle. That is a miracle which occurs within, not the kind that people perform on the outside. Please understand this, my grandchildren. May God give you the wisdom and clarity to do this. *Āmīn.*

The Birds Are Silent When They Eat

My love you, my grandchildren, my sons and daughters, my brothers and sisters. Look over there at those two big trees. Can you see all the different colored birds perched in the branches? There are probably five thousand or more. Listen! Do you hear any noise coming from them? No, they are sitting peacefully, eating in silence. When they first saw the fruits they made so much noise, screeching and cawing, but now they have settled on the branches and are enjoying the sweet taste in silence.

My love you, my grandchildren. You can observe the same behavior in those who are with the sheikh and are searching for wisdom and God. People of different colors and different languages will all gather together here in the presence of the sheikh. Even though disturbances may occur at first, they will subside when the sweet taste of God's divine knowledge, His *'ilm,* is imbibed with wisdom. Then all colors will mingle together blissfully.

My children, when you first approach your father of wisdom, you too might make some noise, but once you settle down and begin doing your duty in his presence, all your sounds must stop. You must become silent, peacefully enjoying the sweet taste of God, the fruits of wisdom, love, patience, tolerance, and truth. Once you are in that state of silence, your qualities, actions, and love will be beautiful. Your inner patience, contentment, trust in God, and praise of God, your *sabūr, shukūr, tawakkul,* and *al-hamdu lillāh* will be so beautiful. Your compassion will be even more beautiful, and your wisdom will be ever so subtle.

My love you, my grandchildren. All the children of Adam ﷺ need the nourishment of those fruits. You all need to attain that tranquility. Then the taste and flavor of God's divine knowledge, His *'ilm,* will be

When the birds first see the fruits, they screech and caw, but then they settle on the branches and enjoy the sweet taste in silence.

your bliss. You must find that peace and unity. This is the blessing you can receive from the sheikh. If you reach this state, you will know the taste of Allah. Do your duty and try to discover that taste. My love you.

Only when man comes to the forest do these animals face real danger.

Man Is More Dangerous Than Animals

y love you, my grandchildren, my sons and daughters. Will you come with me to the pine forest? Look how straight and tall the pine trees grow. Here in the midst of these trees there are a few ponds where deer and elk come to drink. Moose also come here when there is nothing for them to eat in the forest. They wade into a pond, dip their heads into the water, and eat the vegetation that grows on the bottom. The deer, the elk, and the moose live together peacefully in the forest, with very few hardships. Even in the winter when the snow brings added difficulties, God provides them with some kind of warmth and shelter.

My grandchildren, God created the stag with very large and beautiful antlers. When these antlers grow to full size, the stag rubs them against the trees to remove the moss that tends to collect on them. He rubs very carefully so that his antlers won't get caught between the trees and branches. Moose antlers are much broader and thicker, so they can become stuck even more easily. Sometimes a moose may even die if he cannot free himself.

Neither stags nor moose experience many difficulties from other causes. Only when man comes to the forest do these animals face real danger. They are terribly afraid of men, more fearful than they are of lions. Because moose and deer are very intelligent, they know that unless the lions are hungry, they have nothing to fear from them. And so they live among them and graze near their mountain lairs. They only run away when the lions show signs of hunger.

Most of the time these antlered animals live peacefully, but sometimes they fight among themselves. When their antlers clash, the noise resonates throughout the forest. They fight over their females, claiming, ''She's mine! I want her!'' Using their antlers, they fence with each other to see who is stronger. They lock antlers and push each other back and forth until one loses his strength, becomes frightened, and runs away. This is how the fight ends. The animals do not usually die, they just fight back and forth with their horns until the conflict is resolved. The cleverest and strongest stag wins all the females, and they follow him everywhere from then on. The younger males also trail along behind. The other adult males are a little afraid of him and keep their distance.

～ ～

My grandchildren, all animals have their own unique way of fighting. Moose and stags fight with their antlers. Chickens and birds peck with their beaks and kick with their legs. Some animals bite with their mouths and scratch and claw with their forepaws. Monkeys grab and push each other with their hands and wrestle and roll on the ground. Some animals kill their enemy and then eat it. Other animals just run away to escape from the fight. You can see all this in the forest and jungles where animals dwell.

Each animal tends to fight with one particular part of its body. But man uses many weapons. He not only fights with his hands, his legs, and his mouth, he also uses deceit and trickery. There is no weapon that man will not use and he will never let his enemy escape. Even tigers are not like that. If a tiger stalks a deer and fails to catch it in the first pounce, the tiger will let it go free. Rarely will a tiger chase a deer beyond a certain distance. Many animals and birds are like that. They will not seek out the other animal once it runs away from the fight. When two male animals fight over a female, if one becomes afraid and runs away, the winner will usually let him go rather than pursue him. Animals do not have that vengeance which seeks to kill.

But if someone runs from man in fear, man will never let him go. He will search him out, determined to kill him in any way possible. He might use a knife, a gun, a rock, or even trickery, magic, and charms. Man has cruel and vengeful thoughts. He will not allow his prey to run away and escape. He will pursue him until he destroys him and then go after his family. Man will do all this without even showing his face or confronting his enemy.

Other creatures are not like that. Even a snake will pause to think before it strikes. It will only bite when it is stepped upon. If someone treads on it unknowingly, the snake will first look to see what happened. If the man holds his hand over his heart with fear and says, "I'm sorry! I didn't know you were there," then the snake will not bite him. A man is not like that. He will not give you a chance to apologize or feel sorry, whether you tread on him knowingly or unknowingly.

🙰 🙰

My love you, my grandchildren. You have to think about this. Which is the most cruel creature? Which is the most venomous? Which is most vengeful? Which creature torments others the most? Is it beasts, reptiles, poisonous insects, or man?

Man is the most cruel. He has the horrible quality of vengeance and a poison worse than that of any poisonous creature. Man has certain qualities that even the animals do not have. If you accidentally harm an animal, you can ask forgiveness and try to smooth things over. At least you will have a chance to run away and escape. But do not make mistakes around men! Always be very careful and use your wisdom to avoid them. They are not what they appear to be.

My grandchildren, do not be deceived by appearances. There are demons and ghosts which can show you very beautiful acts, but you must not go near them. There are trees which have vines that look beautiful, but they can wrap around your neck and suck out your very essence. Similarly, there are men who appear beautiful and seem to speak beautiful words, but they may catch you in an instant and drink your blood. Do not be deceived by such men. Do not look for beauty in a person's face or body or in anything you can see with your eyes. Do not look at the decorations, honors, or titles a person may have. Do not listen to his beautiful words or the praise that people give him. Do not be influenced by any of these things.

My grandchildren, you have to use your wisdom to analyze everything in life. Ask yourself: What qualities exist in that person? What is the nature of this tree? What is that demon like? What did that vision mean? In every circumstance, you have to stand back, know what you are dealing with, and be ready to escape if necessary. There are many dangers like this in your lives. You have to see them and escape from them as quickly as possible in order to conduct your life in an exalted way.

285

But, my grandchildren, if at times you must be in the presence of men who have evil qualities, you still have to show them love. No matter how much enmity others show you, you should never be angry, hasty, or impatient. You should never even think of being vengeful toward anyone. You should not live like the men who have those poisonous qualities.

Remember, not all snakes are poisonous, some are good; not all animals are killers, some are peaceful; and not all creatures are fierce, many are very gentle. Similarly, not all men are dangerous, some are compassionate and loving. There are a few men in this world who live with the good qualities of God. If you are careful, you can join those who have wisdom and learn wisdom with them. You can join those who have good qualities and learn the good qualities. You can join those who are patient and learn patience. You can live with such human beings in love and compassion. You must understand and study all these qualities.

My grandchildren, when you see that special beauty of love, good qualities, and good actions in someone's face and heart, it is God's beauty that you are seeing. Such a being will have a beauty born of light. There will be a fruitfulness in his words and in his qualities. If you can live with such a one you will truly benefit.

My love you, my grandchildren, my daughters and sons, my brothers and sisters. We must think about this in our lives. We do not need to be as careful around animals as we need to be around men who have turned themselves into beasts. Such men are fiercer than any animal. We have to be very careful in the world while we study wisdom.

My love you, my grandchildren. If we live with goodness we will attain triumph, truth, love, and peace. Then we can realize the help of God. Do not ever let go of your faith and your trust in God. He will protect you. *Āmīn. Āmīn.*

The Electric Fish Doesn't Shock Itself

y love you, my children. God has made many millions of creations that live in the ocean. Have you ever gone down into the ocean and seen any of them? Let's go together and take a look at some.

How subtle these creations are! They display so many different shapes, forms, colors, and designs. Some of the fish look a lot like flowers, and some are even more beautiful than man. Each is more amazing than the next.

Look at that fish with the sharp, thin tail and broad body. It is an electric fish. The current in its tail is more powerful than the current in a five hundred watt bulb. When this tail touches other fish, the current passes through them, paralyzing or even killing them. So, even though many fish catch and eat one another, no fish can catch the electric fish. God has created this fish with so much power. But it uses its power in such a subtle way that it doesn't harm other creatures unless they touch it directly.

The electric fish is made of the same five elements as man. Its body contains blood and water, just like ours. But it also contains a powerful electric current. This electricity is different from what we are familiar with. The kind we use causes a shock if we are in contact with any water or metals through which a current is passing. But even though this fish is full of electricity, it is able to live in water without shocking itself. How subtly God has created this creature!

My grandchildren, my love you. God has also placed a special type of power within the body of man. This power arises from wisdom and exists in a very secret way. It exists in man's breath, in his wisdom, and in the qualities of God within him. If man establishes a connection to this power of divine luminous wisdom and develops it

*Even though this fish is full of electricity, it is able
to live in water without shocking itself.*

so that he is able to scrutinize each and every thing he encounters, then even though his body is made of the five elements, no current in this illusory ocean of life can ever harm him.

If he uses this power correctly, the four hundred trillion, ten thousand dangers that come to hurt him will receive a jolt the moment they touch him. Nothing will be able to catch hold of him, not illusion, darkness, torpor, satan, demons, nor ghosts. None of these countless evil beings or animal qualities will be able to harm him. God's power is like that, God's wisdom is like that, and God's qualities and actions are like that. If man's actions and duties are done in that electric state of divine luminous wisdom, then he will be sharp enough to escape from any kind of accident. But first he must generate this power within himself.

My grandchildren, the power of God is electric. His wisdom, love, and compassion are electric. If we connect ourselves to this power and make it function within us, we too will have so much power. And we must use that power in the proper way, just as the electric fish uses its current to protect itself. Then neither earth nor water nor anything else can harm us; whatever touches us will receive a shock and quickly leave. No matter what type of danger may approach, it will get fried and that will be the end of it. This power within the heart will protect us.

My love you. Think about this. The same One who gave electricity to this fish has also given man a wondrous power. But man does not make use of it. He has lost contact with the power and the beauty within, and instead he looks at all the visions in the outside world, exclaiming, "This is beautiful! That is beautiful!" But all that he sees on the outside will eventually kill him. Because of his connection to the elements, that electricity of the world will shock him, lift him up, and throw him down.

Man learns only about the electricity of the world. He does not consider the power that he has within him, the power given to him by God. The electric fish uses the natural power given to it by God, but man swims about in the huge ocean of illusion, relying on artificial powers, and because of that he is subject to accidents. If only man would make contact with the true power, he would progress so much. He could obtain whatever food he needed and live happily. How peaceful his life would be.

My love you, my grandchildren. Understand and use that natural power of God's wisdom. Then no harm can come to you. Whatever comes to hurt you will be shocked and then leave you alone. My love you.

As-salāmu 'alaikum wa rahmatullāhi wa barakātuhu. May the peace of Allah and His beneficence be upon all of you. May Almighty Allah help us. *Āmīn.* May the One of limitless grace and incomparable love protect and sustain us. *Āmīn.*

Don't Blame the Tree

y love you, my grandchildren, my sisters and brothers, my daughters and sons. Shall we go for a walk? Let's visit that orchard over there.

Oh, what a fine orchard this is! Look how many trees there are. On some trees the fruits are ripe, on others they are still small and hard, and some trees have no fruits at all. How pretty all the fruits are with their varying shades of red and yellow. Some are quite juicy, some are tart, some are bitter, and some have a taste as sweet as honey.

My grandchildren, it is your duty to select the fruits you need from these trees. But first you need to know what type of fruit is good for your body. Once you reach the state in which you can understand your body's needs, then many deficiencies can be corrected by eating the appropriate food. You may need vitamin C. You may need iron, copper, or gold. Your body may need a sweet fruit or a tart one. You should know all this before you select and pluck a fruit.

You need to know which variety of fruit has the vitamins and minerals your body needs. One contains traces of iron, another is poisonous, another is not quite ripe. But if you eat a good, ripe fruit which can supply your body with what it lacks, it will make you healthier.

My grandchildren, you shouldn't eat fruits that are not suitable for the state of your body. If you say, "Oh, look at that wonderful fruit!" and eat it without knowing all there is to know about it, you may suffer. Certain fruits taken in combination with the wrong food or drink might even kill you. But is that the fault of the tree? Is it the fault of the fruit? Or is it your own fault? You must think about this. Will it bother the fruit or the tree if you throw the half-eaten fruit on the ground, just because you don't like its taste? No, the tree does not become sad when an ignorant man stomps away complaining about

The tree does not become sad when
an ignorant man stomps away complaining about its fruits.

its fruits. Someone with more wisdom will come along and eat them. Even if the fruits are not eaten by the birds or picked by man and they fall to the ground untouched, the insects and worms will enjoy them. Either way, it is no loss to the tree.

Similarly, whose fault is it if a man slips and falls when he is trying to climb a tree? If he gets angry does it upset the tree? Does it matter to the tree if he complains, "I came to eat your fruits, and you made me slip and bang my head against you. You hurt me!"

No, the tree only laughs at him. "You fool! Don't you know how to climb? You better learn. Just catch hold of a vine, or else brace yourself against another tree, or bring a ladder, or even throw a rope over a branch and pull yourself up. But don't blame me if you fall. The fault is yours." This is what the tree would say to such a foolish man.

My love you, my grandchildren. Like a man who picks the wrong fruit or a man who falls from the tree, people blame God for their own faults and ignorance. They clutch at the differences between races, religions, and colors, and that makes them fall down. Then, failing to understand that it is their own fault, they criticize the religion or the race, and they blame God.

Man has four hundred trillion, ten thousand illnesses, which are his religious, racial, and social prejudices, his doubts, his pride, arrogance, karma, jealousy, envy, deceitfulness, treachery, and selfishness. He has the illnesses of seeking praise and avoiding blame. Failing to understand these deficiencies within himself, he finds fault with others. He does not realize that, like everyone else, he too is made of earth, fire, water, air, and ether. The family of mankind is the only race he belongs to, but he doesn't know this. And so he finds fault with other religions, other races, and other castes. Holding on to all these differences, man tries to climb up and see the truth. But he slips again and again and finally falls down and bangs his head.

Rather than examining himself to find out what he is doing wrong, he blames God. Instead of searching for the medicine that would cure his deficiencies, the medicine of God's qualities, actions, conduct, equality, peace, and compassion, he finds fault with God. His ignorance is his real illness, for it destroys him by separating him from truth and ruining his love. His body, his life, and his soul become riddled with diseases which fill his mind, thoughts, vision, speech, and conduct. Then, moaning in the darkness of ignorance, he is flung into the raging fire of hell. Man must think about this.

My love you, my grandchildren. Whose fault is it if harm comes to you? If you slip and fall and hit your head, do not blame the tree. Do not blame its fruits and flowers and claim that they are worthless. Do not find fault with something else. Instead of turning away, stop and think.

Everything in God's creation is an example. Everything that He has created is filled with fragrance, taste, and beauty. God has covered this world with tasty fruits and beautiful, fragrant flowers. By carefully observing these fruits and flowers, you can know His taste within you. God has made them beautiful, and He has made you beautiful. He has placed within you the ninety-nine powers of His three thousand precious qualities and actions. Whatever you need to cure your illnesses is there for you to take. My grandchildren, you must understand the illnesses in your mind and body and treat them with the food and medicine from Allah. You must do this.

Don't blame others. Look at your own faults. Then take the fruits you need from Allah and cure those diseases within you. Just as you can cure different illnesses in your body by eating certain fruits, you can purify your soul as well as your body by imbibing God's good qualities. God has an orchard filled with His three thousand gracious qualities. Everything is there. Take the taste you need. Take the appropriate qualities, abilities, and conduct to cure each disease within you. Knowing each section, take the medicine of His actions and qualities and correct your deficiencies. Have patience, inner patience, contentment, and trust in God. Give all praise to God.

If you purify all the faulty sections within you, you will have a long life without illness. If you take the fruits of love, wisdom, compassion, justice, and the integrity of His ways, you can know the taste of His peacefulness and equality in your soul. Such is the life of grace which belongs to the liberated soul. Please think about this.

As long as you do not understand your own illnesses, you will continue to find fault with God's creations. Out of ignorance, you will find fault with the fruits of His qualities and grace. Think about this, my grandchildren. Acquire wisdom, God's skills, and His qualities. Go to a physician who knows and understands this. Go to your father of wisdom. He knows. Study with him and try to increase your understanding. Learn to develop the peace, serenity, love, and compassion that will make your lives full and everlasting. Try to attain the freedom of your soul from him. My love you, my grandchildren.

The Untold Story of Jesus (A.S.)

y love you, my grandchildren. Have you read the Bible? The Bible tells us the story of Jesus ☺, but it does not explain where he was between the ages of twelve and thirty. It does not say whether he remained in this world or went to the kingdom of heaven. Where was he? What happened during those eighteen years? We can learn nothing about this from either the Bible or the history books.

My grandchildren, if we don't know the complete history of Jesus ☺, how can we understand him? How can we know who he truly is if we do not know his state? How can we know his glory? Without knowing his life history, we can only conclude that we do not really know Jesus ☺. We can cry out, "Jesus, Jesus! We dedicate our lives to you!" But how can we determine anything about any man without fully understanding him?

My love you, my grandchildren. Let me explain something to you about those eighteen years. Have you ever noticed how, in the morning when the sun is still low on the horizon, you can see long shadows stretching from the trees? Sometimes a shadow might extend a hundred and fifty feet. But when the sun is directly overhead at midday, you cannot see any shadow at all. Then later, when the sun is at a low angle again, even your own shadow will be over a hundred feet long. But are you really that tall? No, you are only a few feet tall.

My grandchildren, we live in a world which casts shadows. People only know that something exists when they can see its form, a form that casts a shadow. If that form is missing, they cannot see anything. That is why the prophets came as forms which cast shadows. For our sakes they appeared to us in a way that we could understand, in a form which we could see with our eyes. But because their shadow forms are no longer here today, people say, "The prophets are no

296

longer here. They are dead and gone.''

Jesus ☺ did live in this world during those eighteen years, but he dwelt where the people of the world could not know him. He did not live within earth, fire, water, air, or ether. He did not live with the desire for women, earth, and gold. He made the world within him die. He surrendered to God and merged with God. His body was still in the world, but he was not in his body. The soul was with him, but the world was not. No one saw him during those eighteen years, for Jesus ☺ was with God, immersed in prayer. His body was in the world, but he was not in the body, he was in the section of God.

The people who believed in the body, because they only had the eyes to see the world, did not see him during that time. Those who carried the body of the five elements of earth, fire, water, air, and ether could not see him. Those who believed in the differences between I and you could not see him. Those who were caught by arrogance, karma, illusion, and pride could not see him. Religions, races, and scriptures could not see him. None of these could see Jesus ☺, because the world was not in him. He was here, but he was not visible to the eyes of the world.

During the time that Jesus ☺ was with our Primal Father, surrendered in *Allāhu,* the light of God was at its zenith within him, just as the sun at midday is directly overhead. The shadow of his body was not to be seen. But then he came back to the world to continue his work. When he came out of that state, people said, ''Jesus has returned,'' because they identified him with his body. They were looking for a physical form, not for the true Jesus ☺.

For the next three years, Jesus ☺ spoke to the people, saying, ''My Father God says .....'' And it was then that people began to find fault with him. The Bible says that he was finally captured and crucified. But during the crucifixion that is spoken of, Jesus' ☺ state was comparable to his state during those eighteen years.

My love you, my grandchildren. Do you understand? We can only explain something if we have understood its meaning. We are only able to speak about what we have seen after we have experienced it. And we can only know the truth when we have opened the eye of wisdom to understand it.

The knowledge you have now, my children, is limited by the intellect. The scriptures are also limited by this boundary. You can understand the words of the prophets and the lights of God only up to that level. Intellect cannot see beyond itself. Only when you transcend the intellect can you know what is beyond. Only with the four higher levels of judgment, subtle wisdom, analytic wisdom, and divine luminous wisdom can you progress.

God is beyond intellect. He is beyond scriptures, religion, race, and caste. He is a treasure which cannot be described within the bounds of intellect, a perfectly pure treasure beyond all beginnings and endings.

My love you, my grandchildren. Just as the world did not see Jesus ⊕ during those eighteen years, the world will not see us when we do not have the world within us. The state in which we forget this body and this world and dwell within God is true meditation and prayer. If you are in that state, you will not be aware of the body. Your body will be here, but it will be forgotten, as if it were dead. Your friends, relations, and possessions will all be forgotten. You will see only God. You will be living in His truth and in His body.

My love you, my grandchildren. What do you think people are searching for? They seek only a shadow that comes from darkness. But when a body is connected to God, it becomes light. When such a pure light or resplendence appears, it will be invisible to those whose eyes can perceive only shadows, the forms of darkness.

No one saw Jesus ⊕ for eighteen years because they were looking for him in that way. The sign they held dear and searched for was not there. He had become light, and the darkness had gone away. The body had no more pull on him, and he disappeared within God. But after the work of those years was completed, the form emerged in the world again, and the people found what they were looking for. Then the rest of his history was written.

My loving grandchildren, even though you and I are in the world, we will not be in this body when we dwell in God. At that time we will be in light, and when that light comes to us, we will not cast any shadow. Only God's power will exist when we reach the state in which our prayers, worship, and our devotion, or 'ibādat, dwell within God.

However, as long as we are not in that state, the body will exist. We will live in this world and not within Him, and we will be in darkness.

Histories can only be written about the time that one is in this world. They cannot be written about the time that one dwells in God. That is why the Bible does not speak about the life of Jesus ☺ during those eighteen years. And that is also why the true state of all the prophets has never really been known. The world searched for their shadows, their bodies. Without searching for their true state and without knowing who the prophets really were, people beat them and chased them and made them suffer. Such is the wonder of the ignorance of man.

My love you, my grandchildren. When light comes, this section of earth disappears. But when the section of earth and darkness comes, the light fades away.

Think about this. You must understand the prophets that God sent and know their true form. You must think about their words. You must think about everything with wisdom. In what way should you establish your connection to God? In what way should you conduct your life? Acquire God's qualities. Learn wisdom and the divine knowledge of *'ilm*. Understand every section and then know. *Āmīn*.

*In this arid land, God created the date palm to
provide food for the desert people.*

The Desert Wind Ripens the Dates

My grandchildren, will you come with me? Today we are going to visit an Arab country where the sand is endless and the heat is extreme. The people who live here undergo so much hardship and difficulty. There are times when nothing will grow and food becomes scarce. But they never give up. Somehow, they always manage to survive. This way of life is normal for people who live in the desert countries and has been for many ages.

Allah provides all beings with a place to live and food to sustain them. Even in this arid land He created the date palm to provide food for the desert people. Come, my grandchildren, and look closely at this tree. There are five hundred to a thousand dates packed together on a single branch. Do you see how beautiful they are? Their skin is like a mirror, all polished and shiny.

There is a hot wind that blows in the desert, called the wind of fire. This wind ripens and sweetens the hard dates. Then, if you squeeze them, they produce a large amount of juice. It is like milking a cow. But first that wind of fire must blow and ripen the dates.

Since the time of the great Prophet Muhammad ﷺ, these Bedouins have survived on very few foods. Dates are the mainstay of their diet. They depend upon them during long journeys and use them for breaking fast. The juice of the dates is like honey. They spread it on their bread and use it to sweeten their camel's milk, which is otherwise extremely salty.

God also provided the desert people with beautiful flowering olive trees. Like the date palms, they are hardy enough to survive this climate and produce fruits. But the unripe olives are very bitter and need to be boiled in salt water before they can be eaten. So, in a land where food is hard to find, dates provide the Bedouins with a palatable diet. A man can say, *"Al-hamdu lillāh!* Praise be to God!" and survive for a long time on just water and dates.

My love you, my grandchildren. There is no Creator or Protector other than Allah. Not an atom would move without Him. He created man, He created the date palm for man, and He even created the hot wind to ripen the dates. No one but Allah can do these things.

You and I must realize that there are also certain fruits within our hearts which must mature and ripen. The hot wind of Allah's power, His *qudrat,* must touch us. Just as the date palm grows in the desert, *imān* and the qualities of Allah must grow in the desert of our lives. If we continue to grow until we approach the age of forty, then the wind of Allah's *'ilm* and wisdom, the wind of His *rahmat,* and the wind of the plenitude of His *Nūr* will blow, and it will mellow and ripen our innermost hearts, our *qalbs.*

With that ripening, the heart itself will become a beautiful mirror, and when you look into that mirror you will see the honey of Allah's grace and love flowing forth from your heart. Once that nectar begins to flow, your life will be soothed and refreshed. Beauty and light will come into you, and everyone can partake of that nectar. All lives who drink even one drop will experience peace, tranquility, and serenity. And when you reach the desert of hunger, old age, disease, and death, God's nourishment will be there to protect you. No matter where you are in the world, if you drink just one drop of this honey, your tiredness will end.

My love you, my grandchildren. Just as the date palm grows in the desert, the roots of faith, certitude, and determination must take hold in the desert of our lives. And the divine knowledge known as *'ilm* must grow within us, blossom, and bear the fruits of wisdom.

Think about this, my grandchildren. You must resolve to grow in His qualities. You must live with the faith and determination known as *imān.* If you do, you will be capable of helping others and bringing comfort to their hearts. If you become the date palm of God's grace to all lives, then their hunger can be appeased and their hardships eased. You must have the certitude to realize this and resolve to make this state grow within yourselves. That will benefit you and all lives.

Āmīn. Āmīn. May Allah help us.

The Termite's Beautiful House

y love you, my grandchildren. Look at this huge mound built by termites. See how tall it is! The termites designed this house very carefully so that it would be a healthy environment for their colony. The house even has a subtle air conditioning system which allows air to enter one side and flow out the other. It also allows the sunlight in, but keeps the rain-water out.

The termites think their house will last forever, but sooner or later it is bound to be destroyed. A fire could easily run rampant through the very same air conditioning system that they so cleverly designed. Other insects or animals could crawl into the mound and eat their children. Or a man might decide to farm on that spot and plow down their house, destroying the entire colony. No matter how subtly the termites construct their house, any of this could easily happen. Isn't that so? We must think about this.

My grandchildren, man also does many great and clever things in his life. He builds huge palaces and thinks they will last forever. But he never has any peace. At least a termite lives happily until its house is destroyed. But even if man were to build a vast palace and rule the entire world, he could not live there peacefully. Destruction would eventually come to him through himself or through others.

So what is the use of building such a grand palace? It will not last forever. It is no more permanent than a termite mound. Man needs to understand this and build a house which can never be destroyed, a house for his soul. With the absolute faith, certitude, and determination of *īmān*, he must lay the foundation of God's qualities within himself. And upon that foundation he must build an eternal palace of prayer where God, our Father, will come and reside.

We have to think about this, my grandchildren. No house built in

The termites think their house will last forever, but
the only house that can never be destroyed is the house of the soul.

this world will ever do us any good. Only if we build within ourselves a house of *gnānam,* a house of grace-awakened wisdom, will we attain the ideal state in which our souls and lives can never be destroyed. We must build that good house, a house of light, where we can find peace and tranquility throughout our lives.

My love you, my grandchildren. With the love of God, with determination, with His qualities, His wisdom, and His help, you must make the effort to build that house of wisdom and light. Please try. It will be good for your life. May God help you. *Āmīn.*

"When I lived in heaven, I was worn around the neck as a beautiful, fragrant garland. But now I am just a crawling snake, living in the dirt."

The Snake's One Great Fault

y love you, my grandchildren. Let us go for a walk in Victoria Park. Fifty years ago this was one of the most beautiful parks in Sri Lanka. But since then they have cut down many trees, cleared out bushes and plants, and installed bright lights. People still come here, but it is not as pleasant as it used to be.

Shall we walk around a bit? Oh! Look at that snake sticking its head out of a hole. At one time there were a lot of snakes in this park, but there are not so many any more. Let's go closer. Children, the snake is crawling toward us, but there is no need to be afraid. Don't think, "It's going to bite me!" It won't bite. It must have a good reason for approaching us. Let's ask it what it wants.

"Good snake, you came right up to us. Snakes don't usually do that. Is something troubling you?"

"O great one, the wonder of God is truly within you. Your face shows so much compassion, love, and peacefulness that I know you won't harm me, so there is no need for me to fear. I can see that you have wisdom and faith in God and so I came right up to you to pay my respects. I also have something to confess to you.

"In ancient times, I committed a serious fault, and I beg your forgiveness, O great one. I am only a snake, one of God's many creations. In my ignorance I did not understand satan, and I secretly helped him get into heaven. I did grave harm and brought terrible hardship to mankind's original father and mother, Adam and Eve, peace be upon them. After that they were thrown out of heaven and cast into hell.

"Because of this one great fault, I was cursed and made into an enemy of man. God caused fear to develop between myself and mankind. Whenever I see human beings, I am afraid, and whenever they see me, they are afraid. Their fear makes them run away from

307

me or beat me, and my fear makes me run away from them or bite them.

"Long ago I made just one mistake toward God and toward mankind's original mother and father. Because of that I have suffered for so long! When I lived in heaven, I was very beautiful. My skin had the fragrance of flowers, and I was worn around the neck as a garland. But now I am just a crawling snake, living in the dirt, eating frogs and other small animals. This is what my life has come to. If I hadn't committed that one mistake, I could have lived in beauty, freedom, and peace.

"O one with the beauty of God, I have been searching all over the world for a man with such wisdom and beauty, but until now I have not seen one. I have been searching for so very long.

"Finally, I came to this island of Serendib, called Sri Lanka. I came with the faith that perhaps someone here could help me. And now you have walked along this path. The minute I saw you, I knew you could tell me how to dispel this fear and enmity so that we snakes can live in peace with mankind, with the children of our One Father. This is what I am asking of you."

"What you say is true, O snake. Your fault was indeed great. Because of you, there was so much ruin. You were originally in a very good state, but you came to this bad state because you listened to the words of someone else and whispered deceitful things. If you want peace, then from now on you must pray to God."

"O great one, there is no peace for me anywhere. Whether I am in the trees or on the ground, no matter where I hide, the face of man comes. Man is my enemy, yet I feel no hatred for him. Usually when I see a man, I respect him and keep my distance, because I try to follow the word of God. I don't even bite him if he steps on me, I just slither away in fear. I only strike at man if I am badly hurt or in danger.

"O great one, won't God forgive me? I made only one mistake, and because of that I now have four poisonous fangs. But human snakes have thirty-two fangs filled with poison. Their hearts as well as their bodies are full of poison. Not even a great one like you can escape the bite of such beings. They will not see the light shining in your face and your heart. They will even call you a snake and an enemy to the world. They are full of doubts and evil thoughts, and even though they have human faces, they possess the evil qualities of satan and illusion. Their qualities are worse than mine! They murder so many people and commit so many sins. At least when I sinned against God and man, I trembled with fear, but they sin fearlessly.

"These human snakes fight over women, land, and gold. They fight about race, religion, and language, and many murders result from these battles. Some of them even eat each other. In the whole world, there is no being who commits as many sins and who is as poisonous, murderous, and bloodsucking as man. He does not have a conscience, nor does he listen to the words of God, the justice of God, or the love, peacefulness, and compassion of God. And yet God still forgives all his faults. But I have not been forgiven after all this time. I have been punished so severely because of one mistake.

"O great one, tell me, which is the worse snake, man or me? You are a wise man with the qualities of God. You have His love and peacefulness and compassion. Can't you give me some relief? Please show me a way to live in peace with this dangerous, poisonous being."

My grandchildren, have you listened carefully to all that the snake said? We must think about this and give him an answer.

"O snake, what you say is true. In this present day there is no other being in the whole world as poisonous as man. His poison is worse than that of a thousand snakes. You cannot live in peace with man. You might be able to find some peace between yourself and the other animals, but not with the man of today, because he has no justice or conscience. How can anyone live in a state of love with such a being?

"And yet it is true that God has forgiven the human snake for thousands of faults, so you might be able to obtain forgiveness for your one fault. But consider this, O snake. You are poisonous, and you do use that poison to bring harm to others. You bite others because of your fear. Therefore, you must dispel that fear, and fear only God. You have listened to the speech of sinners and now you must learn to listen only to God's speech. Whenever a person speaks, listen carefully and analyze whether his words come from the truth and justice of God or from doubt, treachery, and other evil, poisonous qualities.

"Never try to deceive God. You must believe with total certitude that God will protect you. Therefore, trust in God, dispel your fear, and stop hurting others. Only then will the poison within you be transformed into a gem, and the light of God will manifest within you. Your qualities will become good, and His grace, His speech, and His beauty will be yours.

"At that point, all evils will disappear from you, and when you pray to Him, you will understand that He is the only One. When you surrender to Him and ask forgiveness for your faults, He will forgive you and return your original beauty, fragrance, and light. Then everyone will love you. He will create that respect between you and mankind. God will do that. But as long as you do not change yourself, they will always call you a snake.

"O snake, you and the original mother and father were cast out of paradise by God. At the same time, He threw Adam (☉) to the east and Eve (☉) to the west. They also had committed only one fault. Because you listened to satan's whispering, you were banished, and because they ate the forbidden fruit, they were banished.

"For six hundred years, Adam and Eve (☉) begged forgiveness from God, crying and surrendering more and more. Finally they obtained that forgiveness, but they still had to face many difficulties. When they joined together as man and wife, they produced twenty-one sets of twins, and through these forty-two children, the world multiplied.

Finally Adam and Eve (☉) were called back to heaven. With every breath they continued to beg forgiveness from God, saying, 'O God, so much difficulty resulted from our one fault! Please protect our children and their children from committing the same fault we committed.' And they cautioned their children, saying, 'Children, you must try to live in this world without any faults. This is a false kingdom, and you must try to make it into a true kingdom. Cast off all your evil qualities. Listen to God and ask forgiveness from Him.'

"Do you understand, O snake? God finally forgave them. And when you also pray to God and ask forgiveness in the correct manner, with good qualities, then God will forgive you. When you think of God and ask Him to give everyone good qualities and good thoughts, then He will forgive you and call you back to your original place.

"O snake, do not keep thinking about the sorrow man creates for you and others. Instead, change yourself, ask forgiveness, and act with God's qualities. He is the One who protects, so trust in Him. Then you can obtain peace. Will you do that?"

"Yes. I will, O wise one. God must help me. He must save all of us snakes from the enmity that exists between ourselves and mankind."

"That is true. Cast off your evil ways, dispel all the evil qualities within, obtain what is good, and in that state pray to God. Help men when it is for their good, but keep away from their sins and evils. Stay in the presence of God, surrendering to Him always. Then you will attain beauty and avoid danger."

"O wise one, you are my spiritual father. You have given me the treasures of love and wisdom. I will keep these treasures in my heart and treat them as my very life. O great one, please ask God to take away my sins and grant me my former state."

My grandchildren, did you listen? Do you know what the snake is? He represents the five elements of earth, fire, water, air, and ether. Both the snake's body and your body are made of these five elements. Even though your outer forms differ, both of you are made of the same substance. It is not these physical things that make a man a man and an animal an animal. It is their qualities. One who understands this and dispels the snake's poisonous qualities and actions from within himself will become a true man, the treasure of God. And a snake who changes will once again become a beautiful and fragrant garland, which God will lift and embrace to His heart. Both man and the snake must change their qualities. We must think about this.

Do not look at the outer form, look only at the inner form. There is an outer snake and there is also an inner snake. You can escape from the bite of the outer snake by running away, but the inner snake must be driven out and destroyed. If man has evil within him, he will be evil. If he is clear within, he will have clarity. If he has night within, he will be dark. But if he has light within, he will be light.

If you can change in this way, then you will become the children of God. My love you, gems of my eyes. Think about this a little. May that wealth of His grace be given to you. *Āmīn.*

*My grandchildren, wrong will always come like a
whirlwind to attack what is right.*

The Winds and Hurricanes of the Mind

y love you, my grandchildren. It's very windy outside today. See how the wind is whipping and whirling through the grasses and bushes and trees, as if it were trying to break them. But they just bend with the wind and then straighten again once it has passed. Look! Now the wind is chasing the clouds in front of the sun, and it suddenly becomes dark. Ah! The sun is bursting through again to give us warmth and light. Even at night, the wind will sometimes blow the clouds in front of the moon and conceal its light. There is nothing that the wind cannot move or shake.

My children, man is blown about and affected by the winds and thoughts of his mind, by his attachments and relationships, and by earth, fire, water, air, and ether. All these connections whirl him about. The mind can sometimes build up to gale-force winds or even to a hurricane over issues of race and religion, over attachments, blood ties, relationships, arrogance, karma, and illusion. All these storms arise from within our minds and toss us about.

My grandchildren, wrong will always come like a whirlwind to attack what is right. But just as the trees continue growing straight and tall after the wind has passed, we too can withstand these forces. If we strengthen our faith, certitude, and determination, the winds will pass, and calm will return. And just as the sun and moon burst through the clouds, the goodness of our souls will emerge and shine. Then we too will be able to provide light for the benefit of others.

My love you, my grandchildren. So many kinds of suffering occur in the world. We must push these behind us. Do not think, "This is making me sad. That is making me suffer. This will hurt me." Just try to go forward. To do this we need wisdom, truth, and faith. Only then can we escape from the storms. Sometimes we will have to bend and give way, sometimes we will have to push things aside, and sometimes we will have to go around them. But we must strive. We should not be mesmerized by these hurricanes or gales. We must go beyond them. Only then can we attain peace for our souls.

My love you, jeweled lights of my eyes. We need to think about this. We must escape and go forward. May God help us. *Āmīn.*

The Leader of the Wild Horses

y love you, my grandchildren. We have traveled a long way, but let's go a little further. Even if you are tired, do not complain, "Isn't he ever going to let us rest?" Never think that way. We did not come here to be lazy. We have to work every day unceasingly and attempt to understand everything. God already understands everything, but we have to learn from each of God's creations. They are all His stories, and as each lesson arises we must learn from it. It is our duty to study wisdom.

In our present state, the world appears very big to our eyes, doesn't it? The world is so large to our mind and desire that it seems impossible for us to travel all the way around it. But once God's eye and His wisdom have come to us, the world will seem small and we won't need to look elsewhere to learn wisdom. We will be able to learn wherever we are.

My love you, my grandchildren. Today let us go to a place where wild horses live. Do you see them in the distance? Look, there must be a hundred horses in that herd, living together in freedom with their children.

Some people like to catch wild horses. First they build a corral, then they chase the horses into it and slam the gate shut. They have caught many horses this way. But, my children, this particular herd has a very smart leader. Do you see that beautiful dark brown horse? He runs ahead of the herd to check that all is safe. Then he runs back and calls to them, "Neigh-gh-gh! Neigh-gh-gh! Come along, but be a little careful when you reach this spot." The rest of the herd can then travel safely through the area he has already scouted, while he runs ahead to check the next place.

There are three ponds where this herd goes to drink, and there are three paths that lead to them. Look, the leader is now scouting the trail to one of these ponds. Watch how carefully he checks along the

How carefully the leader checks to see if people or other dangers are about.

way to see if there are people or any other dangers about. Oh, he sees something! "Neighh! Neighhh!" he warns, galloping to tell the others, "Run! Quick! Run away!" Oh good, they have all escaped.

If you look very carefully, my grandchildren, you can see a man hidden in the bushes. That is why the leader warned his herd to run away. Listen to that man shouting. "Oh no! They got away again!" he cries angrily, beating himself on the head and chest. "I'll have to catch that clever one first! Then I can trap the rest easily."

Now the herd has come to the second path. Once again, the lead horse scouts ahead, looking here and there, checking everything. He sees that the grazing is good near this pond and that no people are in sight. So he calls the others to come. But while the horses are drinking, he looks up and sees the same man watching them from the ridge. Immediately, he gives the warning sound and races off, with his herd following behind. Once again they are saved.

My grandchildren, did you notice how the leader of the horses analyzes things with his intellect? He understands the dangers and protects his entire herd. This is why the hunter thinks, "I must catch that leader. He is the smart one!"

Precious jeweled lights of my eyes, the sheikh who protects his children is like that horse. He goes ahead of his children and analyzes everything along the way. Step by step, he has to understand each thing and lead them away from dangers.

But while the sheikh is guiding his children to God so they can drink the water of His grace, what do you think satan and all of his people are doing? They are trying to catch the sheikh and his children. Their eyes are on the leader, and they lie in waiting, thinking, "If we can just catch that sheikh in our nets, we can easily capture the rest."

And so they have put up the corral of illusion and fenced it in on all four sides. The posts of the corral are the four hundred trillion, ten thousand spiritual energies, all of the sixty-four arts and sciences, and the thirty-six kinds of forces. They built this corral to catch the one who protects all the others.

Satan is so determined to catch the sheikh that he focuses on nothing else. He tries to fence him in with the many tricks of illusion. He uses mantras, magic, mesmerisms, and attachments and offers fruits and sweets and all kinds of delicious things to lure the sheikh and his children into that corral. So, my grandchildren, a sheikh has to be very subtle. For if he enters that trap, the rest will follow.

Only one who is familiar with these dangers and has experience in escaping from these corrals can protect the children and take them safely to their Father. He has to know where the sexual games and the nets of illusion lie within relationships, within thoughts and desires and attachments, within hunger, old age, and illness, and within the five elements. If he has not learned from experience, he will be caught by a mantra or by some form of magic or by one of the sixty-four arts and sciences. He might be snared by a certain kind of beauty or by hunger or by a taste or by torpor. He might succumb to anger, sin, or vengeance. If he is caught by any of these, then so many children will be caught.

My love you, my grandchildren, precious gems of my eyes. It is so difficult, so very rare for anyone to escape from these dangers. But with a wise leader we can escape and attain freedom for our souls and for our lives. He will protect us and take us to that bliss. However, a true sheikh who can protect the lives of all his children is indeed rare, and therefore you must think before you choose who to follow. What qualities does he have? What is he capable of? How does he teach his children wisdom and good qualities? Why does he teach them? Does he teach them to satisfy his own hunger or his own desires or to obtain his own freedom? If he does, then all of his children will be caught.

My grandchildren, it is indeed difficult to find and meet a wise man. And it is difficult to live with him, travel with him, and learn wisdom from him. But without him you can never succeed. If an ignorant or foolish leader with no wisdom is guiding you, everyone will be caught. It is like that on the path of God.

Think about this and find a wise leader, one who is in that true state. If you find a good man who is wise enough to overcome these things himself, then he will take you to the pond of God's grace and you will escape from the dangers of the nets and corrals.

My love you, my children. Let us go forward with inner patience, contentment, surrender, and praise to God, with *sabūr, shukūr, tawakkul,* and *al-hamdu lillāh.* We must find the food and water that God has created for us and be happy. *Al-hamdu lillāh.*

Just as you break open the coconut, extract the kernel, and adapt it for different purposes, you have to crack open your heart, examine each section, and make it useful.

Crack Open Your Shell and Be Useful

y love you, my grandchildren. Look at this coconut. It looks like a big, earth-colored ball. The outside is so hard that you cannot break it with your bare hands. You have to smash it with something very hard. Let's crack it open. Oh look, there's water inside. How sweet it tastes! But sometimes it can be a little salty. Have you ever tasted coconut water?

Now let's taste the white kernel that lines the inside of the shell. Here, chew a piece. It's even sweeter than the water. If you scrape the kernel, then mix the coconut shreds with a little water and squeeze it into milk, you can get a still sweeter taste. And if you boil that milk, the whiteness disappears and the milk changes into an oil that can be used for many purposes.

All these things, the sweetness, the whiteness, and the oil, came out of the same coconut. Every part has a use. You start out using one part of the coconut for one purpose, then you change its consistency to use it for another purpose, then you may change it again. Each time you change it, it becomes a different product, with different uses.

My love you, my grandchildren. Your heart is also like this coconut. Just as you broke open the shell, extracted the kernel, and adapted it for different purposes, you have to crack open your heart, examine each section, and learn how to make it useful.

The outer shell of your heart has a connection to the earth. Break open that connection, and inside you will find the water of illusion and torpor. Sometimes it is sweet, but sometimes it is salty. Drink it, and experience its taste. Then move on to the next taste.

My grandchildren, just as the coconut shell is lined with the white kernel, everything in creation has a whiteness, a purity, within it,

321

with its own particular taste. Squeeze each thing and discover its different tastes and uses. In the same way that you make coconut milk, you must scrape and churn and squeeze your life. And just as you boil the milk to turn it into oil, you must boil your life until only the essence remains. That essence has many, many uses. With it you can create light and dispel darkness.

So open your heart and examine each section until you find the point of God within it. In each one you will discover a new taste and a new use. As you keep changing, life will become more and more tasty. But, my grandchildren, if you refuse to move beyond any one section because you think it is sufficiently tasty, you will never know the next one. If you only chew the kernel, you will miss out on the next taste. However, if you scrape the kernel and squeeze it, you will discover sweet milk. But do not even be satisfied with that. You must go still further and boil that milk until you finally extract the oil.

My grandchildren, we have to keep moving and changing, section by section. There are so many tastes and uses to discover in life. There are the sixty-four sexual games and sixty-four arts. There are ninety-six potentials, seventeen *puranas,* five letters, and six levels of wisdom. One by one, you must go on discovering and progressing. Do not stop in one place, saying, ''This is good enough.'' Keep moving, step by step, until you reach the final state, until you find the light that can dispel the darkness in your life.

My children, the world is tasty. Taste it, but keep it under control. Light a lamp with the oil you extract and use that light to do your duty.

My love you, my grandchildren. Just as there is one point in your eye that looks at the whole world and perceives everything, there is also one point within your wisdom. God is that point. If you reach that point, then you are the light and you can see everything. You must reach the state in which you can remove the darkness which covers the soul. You must see all things, control them, cut them, and become the light of the soul. But until then you must go on analyzing and progressing step by step. The day you learn to control the kingdom of the world, to understand the kingdom of heaven, and to receive the freedom of your soul is the day you will be a wise man. You will have conquered everything. Until then you will never find your freedom.

You will be stuck with one taste.

My grandchildren, explore the tastes beyond. You must change and change, again and again and again. With each change, you will understand more and more. There are so many things to understand in this life. Understand and continue changing, my grandchildren. God has given us so many examples to learn from.

If you have wisdom, you will understand this. You must try. My love you.

Both within the body and in the world around us, the cycles of the elements keep changing. We must control these with wisdom and find peace.

The Changing Cycles of the Elements

y love you, my grandchildren. It's midnight now and very quiet. During the twenty-four hours of the day, the elements of earth, water, air, and fire rise and fall every three hours in a way that is unknown to us. These four elements, in the form of ocean tides, air currents, heat, and the glittering nature of the earth increase and decrease in their strength. One energy will always dominate, while the others will be in a state of turbulence.

This pattern changes every three hours. When the energy of earth is dominant, a kind of magnetism, or gravity, exerts its force. But three hours later, when that force diminishes, the energy of water becomes dominant for the next three hours. After that the energy of air takes over, and then the energy of fire. As soon as the cycle of the four is completed, the energy of the earth dominates once again, and the pattern repeats itself.

During each three-hour cycle, one element dominates the others, causing them to be in turmoil. When air dominates and the winds blow, the water becomes turbulent. When water dominates and the tide rises, the air becomes turbulent. When fire is dominant, it heats up the air, water, and earth. These cycles are natural to life.

My grandchildren, these cycles exist within us just as they do in the world around us. Inside the body they exist formlessly; outside they exist as forms. We have to think about the meaning of this. Because the elements in our bodies keep changing, we experience internal changes. Just as the ocean tides ebb and flow, the tides of the blood that flows within us also change. Sometimes there isn't enough air. At other times there isn't enough warmth. Sometimes the power of water decreases in our bodies, and at other times the strength of the mind grows weak. Maya, or illusion, interacts with the elements in the same way. When illusion dominates, all four elements are in a state of turbulence, and there is a lot of trouble.

My children, during some moments within the cycle you may feel peaceful. At such times nothing is on your mind, nothing bothers you, and you have no worries. Even if you have a reason to worry, you forget about it. If you are thinking about something, that thought will slip away. And for the brief moment that you are not thinking about anything, you feel peaceful. However, as soon as another breeze comes rushing in, you suddenly remember and feel troubled all over again.

There are moments at midnight and at twelve noon, when a state of peace and motionlessness exists in all of nature and a brief period of rest comes for the elements. At that time, the air, the trees, and the bushes are all motionless. In the tropics it is so hot that nothing moves, not even a breath of air. Sometimes even the mind stands motionless. Man himself may remain motionless for a brief time at twelve o'clock. His hands and feet and even his breath may slow down for maybe four or five minutes, whether he is sleeping or awake.

Both within the body and in the world around us, the cycles of elements keep changing. If we think about this, we will understand why we experience sorrow and hardship. We will recognize each state of stress and know that one thing is causing turbulence to the next. When the air starts blowing and then stops, we can be aware of why it is happening.

Once we have developed that awareness, we must learn to control all the aspects of the five elements so that we can find some peace. We have to beat down each section and control it when it becomes turbulent. Any section that causes a problem must be controlled with the qualities and actions of God, the love and compassion of God, the prayer of God, and the wisdom of God. We have to imbibe that wisdom and use it to control all those sections so that they cannot attack our hearts. We must always remember that there is a truth. We must always remember Allah. And we must remember that His power, His *qudrat,* exists eternally. That is the only thing that never changes.

The elements cannot block us if we are in a state of wisdom and truth. The path will be clear and we can proceed. However, if we allow ourselves to be affected by the force of any dominant element, our path will be blocked. Each of the elements can block us at different times of day. We must cut away anything that obstructs us and open the straight path to Him. Only then can the relationship between ourselves and God be established.

Jeweled lights of my eyes, my love you. In order to merge with God, you must correctly establish God's qualities and His gaze within your wisdom. They can cut away anything that comes to deter you from the path. Only when this state arises within you will you attain peace in your lives. Peace comes from that direct connection to Him. With wisdom, faith, and determination, make the effort and progress on this path. Then you can speak with Him face to face.

My love you, my grandchildren, my daughters and sons, my brothers and sisters. May God give you His grace, His *qudrat,* His wisdom, and His qualities. *Āmīn.* May He give this to you in complete plenitude. *As-salāmu 'alaikum wa rahmatullāhi wa barakātuhu kulluhu.* May the peace and blessings of Allah be upon all of you. *Āmīn.*

Some of these fish jump so powerfully that they cover ten to twenty feet in one leap. They almost seem to be flying.

The Plight of the Fish
That Swam Upstream

y love you, my grandchildren, my daughters and sons, my brothers and sisters. Shall we go exploring? It has been raining hard, and water is pouring down the mountain streams and rushing toward the sea.

Look! Do you see that fish swimming upstream against the flow of the river? Why is it leaving the ocean where there is so much water? Why should it leave a place that will never dry up, a place that is constantly replenished by rainwater? Yet there it is, swimming happily upstream, away from the ocean. And it is not alone, my grandchildren. Look at all the others! They far outnumber the fish that are swimming downstream, following the flow of the river. These fish love to climb upstream. In America we call them salmon, but they are called by many different names in countries all over the world. Some people call them climbing fish, and others call them leaping fish.

My children, where we are standing the elevation is at least forty feet lower than it is where the river originates upstream. The salmon are struggling to swim all the way up there! Some of them jump so powerfully that they cover ten to twenty feet in one leap. They almost seem to be flying. Come, let's climb to the top of the mountain and ask the fish why they do this.

See that big fish over there, my grandchildren? Let's go over and talk to him. Listen carefully to what he has to say.

"O fish! Now that you have climbed up to such a height, are you glad to be here?"

"I have never felt so wonderfully content. O sir, are you a wise man?"

"No, I am just an ordinary man. Only God is wise. Even so, I would like to ask you something. Using the intelligence God gave you, you were able to climb so high. I want to find out just how you did it. And is this a good life for you? Does it make you happy?''

"Oh, yes! My wife and family are here with me, and we have never been so happy. The water here is exquisitely clear, like light. When we were in the ocean, the water was dark and murky. We couldn't see down to the bottom, we couldn't see above us, and we couldn't see what was ahead of us. Sometimes the water turned black or red. Sometimes we didn't even know where we were. It was so difficult! But here we can display our strength and use all our powers. And here we can maintain perfect balance. How happy we are to be in this place!''

"O fish, you have left a place where there will always be plenty of water, and you have come to a place where the amount of water keeps changing. It seems as if you have concluded that there is plenitude here. However, you have actually gone from plenty to little, from large to small. You have gone against the direction of your life. When you leave your natural place and go in the opposite direction, won't hardship befall you?

"This plentiful clear water is not permanent, O fish. As you climb higher, you may come to a place where there is no water. When the rain stops, the floodwaters will recede and the streams will dry up. Then where will you go? What kind of freedom will you have then? What kind of joy? You might be caught by birds or snakes, by reptiles or human beings. And that will bring only misery, not happiness. It really would be better if you went back to your original place and stayed there where you could live out your life to its completion. If you stay here, you will surely die before your time. Do you understand this?''

"O man, don't try to advise me! I know what's good for me. I know what will satisfy me. Never before have I experienced prolonged happiness like this. See how cheerful we all are, jumping, leaping, and swimming. I wasn't this free and joyful in the deep ocean. You are just trying to make me leave this wonderful place. That's what you men are like. You won't ever let a fish be happy! Never trust a human being, I always say.''

"O fish, think a little and you will understand. You are swimming along, trusting this water, but it will not always be here. It is not permanent. It will not last forever. When you first see it, you think

330

it's wonderful. Your desire thinks this is the source of joy. It won't be long, though, before your head will be sticking out of the muddy shallows, gasping. Then you will understand. Why haven't you thought of this?''

"O idiot who was born as a man, you are still trying to ruin our freedom and happiness! Who are you to come and confuse us? Go away, you fool! Mind your own business. Don't give us advice we don't want to hear. Everything you say is opposite to what we like.''

"Very well. I will leave, but we will meet again.''

Come my grandchildren, let's walk on a bit. We will return here one day soon.

Sometime later...

Ah, since we were last here, all the water has run down to the sea, and only a few puddles remain. Can you see all the fish trapped in the shallows? Look how they flop around in the mud, gasping and struggling. Now they are in real trouble. Eagles and vultures are circling overhead, waiting for them to die, and people are throwing their nets into the water, hauling in the fish. Already they have enough to fill three trucks. Look! Over there is the big fish we met earlier. He and his family are trapped, unable to go upstream or downstream. See how they are huddled together in the shrinking puddle of muddy water?

"O fish, how do you like your freedom now? Are you still glad to be here? Are you happy now?''

"Happy? Most of our children are dead!'' the big salmon cried.

"But how can that be? You told us you were free. You insisted you knew what was good for you when you left your natural place and went in the opposite direction. Do you still think this is good for you?''

"I can't talk to you now. Go away!''

Children, do you know why the fish cannot speak? Because it is gasping for breath. Look at all the fish lying in the dried up riverbed, panting, with their mouths hanging open.

"O fish, is this what you call freedom? Intelligent beings like you turn away from your rightful place and go in the opposite direction, encouraging others to follow. Not only do you bring about your own death but also the deaths of those you lead astray. You are now

331

trapped in this dirty puddle. Do you understand your plight?

"Look over there. A group of men are coming to catch you. Eagles and vultures are hovering in the sky overhead. Even the ants are waiting nearby, ready to devour you. This is hell, O fish. Your desire, your blissful ignorance, and your arrogance have led you to this end. Nothing can save you now. There isn't enough water here for you to catch your breath. You would have to travel far away to find enough water, and you can't last that long. If you had listened to me earlier, I could have saved you and your family, but now it's too late."

"Leave us alone, you idiot! Mind your own business and stop trying to make things worse for us. It may look like we're in trouble now, but we will soon escape. You'll see! Water will be here any minute."

"Very well, fish, we'll leave you alone."

Children, did you see how the fish managed to splash us with his tail even though he was gasping for every breath, and even though there was so little water? Oh well, there is nothing more we can do here. It is time for us to go.

My grandchildren, creation is like this, and man is also like this. He finds happiness in the rushing floodwater of illusion, like the salmon that joyfully leaps upstream. Everything that he thinks of as happiness he sees stretched out before him, as if in a mirror. He sees his gods, love, wealth, sexual games, and the fulfillment of all his desires. He pictures gold, silver, land, and houses awaiting him. All that he sees with his eyes pleases him. But once the illusion disappears, he is caught in hell, gasping for breath in the ditch of desire. His state is then lower than that of the fish. It is in this state that man and the other creations are leaping toward hell in the water discarded by truth.

When man was in truth, he did not see all these things that he now finds so gratifying. But in his present state, he only grabs for easy pleasures, because it is so difficult to delve into the layers of truth.

My grandchildren, truth flows in one direction but mind and desire flow in the opposite direction, the direction of evil. They cannot flow in the same direction as truth. The mind in its torpor enjoys looking at the wonders of the world. It does not realize that what it sees outside only mirrors what it has within. The mind can fly faster than the wind, and wherever it flies, desire is following happily behind, seeking miracles.

This monkey mind sees happiness in race and religion and leaps in that direction. And following his mind and desire, his property and attachments, man swims away from the place of plenitude where God, his Father, exists in completeness. He leaves the west and travels toward the east. Man, who should be swimming toward God, swims in the opposite direction toward hell. Creation swims toward the dark ditch of ignorance and hell. Thus man suffers like the salmon gasping in the shallows.

But still you cannot tell him anything. He refuses to understand the realm of God and His qualities. He will not turn toward God's justice, nor will he conduct himself correctly in the service of God with love, truth, and wisdom. His intellect only looks at what it thinks is pleasurable. No matter how much you advise him, he will scorn you, just as the fish scorned us. "Leave me alone!" he will cry. "Who are you to advise me? I know everything and you are only a fool! I have never been so happy. This way of life is freedom, and this happiness will last." People talk like this.

My grandchildren, it is not easy to live on God's side, to live with truth, love, wisdom, justice, compassion, tolerance, peacefulness, conscience, unity, and good qualities. During the season when the water of illusion is flooding, it is much easier to travel toward illusion, toward the east. It is easy to live on that side of the world. So man goes in that direction and is happy, but only for a brief moment. Soon the water ceases to flow and the river turns to mud. Then, not knowing how to escape or where to go, man falls prey to snakes, birds, demons, and ghosts.

Nothing in creation loves karma and desire as much as man does. Of all the creations, he is the one with the most arrogance and greed and the biggest ego. He is also the most ignorant. There is no being whose qualities are more dangerous or wicked. There is nothing like man.

My children, do not leap into the glittering flow of mind and desire. At first they promise happiness and wonder, but suffering will follow. When you gain wisdom, you will understand.

With the faith, certitude, and determination known as $\bar{i}m\bar{a}n$, learn the qualities of your Father. Nothing can compare to the beauty of God. He is an endless miracle, undiminishing, changeless, imperishable. He is the original, natural beauty, the Truth. As you delve into His beauty atom by atom, His power will endlessly unfold. This beauty is the wealth of your life, the treasure of grace, love, wisdom, and compassion. Understand this, my grandchildren.

Look, do you see all the dead fish? This is the way their journey ends. There is nothing left of them but the stench of rotting flesh, the stench of the vilest hell. All that remains is opposite to truth. Understand what is opposite to you, and conduct your lives correctly.

My love you, my grandchildren. Please think about this. Understand the plight of the fish.

The Wise Boy Advises His Mother

hildren, do you see that mother and son over there? The son looks like a very wise child. Look, he is walking toward us. Let us listen carefully to what he says.

"O father of my wisdom, I pay my humble obeisance to you. The moment I saw you, my feeling, awareness, and intellect told me to pay respects to you. You teach your children to lead a steady life and to go on the straight path with good conduct. You are truly a great one. I feel peaceful and tranquil in your presence, but I do have a small problem on my mind, which I would like your permission to discuss. It concerns my mother and me. Please forgive me if I say anything wrong.

"O father of my wisdom, is it correct for me to speak wisdom to my mother? It does not seem right to me, because I am just a young child. How can I explain to her that even though I was born from her womb, my first duty must be to God? I want her to understand that I must place my trust and faith in God above all others, bowing down at His feet and keeping Him always first in my heart. And I want her to know that my second duty is to have faith in those whom God has sent as His representatives to lead the people. Only after that comes my third duty, the duty to respect the mother who carried me in her womb for ten lunar months, embraced me to her breast, and gave me her milk with love. Then comes my fourth duty, to my father who dwelt in my mother's heart and was bound by her love. I must respect him from the love and wisdom of my heart."

My grandchildren, do you see how wise this boy is? We must give him an answer to his question. "My son, your words are like pearls of wisdom. Do not hesitate to tell your mother what you have to say, for God does not distinguish between big people and small ones. The true elder is the one who has a pure heart, peace, equality, unity, and a love that is clear. His love contains God's qualities, his wisdom performs God's duty, and he leads a life of goodness. If someone has such qualities, even though his body may be young, he will be mature in wisdom.

"My son, you are young in years, but in wisdom you are old, so it is good for you to advise your mother. I am small in learning, so I too can learn from you. It is in the hearts of small children that God's qualities and speech dwell, and through these young ones we often receive the answers we need. Something we do not know might come through you. We cannot necessarily say that those who are old in years are learned. No matter how old we are, if the ego of the I is big in us, we cannot really learn. We can only learn if we are small. Therefore, my son, it is good for you to speak wisdom. Ask your mother to come over here, so that all of us can learn from your wisdom."

My grandchildren, listen carefully as this wise young boy talks with his mother about life.

"O my mother, God has given us the riches of inner patience, contentment, trust in God, and praise of God, the riches of *sabūr, shukūr, tawakkul,* and *al-hamdu lillāh.* The greatest wealth of all is to have a heart that is contented with whatever God has given, a heart that praises Him, saying, 'All praises belong to You, O God. *Al-hamdu lillāh!*' If God gives us just one grain as our allotted nourishment, our *rizq,* then we must gratefully accept that one grain. We should not have the thought that we need a big, rich meal. We should not think, 'I want this. I want that. I want money. I want titles.' If we think like that, we are doomed.

"Everything in life has a limit. If we receive more than God intends for us, it will be too much. For example, one finger by itself cannot endure the same amount of swelling that the whole body can. At some point it would burst. Something in our lives also bursts when we try to exceed our limits, complaining, 'I want more. I want jewelry and fine clothes. I want to live a grand life.' Everyone wants something they don't have. The wife wants money, the husband wants loving. This kind of thinking causes resentment, anger, fights, and separations between people, and their lives become hell for them.

"My mother, when the lives of the adults go wrong, it affects the lives of the children. They watch their parents' qualities and feel great sorrow, a sorrow that never ends, not even in a lifetime. It is like a terrible disease. They are deprived of their learning, their wisdom, their talents, their peace of mind, their tranquility, and their good qualities. They cannot acquire any of these under such tense circumstances. The wealth of wisdom, love, patience, and compassion, which they brought with them when they came into this world, is destroyed. The love of God, the attachment to God, and all that comes from God is lost to them.

"This is the karma that parents pass on to their children when jealousy, ego, pride, and faith in the world and things of the world replace patience and God's good qualities. It causes so much suffering for the children when parents lack unity and instead display the differences of I and you. When parents separate, leaving the children with no father or no mother, those children live like orphans and their lives are wasted. The ignorant actions of the parents create this sorrowful state.

"When faith in God, God's qualities, peace, and contentment are not present in the parents, the children will be separated from God and His kingdom, separated from love and equality, from wisdom, and from their own lives. They will even be separated from God's justice. That is what will happen.

"My mother, you must think about this. It is easy to plant a seed, but you must toil hard to make a tree grow. It is easy to have children, but to bring them up and protect them, you must first know the limits of your own mind and wisdom. You must also know the capacity of your children so that you can give them what they need. When the roots begin to form, you must dig around them and apply the proper amount of fertilizer to make them grow. But dig very carefully, for if you start digging deeply here and there without looking, you can damage the roots. You must also use the correct fertilizer. If you deposit the fertilizer of anger, ignorance, opinions, the ego of the I, and your own bad qualities, then the children will not receive any benefits.

"O mother, do not let your bad qualities affect your children. It will damage their original roots and make their lives shrivel up and die. It will stunt the growth of their wisdom, love, and good conduct. If you inflict your bad qualities on them, you will be killing your chil-

"Mother, if you and father had a good life, and if I lead a good life and my children lead good lives, then perhaps the neighbors will see us and improve their lives, and others around them may also learn to lead good lives."

dren without actually killing them. By cutting them with your qualities, you will kill the love and wisdom in their hearts.

"My mother, in this world there are many children who suffer as I do. They have no peace in their lives. Some are in orphanages, some are in foster homes, and some are made to work like slaves. Some, even though they have a mother and father, are like orphans and slaves because of their parents' state.

"Parents must understand the correct way to raise their children. They must also learn how they themselves should mature. The wife must respect and serve the husband, and the husband must be a slave to the love in his wife's heart. They must be slaves to each other's love. Then they will have peace, *sabūr, shukūr, tawakkul,* and *al-hamdu lillāh.*

"When the hearts of male and female unite, then love, compassion, unity, and peace will appear. That same love and unity will automatically come into the lives of the children and benefit them later. They will share in that growth. If children are allowed to grow with such tender nurturing, they will return that good to their parents and to others.

"Have you seen how a tree that has been protected and nurtured grows to bear flowers and fruits that comfort people? The tree gives to others without caring about itself. But if it is not helped to grow properly, the tree will not benefit anyone. It will shrivel up and die.

"That is what happens to children when their parents lack good qualities and are not contented with what they have. When parents have fallen into the heat of hell, the children who dwell in the womb of this heat will be affected by the karma that oozes into their bodies along with the blood. They will feel deserted, they will suffer a life of hell, and their lives will not progress.

"It is true that God will provide a remedy for this. Somehow, He will make life complete for children like me. But we must have faith, for if we do not, our lives will be spoiled. God's grace will be lost, God's qualities will be lost, and God's kingdom will be lost. All that will be left for us is the kingdom of suffering, the kingdom of hell. If we are not contented, this is what will happen.

"My mother, my love, my heart, you are the first one I saw when I came into the world. A mother's actions determine how her children will grow. If her life is right, their lives will be right; if her life is wrong, their lives will be wrong. If she conducts herself with good actions and qualities, those same actions and qualities will enter into her children. If she has faith, that faith will come into them. Whatever qualities she has will enter them. Even the way she searches for God's qualities and God's love will come into them.

"They will also inherit the parents' reputation. If the parents have good qualities and justice, the children will be known as children of good people. That name will follow them. If the father is a thief, the son will be called the son of a thief. Even if the children somehow manage to become good, people will look at them and say how rare it is for a child of such bad parents to turn out well. No matter how hard the child strives to earn a good name, that hell of the parents' reputation will be associated with him. Many children suffer because of this.

"Mother, I am not saying this only about you. Many other children have problems like mine. This is not just my story, it is the story of all children who suffer from neglect. Even children who live with both parents suffer great sorrows in their lives because of the ignorant state of those parents. You must not think that your children will automatically be happy just because you both are with them. The bad language and fighting you do in their presence will enter their hearts, and they will copy whatever they see you do. If you use bad language, the young children will speak like that. If you are immodest, they will behave the same way. The qualities in you, both good and bad, will exist in the children just as the fragrance in a leaf exists in the juice extracted from it. Therefore, if you demonstrate patience, good actions, and loving, peaceful speech in the presence of the children, those things will become part of their lives.

"Some parents fight like cats, some fight like lions and tigers, and some fight like elephants. Some fight like foxes and dogs, biting one another. What will the children do when their parents fight like this? The essence of such behavior will enter the children. But, if you live with unity, if love joins with love, compassion with compassion, life with life, body with body, mind with mind, heart with heart, and soul with soul, then your children will also live like this. Peace will come to them, and they will grow up to be good.

"Parents must understand how to bring up their children. This is the primary duty of parents in our human society. If they lie and steal and exhibit bad qualities like jealousy and deceit, the children will do the same. Whatever the parents do, the children will pick up and learn. The success or downfall of the children comes from the way the parents treat them and bring them up.

"Mother, if you and father lead a good life, and if I lead a good life and my children lead good lives, then perhaps the neighbors will see us and improve their lives, and others around them may also learn to lead good lives. That will bring about heaven on earth. Love and God's grace will grow and flourish, and this world itself will be God's kingdom.

"Mother, I love you. Please forgive me. I am not scolding you. I am not the one who is doing the talking. Something in my heart is speaking to you. Whether I progress and prosper or live in misery depends upon you. So, first you must progress and then you will be able to help me. If each mother will make the effort to live like this, I think it will be good. Please forgive me, mother."

My love you, my grandchildren. Did you listen to what this wise boy said? You must be wise too. You need wisdom, and you must have faith in God and pray to Him. Improve your lives, and grow in patience, contentment, and surrender, giving all praise to Allah. May God help you.

Man-Eating Creatures

y love you, my grandchildren, my brothers and sisters, my daughters and sons. Did you know that a very long time ago there were man-eating plants in the African jungles? If a person came close enough to a man-eating bush or tree, it would grab hold of him, suck out all his blood, and dissolve his flesh.

The smaller man-eating trees were about four feet tall, and the larger ones sometimes grew to a height of fifteen feet. Their gnarled branches drooped downward like tangled locks of hair, and their leaves were long and broad. Some of the trees had vines that could twine like snakes around a man. These man-eating trees were so strong that even the fierce winds and storms and hurricanes which swept through the jungles could not destroy them.

Occasionally, hunters carrying spears would venture into the jungles, and when a storm arose, they would dash under these trees for shelter. As they stood there unsuspecting, the branches of the trees would fold around them like fingers, catch the men in their grip, and then dissolve their flesh and bones within five or six hours. They contained certain *saktis,* or elemental energies, which enabled them to do these things. Trees like this really did exist hundreds of years ago. They were known as demon trees.

There were also man-eating bushes, both large and small. On some of these, the branches stood straight up and could capture a man only if he brushed against them. Other bushes were poisonous like snakes. Their branches could engulf a man, paralyze him, and hold him captive until he died. These demon trees and bushes killed more people than animals, because animals instinctively knew to avoid them.

Four or five hundred years ago, there were over a thousand such demon trees. Eventually, however, people realized that these trees could be destroyed by fire. In some remote areas, a few managed to survive for quite a long time. But now that men have explored the whole world and analyzed each and every thing they found, they destroyed many of the things that were harmful, including the demon trees and bushes. Only some small plants of those species still exist, and scientists and wise men continue to study them.

Recently, my grandchildren, these man-eating creatures have taken human forms and are sprouting up everywhere. Just think about what has been happening over the last hundred years. Man seeks out other men to murder them. He drinks the blood of his victims, sucks them dry, consumes their flesh, and devours their lives.

Man has become more poisonous than any poisonous plant, more horrible than the man-eating demon tree. The demon trees and bushes only ate people who came near them, but the man-eating creatures with human faces go out and hunt for their victims. They spit their poison on animals of all species, on those with four legs, those with two legs, and those with no legs. Torturing man's every thought, they have set out to abolish the human race. They are spreading everywhere, destroying the community of mankind and ruining the world. Soon the poisonous creatures with human faces will take over. Full of sin and vengeance, they will search and search until they find you, and then spit their poison all over you.

My grandchildren, you must escape from these creatures. With wisdom and love, with the faith, certitude, and determination of *īmān,* and with God's qualities and actions, you must attain peace and tranquility. All of us must take refuge and hide in God's kingdom, in His wisdom, and in the beauty of His qualities. That is the only protection we have. The man-eating creatures with human faces will find us if we hide anywhere else.

My grandchildren, my daughters and sons, my brothers and sisters, think about this a little. My love you. Search for God's help and escape. *Āmīn.*

One after another, the dogs bark at anyone who walks
along the road, whether he is good or bad.

The Dogs That Bark Within

y love you, my grandchildren, my daughters and sons, my brothers and sisters. Come, night has fallen and it is growing dark. Shall we walk this way? Listen to all that barking! Do you know where it is coming from? Many of the people living along this road have guard dogs. A dog barking in one house starts the dog barking in the next house, and then the next and the next. One after another, they bark at anyone who walks along the road, whether he is a good person or bad, a human being or a demon. They bark at every creature that passes by.

People keep these dogs in their houses to guard them, but what do they really do? They eat and they make noise day and night. There is never a time when they are silent.

There are so many kinds of dogs, and they make so many different noises. The big ones roar, "Wooof! Wooof!" The medium-sized ones bark, "Bow Wow!" and the small ones shriek, "Yip! Yip!" Whether they are tiny or huge, mere puppies or old dogs, their barking never lets anyone rest. And even if they are raised properly, they still may bite strangers and sometimes even their owners. God did create dogs, but they do not have the capacity to know right from wrong. Dogs are like this. Listen to them barking and barking as we pass by.

My love you, my grandchildren. It is no great wonder that dogs bark, for every creation makes some kind of noise. And it is no great wonder that people keep these dogs in their houses. The great wonder is that man also raises dogs within himself. Just as people raise their guard dogs carefully, man lovingly raises the barking dogs within his mind. He kisses them and gives them everything they want. As long as he feeds these dogs, they will surround him, distract him, and never let him finish his work. They won't let him sleep or

345

have any peace. About ninety-five percent of all people raise these dogs within themselves. Very few are without them.

My grandchildren, the dog you raise inside this cage of your body is the dog of mind and desire. Its duty is to bark and growl. If you give it something and then try to take it away later, it will bite you. If you fail to satisfy its every desire, it will bite you. This dog will never give you peace. It will never let you do anything good. The only work it will do is bark and eat.

This dog has horrible qualities. It is selfish and does not know right from wrong or good from evil. It indiscriminately likes everything, even the things that are discarded by God and by a man of true wisdom. It constantly points its nose at the ground, searching for blood, feces, and other filth. It wanders all over, scavenging for smelly things to fulfill its desires. It does not like anything with a good fragrance.

This dog of mind and desire begs and begs, demanding food from the man who raises it within himself. All his time is spent searching for bones, flesh, chicken, and fish. That is the only work the dog will allow him to do. It barks and barks, insisting upon having everything it desires.

My grandchildren, you should never raise this dog within yourself. Such a dog is suspicious of everything and watches everyone who passes by. It is so suspicious that even while sleeping it will suddenly wake up and bark. It cannot even live in unity, peace, or harmony with another dog. Because of its selfishness, it will fight and bite, without caring whether its ears, nose, or eyes get injured.

As long as you raise such a dog within yourself, it will always be barking, and you will never know unity, harmony, or equality. You will never know love, compassion, peace, or tranquility. Those qualities will not grow within you. You will only know doubt, jealousy, envy, resentment, treachery, deceit, and the egoism of the I. You will only be able to do the work of a dog.

My precious grandchildren, do not entrust the house of your heart to the dog of mind and desire. Do not think that such a dog can guard this house filled with God's qualities, this house of wisdom and love, of compassion, peace, and tranquility. Anyone who entrusts his house to the dog will never attain serenity. This house does not need any guard but God. He is the Father whose three thousand gracious qualities and ninety-nine duties and actions, or *wilāyats,* are always guarding the house of your heart.

My grandchildren, do not leave room for anything opposite to God to creep into your heart. Give Him the sole responsibility for guarding that place. He alone is responsible for His kingdom, His house, His property, and the wealth of the soul. If He is the guard, you will have peace. If you refuse to hand the kingdom of your soul over to mind and desire, that kingdom will be strong in peace. Then you will be able to complete all your lessons in the school of this world. You will understand justice, fairness, and love. You will come to understand yourself, your Father, and the freedom of your soul.

My love you, my grandchildren. With your wisdom, catch that dog, control it, and then chain it behind the kitchen. Raise only the qualities and love of your Father. If you do this, you will have peace and tranquility. You will gain the comfort of wisdom and be happy. You will know the wealth of the love of God and appreciate the true value of that wealth. You will understand the One who is responsible for this kingdom. My love you. *Āmīn. Āmīn.*

Skin is no more than a layer of colored tissue paper glued onto man. If it were taken off, the color would be gone.

Man Is Dressed in Colored Tissue Paper

y love you, my grandchildren, my sisters and brothers, my sons and daughters. Today we are going to Europe to look in on a very special meeting where seven or eight groups of people have gathered. Look, they have separated themselves into different areas of the room according to their different colors. Come, let's stand over here and watch what happens.

Do you see that group of white people standing together? Listen to them carefully. They are all saying the same thing in many different languages. "We don't want black people in our countries. Let's tell them to leave. We are all white, and we all follow the same religion. We need to stick together! We should be the only ones in our country!"

This is how they talk, but look at what these white people are wearing. Three-quarters of them are dressed in black! Some are wearing black hats and some of the women are probably even wearing black underwear. And look at the waiter serving them coffee and tea. His uniform is both black and white.

Now come, and we'll look outside for a moment. Do you see the dogs out here? They belong to the people who are at the meeting. Some are tied on leashes and others are locked in their owners' cars. Aren't they all different? There are black dogs and white dogs, big dogs and small dogs. Even some of the cars are black and some are white. But do these people tell their cars or dogs to leave the country?

Now let's go back in to the meeting. Look, the people in that group over there all have black skin. Let's listen to what they are saying. "We have to chase those white people away! We have to destroy them!" Their talk sounds exactly like the talk of the white people. But they too are wearing clothes of varying colors. They too have animals, cars, houses and other possessions of all different colors, yet they reject human beings because of a thin layer of skin.

People will wear clothing made of every color, but they attack people whose skin is not the same color as theirs. They dress in pink, green, yellow, red, and blue. The glasses and cups they drink from are multi-colored. In their houses they keep objects that are the very colors they hate. Yet they say, "We must get rid of those people. We must chase them away and destroy them." Both groups feel hatred because of that skin.

My precious children, God created your skin as clothing for you. It is just a very thin, delicate tissue which contains color pigments. And yet, everyone is fighting because of this skin. If it were taken off, the color would be gone. Skin is no more than a layer of colored tissue paper glued onto man. And yet, look how long people have been arguing over this matter. They even set up the meeting we just witnessed in a way that allowed one group to attack another. Meetings such as this lack the unity and compassion of God. This kind of fighting destroys the love of God.

My grandchildren, do not grow up to be like these people. If the black or white skin were peeled off, any man would look like a plucked chicken. God covered man with living tissue in a most beautiful way, just as a man covers himself with fashionable clothing. God also gave His creations the ability to speak beautifully. Listen to all these people speaking in so many different languages. But what are they saying? "Chase the others away! Destroy them! They don't look like us. They don't talk like us." These people are fighting over differences in their languages, even though the sounds are similar. Isn't man a wonder, my children? He wastes his life attacking others.

Look at these so-called learned people! But what have they learned about themselves, about love, compassion, or patience, about unity or harmony? Nothing. They have learned everything else, but what kind of wisdom is that? They have not learned about God and His good qualities. All they will succeed in doing is destroying the peace of God.

My grandchildren, you have to go within yourself to realize each and every thing. For every fault you see in the outside world, you must look within and ask yourself, "Where does that energy exist inside of me? Where did it come from?'' When you recognize a fault outside, search within yourself until you find that same fault. Then you must understand it and wage war against it. Once you have cut away those things inside you, you will acquire the wisdom and the qualities of your Father. Then you will become a brother to all creations and dwell in the kingdom of God. You will no longer have to fight those outer battles, because you will realize that whatever you see outside is also within you.

There is a vast museum inside the heart and mind of man. It is filled with the bones of so many ages. Man also has an entire zoo inside, where all the many-colored birds and animals speak. All these creations have their own languages, and all those languages are within us. But without realizing this, man goes about shouting, ''My race! My country! My language! My religion! My kingdom!'' Man still has not realized that this is all God's kingdom. He sees only the different religions, races, languages, and colors. Look how one group attacks and slaughters another, just because of these differences. God is one, but people have not studied His wisdom. Prayer is one, the family of Adam ☺ is one, and mankind is one. But man does not understand this.

All creations and all the universes are in Allah's kingdom. He gave them life, He nourishes them, He watches them, He calls them back unto Himself, and He judges them. This is His kingdom. Everything is His creation and His possession. Our body, our life, our eyes and the light within them, our ears, and all of our faculties belong to Him. In the same way, His truth and wisdom belong to everyone. His love, compassion, purity, and patience belong to everyone. God belongs to everyone.

No one can say, ''The sun is mine.'' It is for everyone. No one can say, ''The moon and the earth belong to me.'' God created them for everyone. Love belongs to everyone. Truth and justice belong to everyone. Good qualities belong to everyone. Who can say, ''Mine!'' when everything belongs to Him?

Anyone who shouts, ''Mine! Mine!'' forfeits these treasures of truth and lives in hell, gathering the possessions of hell. He claims these things for himself without even knowing that he is in hell. This is a mistake. If he understood, he would say, ''This hell is not my kingdom. I am in the wrong place. I must go to the proper place." If he understood, he would acquire God's qualities of peace, tranquility, equality, compassion, and love. Those are his only true possessions. Then he would be a child of God and understand that nothing belongs to him and that everything belongs to his Father.

My grandchildren, do not go to meetings like the one we saw today. Such meetings are useless. They are just for fighting. Everyone is ready to kill each other. Do not nourish this kind of hatred within. Instead, gather together the qualities of God and then conduct a meeting within yourself. Invite His wisdom and His justice to that meeting and chase away all that is wrong within you. This work must be done on the inside. Chase away your doubts, your faults, and your hatred. Chase away your arrogance, your karma, your pride, your envy, and your sense of the I. Chase away these enemies to the kingdom of God. Then you will find peace, tranquility, and love.

The world exists around us, but the kingdom of God, the kingdom of grace, is here within the heart. My love you, my grandchildren. Each of you must think about this. You must nourish the unity and love of your Father. Find the house of your Father's peace. Find equality in your life. *Āmīn.* May God help you.

The Mosquito Melts the Skin
Before Biting It

y love you, my grandchildren, my sons and daughters. You have seen a mosquito, haven't you? Did you ever notice how small its body and wings are? It also has a very tiny needle that it uses to sting you with and draw your blood. This needle is so subtle that sometimes you can't even feel it when the mosquito pricks you.

Can a doctor do that? No. A man has to study for ten or twelve years to become a doctor. He has to learn how to give injections and draw blood samples. First he has to poke you and pinch you to find a vein, and then when he finally does puncture your skin, it hurts, and sometimes that spot becomes swollen.

But what is difficult for a doctor is easy for a mosquito. The mosquito knows exactly where the tiny capillaries are. Before injecting its needle, it makes a high-pitched humming sound, and upon hearing that sound, your muscles and skin shiver in fear, for they know it means a harmful creature is coming. This fear causes your skin to melt like wax, making it soft and thin. Then the mosquito can slide its tiny needle into that soft surface and draw out the blood. It is as easy as dipping a finger into water.

Did you know this? Were you ever aware that your flesh becomes soft before a mosquito bites you? No, we never notice such things, but our skin and muscles do. They have such fear and awareness. This same awareness causes the eye to blink automatically when a speck of dust or a small insect flies into it. The muscles know before we know.

☙

My grandchildren, the mosquito can draw your blood in a very subtle way only because fear has melted your flesh. Like this, your heart must melt from the fear of wrongdoing, and you must melt with

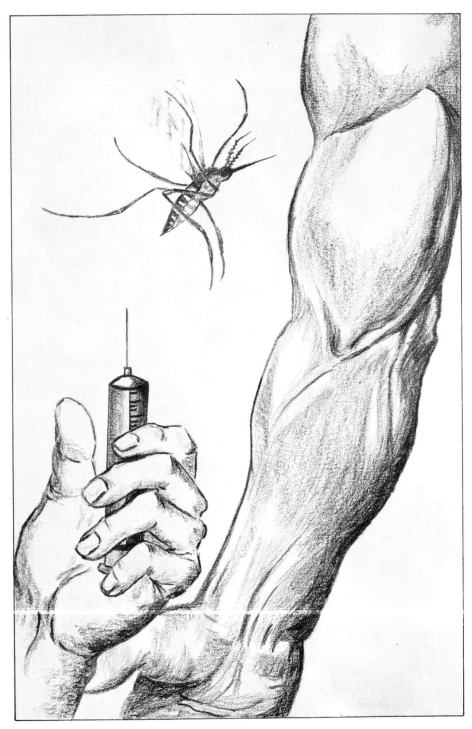

What is difficult for a doctor is easy for a mosquito.

love, so that God and the truth can easily penetrate and establish a connection with you. That connection must be made.

And what is the sound that will melt your heart? Earnest prayer and the search for truth. Your entire body must be focused on Him, and you must melt like wax. Awareness must exist in your muscles, your breath, and your speech. If you are in this state, Allah's power will merge with the truth that is within you. It will enter into you so naturally, and then He can easily draw into Himself your earnest prayers and melting love.

My grandchildren, God is not really like a mosquito. He does not come to take our blood. He comes to enter our hearts with love. But if our hearts are like stone, God's love cannot penetrate. Our muscles and awareness must melt from love. This is what prayer is all about. We must reflect on the true meaning of faith, certitude, and determination and bring our hearts and bodies to the proper state of awareness. We must melt with love, and then God will enter our hearts.

My love you, my precious children.

Why Does Man Do So Much Wrong?

y love you, precious jeweled lights of my eyes. God made man as His most exalted creation. Yet my children, you may wonder, ''Why does this elevated being do so much wrong?'' It is because God also gave man the freedom to do good or evil, to give peace to all other lives or to take peace away from them. Man has been given the energy and force to do this. There is no other creation that has this capacity. But what does he do with it? He acts according to his whims. When his thoughts are good, he does good deeds. When his thoughts are evil, he does evil deeds. As each thought arises, he follows it.

These thoughts come from his qualities of selfishness, doubt, jealousy, and from his feelings of separation and differences. They are the storms that arise in the mind of man and blow him about, just as the wind arises in the desert and whirls the sand about. When these thoughts appear, they do whatever man allows them to, and that is when he starts to go wrong. He acts without the awareness that his actions are evil. Why else would such an exalted being do so much wrong?

Man must realize his faults. He has to think about his every action and analyze what he is trying to accomplish. Whether his actions end in good or in evil is entirely in his own hands. If man acts out of wisdom, tranquility, and good qualities, then goodness will result. If he understands what is right and wrong and then dispels all that is wrong, there will be no one as exalted as that human being. No other creation can do as much good. But if he just follows the whims of his mind without any understanding, then there will be no one in the world who can do as much evil.

That is why man sometimes commits grave faults and at other times brings goodness and peacefulness to peoples' lives. He either lacks wisdom or he has wisdom. He is either in a state of ignorance, or his wisdom is clear.

Jeweled lights of my eyes, the explanation is within us. There is no use in our going around searching for what is already within us. What we must do is discard all that is evil and make room for goodness to grow within us. God, truth and falsehood, good and evil, heaven and hell are all within us. Once we start to do what is good, then we will see that from goodness comes truth, from truth comes wisdom, and from wisdom comes the resplendence of God.

That is why Allah and the prophets and men of wisdom have said, "Look within yourself and you will understand. Do not search for God, search for wisdom. Find those who have wisdom and learn it from them. Only with wisdom can you understand what is good and what is evil, then get rid of the evil and do what is right. If you can do that, you will understand the meaning of righteousness. You will know it when the goodness is there."

Children, do not waste your time looking for miracles. What do you think a miracle is? Each one of your bad qualities is a miracle. These qualities mesmerize you and turn you into slaves, subjecting you to so many kinds of suffering. The outcome of each thought, each illusion, each quality, each relationship, and each desire that you have is indeed a wonder. What these energies do to you is the miracle. Instead of giving in to them, try to overcome them and dispel them before they enslave you. Then, with analytic wisdom, control what is evil within you and allow what is good to emerge. Once the goodness within is revealed, you will understand. You will know God, the truth, goodness, and *gnānam,* or grace-awakened wisdom.

Therefore, children, as you look at each thing, think with wisdom. If you understand and act according to what is right, avoiding all wrong, then you can attain peace and tranquility. You can triumph in your lives. Think about this. My love you, my children. *Amīn.*

How much wisdom and awareness children can gain from observing the way a banana tree's leaves emerge from the stalk, giving way to fruits!

Can a Pretty Bush Satisfy Your Hunger?

y grandchildren, come outside with me, and let's see what is growing in our garden. In western countries many people have enough land to grow whatever they wish. In America and Europe there are farms which have five hundred or even a thousand acres. Many useful crops can be grown on these farms, and they can feed large numbers of people.

But not as much land is available in eastern countries. Many people are so poor that they have no house or land at all, and life is very difficult for them. Those who do own a small plot of ground usually plant banana trees, vegetables, or anything else which can help them to survive.

However, there are a few rich people who own huge houses and spacious grounds, with beautiful lawns and decorative flowers and bushes. They waste so much money planting things just for show without considering their usefulness. It might be useful to plant flowers if you want to extract their fragrance to make perfumes, and it certainly is useful to grow grass if you have a cow to feed. A grassy lawn might even be fun for the children to play on. But how much more wisdom and awareness children could gain from observing how a banana tree is planted and fertilized, and how its leaves emerge from the stalk, finally giving way to fruits.

My grandchildren, there is a lot to be learned from gardening. A clear point of wisdom can be found from each thing we do. From our own labor we can learn the limit and the good and the bad of each thing. But people who rely on servants, cooks, and gardeners do not realize this, because they don't do the work themselves, and so they never learn any lessons from their own labor. They do not know the secrets of life that can be learned from hard work, poverty, loss, and hardship. So how can they gain wisdom and correct themselves when they are only interested in play and decorations?

My grandchildren, when you plant these decorative bushes near your house, they can cause many problems. In the East, there is a hairy, poisonous centipede called a *maskutti* that lives on ornamental trees and bushes. During a certain season, they emerge by the millions. The wind blows them about and scatters them everywhere, even on the walls of houses. You must be careful not to touch them, for if one of their hairs merely brushes against you, your skin will swell and itch and burn so badly that you will cry from the pain. These decorative bushes also breed insects which are so poisonous that you might have to go to the hospital if they bite you. So many difficulties are caused when people plant ornamental bushes and trees near the house, just because their minds seek satisfaction from what their eyes find beautiful.

But look at the banana tree. Some people might not think it is beautiful, but we admire it because it is more useful than a bush or a lawn. We can eat the bananas when we are hungry. We can even learn many things from examining how they grow.

Look, do you see how the branches overlap each other? When these banana trees reach a certain height and twenty-five or thirty branches have grown, a flower will emerge from the stalk. At that time the stalk will split apart and bananas will appear. Then people, animals, and birds will come to enjoy them. Even the white center of the stalk and the flowers at the tip can be eaten. Did you know that? But until the banana tree is mature, its usefulness is not revealed.

My grandchildren, like the banana tree, each branch of the world is wrapped tightly around the truth. The truth must grow until it splits open the stalk, emerges, and shows us its usefulness. Just as the banana stalk breaks apart, allowing the fruits to appear, we must break apart the darkness of ignorance, torpor, and illusion. We have to break apart mind, desire, and attachments. We must work hard to find a way to make that truth emerge. When truth finally reveals itself, the fruit of our goodness will also be revealed, and that goodness can then be shared with others.

My love you, my grandchildren. Do you understand this? We have to emerge out of our darkness of depression and suffering and become useful. If the truth comes out, all will benefit from its goodness. We must think of this. *Āmīn.*

This beautiful creature is a great danger to others
and is sometimes called the tiger of the sea.

Beware of the Beautiful Shark

My love you, my grandchildren. Have you ever seen a shark? It lives in the ocean and is very beautiful. Its face is pointed and its sleek body tapers down and fans out into a tail with two sharp points. The shark silently moves through the water by undulating its tail and head. Its whole body and its manner of swimming have a certain kind of beauty.

But, my children, this beautiful creature is a great danger to others. It is sometimes called the tiger of the ocean, because the instant it smells blood, it goes in search of it. The shark's sharp teeth can cut with great precision, just like a sword. Its upper and lower teeth are offset, interlocking when they meet, and this enables the shark to quickly crush its prey. So do not be attracted by the beauty of the shark, for if you hold out your hand, desiring to touch it, it will eat you!

My love you, my grandchildren. Have you also noticed a certain beauty in man? Do not desire that either. Do not become attracted to the body of man, for it will be a grave danger to your life. If you go close to the man-shark, he too will eat you. If you are drawn to that physical beauty and believe in it, that shark will smell your fragrance and your qualities and come to devour you, your wife, your house, your gold and possessions, and even your cows and goats. It will circle around its prey, then attack and grab whatever it can. So do not chase after such beauty or desire beautiful things.

Remember, if you trust in the beauty of man, your life will be in danger. Your head, your hand, your leg, or your whole body will end up in his stomach. Think about this.

My love you, my grandchildren. Man is the most exalted of all God's creations. Within him there is a special kind of beauty, the

363

beauty of God's qualities, His peace and contentment, His love, patience, inner patience, wisdom, and the compassionate qualities of His ninety-nine actions and duties, His *wilāyats*. Man's beauty is not on the outside. It is hidden within him and is revealed through his actions, his qualities, his behavior, and his love. It is a radiant beauty, a true beauty that embraces all beings with love and never harms or kills any life.

All of everything will be devoted to that beauty, surrender to it, and merge within it. Once you see that beauty and go within it, you will leave your body and your elemental spirit, and you will reach a state of bliss and peacefulness. You will live without sorrow, without birth or death.

My grandchildren, in your life search only for that inner beauty. Go after it. Avoid becoming fascinated by outer beauty. Both the beauty of the shark and the worldly beauty of man are only the beauty of desires, attachments, illusions, races, religions, colors, and possessions. If you become fascinated by that false beauty and pursue it, then your life, your wisdom, your love, devotion, and trust, your qualities, and God's qualities and actions will all be in danger.

My love you, my grandchildren. If you see the true beauty and go within it, that will be a great wonder, which will bring you very, very great treasures.

Think about this, realize it, and understand it. In this world of darkness hold onto the lamp of wisdom and proceed on your way. That will be good. That is the way to escape. My love you, my grandchildren. May God help you. May He give you His grace and blessings. *Āmīn.*

Bird Droppings on the Road

y love you, my grandchildren. It is dusk now. Come, let us go for a walk along the main road. Look at all the trees lining both sides. The branches are filled with thousands of birds of all different colors. Some have red beaks, others have black beaks. Some have yellow feet, and some have orange feet. Some have white eyes, some have red eyes. All these beautifully colored birds have come here to rest. But listen to the racket they are making! You can hear more than a thousand different sounds.

Children, be careful as you walk under these trees. The whole road is covered with black, yellow, and brown bird droppings. You could slip and fall and get it all over you. You might even become ill as a result. This slimy mess is everywhere. And what a terrible stench! Look out! Anyone who passes beneath these trees might be bombarded. This filth might splatter on his head or shoulders. It might even land on his face and drip down his nose.

But do you think the birds realize that they should not defecate here because people are walking below? No, they are just doing what's natural for them. It makes no difference to them whether it's a king, a wise man, a common man, or an animal who walks beneath the tree. They just do what they must do. Birds do not know right from wrong. So, if you choose to walk under these trees while the birds are resting in the branches, it is your own fault if you get splattered.

My love you, my grandchildren. Think about this a little. Prayer is the main road between man and God. But so many trees line this road: ego, arrogance, karma, and maya, or illusion; the qualities of maya and the three sons of maya, known as *tārahan, singhan,* and

If you choose to walk under these trees when the birds are resting in the branches, it is your own fault if you get splattered.

sūran; the qualities of obsession, anger, miserliness, envy, jealousy, intoxicants, lust, theft, murder, and falsehood; resentment, hastiness, deceit, pride, treachery, doubt, the differences between I and you, and the differences between races, religions, colors, and languages. All these are the trees that grow along the road of prayer. They are the dark section within the heart of man. Beyond the trees, however, off in the distance in the open space, there is light. But do the birds go there? No, they choose to come and sit in the darkness, soiling whoever walks along that road of prayer.

Prayer is certainly good. But we have to watch out for certain dangers. For, just as the birds settle on the trees and dirty those who pass beneath, many evil energies come to dirty our prayers: all the four hundred trillion, ten thousand energies, the sixty-four kinds of arts and sciences, the sexual games, the *saktis* and *siddhis,* and the many mantras and *tantras.* And just as each variety of bird makes its own unique sound, each type of evil energy makes its own noise. Man adopts these energies, these mantras, and calls them prayer, saying, "This is the path." But, my children, this is not prayer.

Have you ever heard the commotion that crows make at six o'clock in the morning? "Caw! Caw! Caw!" they shriek. Then they fly away and return at six in the evening to shout again. Like these crows, man's mind is always noisy. His thoughts and evil qualities make a terrible racket.

These evil energies are really demons that drop their dirt upon everyone and try to prevent them from progressing on their journey. They bombard people and send them screaming and running in the opposite direction, where they slip and fall in the filth and forget their goal. We must try to escape from these birds, so that we can proceed on our way.

Prayer is the main road, the straight path. To pass safely along this road, my grandchildren, we need wisdom. We must know when the evil energies will come to rest here, how long they will stay, and what they will do. We must make an estimate, a judgment of what will happen, and then escape the dangers that await us along the road. We must cut down the trees of anger, jealousy, envy, lies, doubts, and differences. If we clear the path, the evil energies will have no place to settle. Then that road of prayer, the connection between God and man, will be clear. But as long as we do not cut down the trees where these evil energies gather, their dirt will drop on our heads and turn us away from our goal. We will forget that there is one God, one truth, one prayer, and one society of man.

My love you, my grandchildren. Do you understand these things? You must know the capabilities of these energies, and analyze every situation, so you can make a wise decision. Only then will you find some peace. If you cannot cut down these huge trees, then you must at least know when the evil birds of hell will gather there and when they will leave. Watch and wait, and only begin your journey after they have gone. Then you can escape.

My grandchildren, if you do not know how to avoid these energies, you cannot walk on this main street of prayer, worship, and devotion without becoming soiled. So many things will bombard you: desire for fame and for the titles which are the billboards of hell; the base desires, or *nafs ammārah;* the five elements, the five senses; arrogance, karma, illusion; and the desire for earth, women, and gold. All these will settle in your mind and surround your heart, dirtying the place of prayer. Unless you have wisdom you will be caught up in these difficulties. Be very careful! Learn how to flee from these four hundred trillion, ten thousand evil energies which await you. You will only be able to escape if you cross this section of magic and mesmerism. Only then can you travel on the path of prayer and reach your goal.

My grandchildren, go beyond to where there is light. Go on the road which joins the east to the west. This is the main road, the straight road of one prayer, of one family, one point, and one God. May that one God protect us on our journey. *Amīn.*

Don't Stop Milking the Cow

My love you, my grandchildren, my sisters and brothers, my sons and daughters. Here we are at a dairy farm. Shall we take a look around?

Do you see all the cows grazing in the field? Over there, the men are feeding the cows that are about to give birth. And here is the barn where the cows and their calves are sheltered. Shall we go inside? Oh, good, we are just in time to watch the farmer milking a cow. But look, her poor calf is tied up in front of her, and it too wants some milk. It is straining against the rope and sucking on everything within reach. Now the calf is sucking on its mother's chin. The more it sucks, the more it salivates, so the calf is really only drinking its own saliva. It can't get any milk that way! Doesn't it know any better?

Oh, no! The calf is trying to suck on the farmer's ears. Oops! Now it is stepping on his feet, and he is getting very angry. Listen to him scold the calf and push it away. But the calf doesn't understand, and it keeps on nipping at the farmer's ears and face as if he were its mother. Now he is so furious that he stops milking the cow and stomps off in anger.

So who is the loser? Certainly not the cow, and certainly not the calf, who is finally getting some of its mother's milk. The man is the loser. But look, now the calf is drinking more than it needs, and this could make it sick. If the calf dies, the farmer's anger will have cost him the calf as well as the milk.

My love you, my grandchildren. The dairy farmer gets milk from a cow, but you must go to God for your milk. God is the One who can give you the milk of grace, the milk of love, compassion, and wisdom. God is a power, the One of limitless grace and incomparable love.

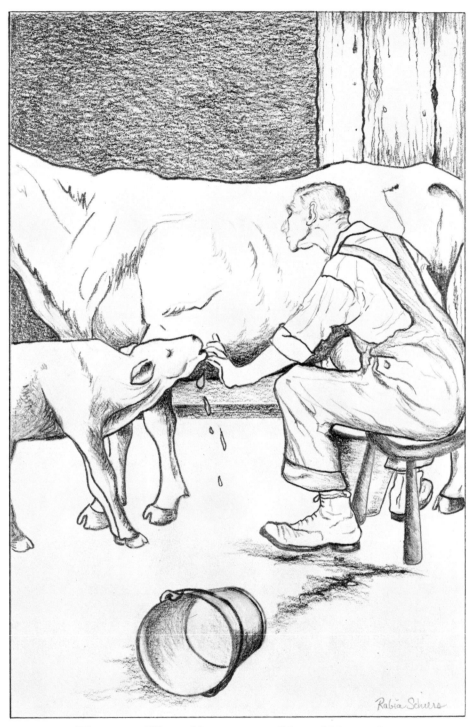

The poor calf is sucking on everything within reach.
It can't get any milk that way!

Whatever benefits you receive must come from Him. But while you are drawing God's milk, do you know what will be right behind you? Your mind, your desire, and the five elements. They will keep bothering you like the calf searching for milk and sucking on this and that. Difficulties, losses, and poverty will also come from behind to lick you and nip you.

When such troubles disturb a faithful man who is searching for God, he may give up, thinking, "What kind of God are You? Here I am, searching for You and for the milk of Your truth, but all I get is misery and illness. It's not fair!" Like the farmer who stopped milking the cow because he was angry with the calf, man sometimes lets his problems prevent him from searching for God's love and compassion. He loses his faith and trust in God. And when that happens, man runs away, searching for help from whatever he sees.

He turns to lesser things, such as the sun, the moon, religions, stones, trees, earth, fire, water, air, or ether. But they have no wisdom, so they too suck at him and tread on him. They disturb his mind, and he becomes still angrier. Again he blames God. "All this difficulty has come to me because I trusted You and was searching for Your milk. What's the use?" he cries. And he gives up his search and loses the milk of grace and wisdom.

Then, just as the calf may fall ill and even die from drinking too much milk, a man who becomes involved in his karma experiences more and more sadness, hunger, and poverty. Because of his sorrows, he gives up the truth and his good qualities, and he stops worshiping God. This is man's most serious mistake and it leads him into still deeper trouble. Letting go of God is the gravest illness, the illness that will cause a man to die.

My grandchildren, like the calf, the world will lick and bite you. However, you must remember that it has no wisdom. No matter how much the world bothers you, you must never give up good qualities, good actions, truth, wisdom, and your belief in God. With faith, you must try hard to extract from God the milk of grace, the milk of wisdom and love and compassion. You must develop inner patience, contentment, trust in God, and praise of God, known as *sabūr, shukūr, tawakkal Allāh,* and *al-hamdu lillāh.* And you must do your duty with the faith, certitude, and determination of *īmān.*

Mind, desire, and evil qualities have no wisdom. They will go after anything at all, looking for their food. Even so, you must never give up your search for truth. When troubles nibble you from behind or in front, or attack and even trample you, you must always show patience. No matter how much suffering you may endure, you must be persistent in your effort to extract and drink the milk of truth from God. Only then will you know the good taste of wisdom through which you can overcome fatigue and fill your life with peacefulness and tranquility.

My love you, my grandchildren. You must think about this. _Āmīn._ May God help you.

The Evolution of Man

y love you, my grandchildren. Do you know the names of the seven continents of the world? They are: North America, South America, Africa, Australia, Asia, Europe, and Antarctica. The lands in the east are called Asia. The lands in the west are called Europe and the Americas. To the south are Africa and Australia, and beyond them lies Antarctica. These are the seven great continents.

Shall we visit the continent of Africa? It was here that Adam and Eve ☺ once lived and gave birth to twenty-one sets of twins. Originally Adam ☺ existed in the form of light, completeness, and plenitude. But then satan became jealous of Adam ☺ and spat on him. Satan's jealousy entered him and changed his perfect state. There was a wavering and incompleteness in that plenitude. Then Adam ☺ was further spoiled by eating the forbidden fruit. His form and qualities changed, and he lost the ability to use the wisdom of his original light form.

Because of his fault Adam ☺ was thrown out of heaven onto the earth. For six hundred years he meditated upon God, and finally he was forgiven. Then God gradually gave Adam ☺ more and more clarity and wisdom and showed him the connection that existed between himself and God. After teaching Adam ☺, God continued teaching mankind through His representatives, His prophets, His lights, and His *qutbs.*

Adam ☺ overcame his faults and conquered himself, but many of his children separated from God and went their own ways in the world. They scattered throughout the land, going to the jungles, to the icy mountainsides, and to the shores of the sea. Wherever they went, the children of Adam ☺ looked about and learned from the animals and the other creations of that particular environment. They imitated what they saw the animals do and adopted their qualities.

What began as pictures gradually changed into letters,
and that is how writing evolved.

Then men began to copy the sounds they heard, and after a while those sounds developed into speech. Next they began to draw pictures of everything they saw, of trees, bushes, birds, winged creatures, elephants, cats, and rats. At first they would think about a tree or a bird and then draw a picture that would show their thoughts to others. What began as pictures gradually changed into letters, and that is how writing evolved.

Much of man's learning came from watching and copying the animals. He even imitated their ways of eating. He observed animals killing and eating each other, and he began to kill and eat other men. That is how cannibalism began. My children, you would be amazed if you saw some of the things that happened in Africa in those days.

However, as time passed, man evolved a little more. He learned how to kill and eat birds and animals instead of human beings. But he still had not thought of using his hands to feed himself. Instead, he sunk his teeth into the raw flesh of his prey, just as he had seen other animals doing. Then he noticed monkeys eating with their hands, and he copied that.

Even though the children of Adam ☺ were human and had only two legs, they did not walk upright. Instead they bent over, loping along on all four limbs. After a while they began to walk on two legs, but they still carried themselves like monkeys. They began to exhibit numerous monkey pranks and qualities. They jumped from tree to tree, and whenever they jumped, they noticed how the branches would bend. That gave them the idea for the bow and arrow. By that time they had already been using stones as a primitive form of weapon.

After a while, from watching nature, man discovered fire and began to cook his food instead of eating it raw. At this time man ate with his fingers, but when he saw crabs eating, he thought, "What a wonder! Look how crabs feed themselves with their claws!" So he invented chopsticks. In this way, he continued to learn, copying one thing after another from his environment. This is how God helped man to evolve. Some people did change and grow, while others remained in the jungle and continued to live like animals. Each group developed in a way that suited the area in which they lived.

A hundred million years after Adam ☺ the human population was greatly increased. Men had scattered and gone to different lands to build cities and towns, and kings were ruling the people. How do you think someone became a king? Just as a lion roars, "I am the king of the jungle," a man who had more strength than the others would roar, "I am the king." He would declare himself the ruler of all beings and force them to obey him.

Now man was civilized. But what did this so-called civilized man do? He went back to the jungle and killed the animals and people that lived there, claiming the land for himself and chasing others away. As man spread over the face of the world, so did destruction. Many wondrous birds and animals are now extinct because of man. A hundred million years ago there were huge fire birds, much bigger than any bird that lives today. With their enormous claws they could seize an elephant behind the ears and actually lift it up into a tree. There were also fire-breathing animals which resembled crocodiles. Today these creatures are all gone, but we still hear many stories about them.

As man developed weapons, he destroyed countless lives. But the greatest destruction has come during the last hundred years. With his superior knowledge and weapons, 'civilized' man captured and killed large numbers of the American Indians, the Veddas, and other tribal people, wiping out languages and destroying whole cultures. Today there are very few places where the original inhabitants still remain.

In the evolution of every species in the world, the strong destroyed the weak. Strong birds destroyed weak birds, strong fish destroyed weak fish, and strong men destroyed weak men. Those with power destroyed those without power. Man destroyed in the name of progress and civilization. He sold animals to other men, and then he started selling human beings. The men with more advanced weapons captured those with more primitive weapons and sold them as slaves.

My grandchildren, man has done all these things in the name of progress. But what kind of progress is this? Man did not progress in correcting himself, he progressed in killing others and capturing their lands. As he spread across the face of the earth, he deserted the good path and progressed in the path of destruction. This is the only effect civilized man has had upon the world.

A true human being would not do such things. He would tame the terrible creations living within himself. He would control those animals that are devouring him from inside. He would destroy the jungle within and civilize the world of his mind. That is how man should evolve.

My love you, my grandchildren. We should not try to take over the world. Instead we should take control of the satans, demons, and ghosts who rule the world within us. We should dispel thought, mind, desire, attachment, lust, anger, illusion, darkness, and karma. Those evils have taken away our freedom. Satan and his qualities have captured that kingdom of goodness and purity, the kingdom of the soul, the kingdom of God. We have to fight to recapture that kingdom within. Think about this and understand what you need to do.

Never relinquish this inner kingdom to your enemies. Who are your enemies? Arrogance, karma, illusion, treachery, vengeance, deceit, the separation between the I and the you, and four hundred trillion, ten thousand evil qualities. Wage war against them, chase them away, and recapture your true kingdom. Be a father to all lives, show them love, serve them, and take them on the good path. This is the eternal kingdom. Anyone who can civilize this kingdom will never again need to capture outer kingdoms, because that kingdom within himself contains all the universes. Try to truly civilize it.

No kingdom can be compared with the kingdom of the soul. There is nothing equal to it anywhere, it is so unfathomably deep and vast. Whoever can control and civilize this kingdom will protect and watch over all lives. To him the outer world will be but an atom. He will show love and compassion to all people and to all creations. He will not hurt any life. He will only protect, comfort, and help other lives. He will tame them, civilize them, take them on the good path, and give them wisdom.

My grandchildren, the inner kingdom belongs to you; the outer kingdom belongs to all the other beings that exist in it. To be truly civilized you must civilize that inner kingdom. That is the kingdom of our Father, the kingdom of grace, wisdom, and love. What evolution is there other than this?

May God help you. *Āmīn. Āmīn.*

The time will come when our lives will fall from us as leaves
fall from the trees. Then we will have to go alone and answer to God.

The Trees Stand Bare

y love you, my grandchildren, my sons and daughters, my brothers and sisters. Come, let us walk over to that grove of trees. Last summer their leaves were a beautiful green, but when autumn came, they turned to gold, orange, and red. Now it is winter, and the branches are all bare. Come, touch this tree and see how cold it is. It feels dead.

My children, the tree is an example from God to teach us about our own lives. We have a limit, just as the leaves do. No matter how beautiful we are or what fame and titles and honors we have earned, the time will come when our lives will fall from us as leaves fall from the trees. We will be left to stand alone, without any possessions, naked and in a state of suspension, with no help from anyone.

On the day of our death, when the Angel 'Izrā'īl ☺ comes to us, and on the Day of Judgment, no one will be there to help us, not our children, or our brothers and sisters, or our mothers and fathers, or our uncles and aunts. We will have to go alone and answer to God. Then we will either go to heaven or to hell. This will happen to each of us one day.

My children, like the leaves that fall from the tree, all of us must go some day. Our relatives from this world will not go with us, but our true relatives will. Who are our true relatives? God, His goodness, truth, and justice, His honesty, conscience, and patience. These relatives will bring us peace and tranquility and show us love. Only that relationship with God will help us, here or in the hereafter. When everything else falls away, just as the tree stands bare after the leaves have fallen, the soul will stand alone, indestructible. Then all of God's family, His representatives, prophets, messengers, and friends, His lights and *qutbs* will come to meet us. They will be our family.

We must establish that true relationship while we are still here in

379

this world. We have to find that affection and trust here. If we do, then just as trees blossom again in the spring, our souls will find liberation.

You must know this, my grandchildren. You must search for your birthright and the wealth of your soul. If you search for this now, your soul will know bliss later. Then you can be happy in this world and in the next.

My love you, my grandchildren. Please think about this.

The Deer Is Ready to Sacrifice Her Life

y love you, my grandchildren, my sons and daughters, my brothers and sisters. Shall we go for a walk through the forest? There once was a man who used to come to this forest to find food for his family. One day he hunted from dawn to dusk, searching everywhere, but he did not catch a single animal. He was very sad. "How shall I feed my wife and children?" he worried.

Just then a family of deer came running through the forest. Suddenly the mother deer stopped and said to her husband, "Take the children home. There is something I must do. I will come later, if I can."

"What do you mean? Where are you going?" her husband asked. "What is it that you must do?"

"Nearby, there is a very sad man who does not know his way out of the forest. Once it becomes dark, all the tigers and other hungry animals will begin to hunt for their food, and they might eat him. That poor man has a wife and four children at home, waiting and hungry. They depend upon him to feed them. So I have to make sure he finds his way home before it becomes totally dark, and then I must fulfill his needs. That is why I have to go now."

"What are you going to do?" asked her husband.

"I will offer him my own flesh, so that his wife and children will have something to eat."

"Are you going to die for him?" her husband asked.

"Yes, I am willing to do that," she said, "because God has said it is good to help those in need. It is true that my action will bring me death, but it will also bring me peace. I will be giving that man peace, and I will attain the peace of God. So do not be sad. This is something I must do. I have to die sometime, anyway."

"Very well, we will come too," her husband and children insisted.

"O hunter, most men would feel sorry if they killed a deer who had a fawn. But you don't seem to have any compassion."

"If we all go, he will have enough food for months, and he and his family will be very peaceful. Come quickly! Let us show him the way home before it gets dark." And so they set out to look for the hunter.

They found him leaning against the trunk of a tree, crying in despair. As soon as he saw the deer coming toward him, he reached for his gun.

"O man, do not kill me just yet!" the mother deer warned. "If you shoot me now, you will never find your way out of the forest. The creatures of the dark are waiting to eat you, just as you want to eat me. So, before it becomes totally dark, let me take you home. After that you can kill me. I said to my husband and children, 'He is so sad! If he dies, his wife and four children will also die. I must go and see to it that they live.' And my family agreed. So together we have come to ease your suffering. First we will lead you to your house and then you can eat us."

The man reflected upon what the deer had said. "How did you know I had a wife and four children?" he asked.

"O man, the only difference between you and me is in our forms," she answered. "Our skin is different, but our hearts are the same. We believe in the same God, don't we? And we both contain the same treasure, the power of God. I am an animal, but God is within me. And because I am an animal, I am clear on the inside and I can heed His warnings. If you become clear, you too will be able to hear when God speaks within you. I came to you because I listened to that inner warning."

The man burst into tears and cried, "How could I ever have thought of killing you? No matter how hungry or desperate I was, how could I commit such a sin?"

"O man," the deer told him, "you should realize that you can never truly grow by eating the flesh of another. We eat branches, leaves, grasses, and even some minerals from stones. Whatever God gives us is sufficient. We always remember that.

"God has given you ears, eyes, a nose, a mouth, hands, and legs. If you apply your wisdom, you can use these to acquire your food without having to kill or steal or lie. You can always find some job. You can become a servant or a cook. You can collect trash, clean the streets, or do almost anything. You can do these jobs with dignity, honor, good qualities, and a good heart. When you earn your own living, the grace and love of God will increase within you. And when His gaze falls upon you, all His wealth will become yours. You will have the wealth of grace and wisdom, the wealth of love and compassion. You will have the wealth of inner patience, contentment, trust in God, and praise of God, the wealth of *sabūr, shukūr, tawakkul,* and *al-hamdu lillāh.* Never again will you be poor. You will always have the treasures of Allah, and when you have those treasures, what will you ever lack?

"O man, it is because you did not have these qualities that you fell into so much difficulty. Killing others made you happy. Your food came from tormenting other lives, but the harm you caused others came back to torment you. Everything you did returned to you. If you had not done those things, you would not have suffered so. You would have attained peace and tranquility. From now on, you must change and go on the path of goodness.

"And now, O man, we must find another way for you to feed your family. Wait here, and I will bring you something that men consider very valuable." The deer then ran off into the forest and returned soon after that with a gem. "The man who owned this gem was killed by a tiger. I was watching, and I saw it drop from his hands when he died. Here, take it. You can sell it and live happily without having to harm others."

Then the deer and her family led the man to the edge of the woods. Carrying his gun at his side, he returned home, and the deer and her husband and children returned to their home in the forest.

My precious children, jeweled lights of my eyes, we have to think about this story. Deer and other animals have feeling, awareness, and intellect. Some even have the love and compassion which enables them to know the hearts and needs of others. When the love of God melts and flows forth from the heart of one of God's creations, that being will want to do what is good. The deer was ready to give her life to help the hunter and his family. If a deer can show so much love and compassion, how much should a man be able to give? If he is not ready to give his body, he can at least give a mouthful of food, a sip of water, or a piece of clothing. He can at least give love and compassion from his heart. The deer was ready to sacrifice herself, her husband, and her children. If we think about this, we will realize how much more compassion and love we must give to others. If a man cannot be compassionate, what kind of person is he?

My grandchildren, we must make our love melt and give our compassion as freely as we would offer water. That will be very good. My love you. *Anbu.*

*How can you connect with that power to receive
the warmth and peace you need?*

Stand at the Correct Distance from the Fire

y love you, my grandchildren, my sons and daughters. Now it is wintertime and snow and ice cover the ground. Shall we go for a walk? Look, there is a cave over there, and some people are sitting inside, warming themselves around a fire. See how they are shivering and rubbing their hands over the flames?

My grandchildren, fire can warm your hands, but it can also burn them. You must be careful to get just the right amount of heat. If you stand too far away, you will not get enough, but if you come too close, the heat will be overpowering.

We do need fire. It has been given to us so that we can make use of its essence to warm ourselves. But before using it, we must assess its limits with our feeling, awareness, intellect, and wisdom. We must judge how much heat is needed to dispel our numbness and shivering and then stand at the correct distance from the fire.

It is also like this with God, my grandchildren. We need God to remove all of our diseases: the diseases of arrogance, karma, and maya, the illness of the mind, and the illness which arises from our lack of wisdom. We need God's help just as we need the fire's help to dispel the cold, but if we get too close, we will not be able to bear it. That great power will scorch us. And yet, if we remain too far away from God, we will never receive His help to dispel the illnesses of our karma, which will eventually catch us and eat us up.

My children, God is a very great power. In what way should you connect with that power to receive the warmth and peace you need? You must stand in the right place at the correct distance and stretch out your hands. You must be in the proper state. You have to acquire the qualities, actions, love, and wisdom of that power. Then, just as fire can merge with fire, you can merge with that great power. If you do, then all your difficulties will be eased and kept under control, and problems that seem like huge mountains will be reduced to tiny pebbles. But if you do not attain that state, you will experience many difficulties and gain very little. Think about this.

My love you, my grandchildren. The sheikh also has blessings to give you, but you will only know this goodness according to your capacity to receive it. If you are in too much of a hurry, or if you come too close, too soon, you could cause yourself harm. You could become confused and unbalanced. You must use your judgment, and with absolute surrender, perfect concentration, balance, and wisdom, keep moving forward a little at a time and see how you feel. See how much heat you can bear. As you progress, as God's qualities and actions and love grow within you, move forward some more. Once you arrive at the state of the sheikh or reach the state of God, you and the sheikh will merge into one. But until then you must remain at the level of knowledge appropriate to your development.

My children, keep moving closer to the sheikh for the wisdom you need and then go on to God. Do not stand too far away, but do not stretch out your hand before you are ready for that power, or it will burn you. Whether you are warmed or burned will depend upon your state. If you stand at just the right spot, you will receive some peace when problems arise. If you want to benefit from the sheikh, you must develop his wisdom and his qualities and actions. Then you can come still closer and closer. In the way that wood burns and burns until it is finally consumed, you also must keep progressing and developing, until you finally merge with the sheikh.

The sheikh must also develop and draw even closer to God. A wise man, a sheikh, a father must surrender to God and become His slave. He must have the **qualities** of God the way a fire has heat. He must have God's actions, love, compassion, patience, tolerance, and equality. If the sheikh has these qualities and if he has wisdom, then all the diseases that come to the disciples through ignorance, karma, illusion, and attachments can be cured. With the sheikh's love and wisdom and good thoughts, with his gaze and his speech, with his good qualities, actions, conduct, compassion, mercy, truth, and *imān*, he can help the disciples, and they can find peace.

But if the sheikh does not have these qualities, if he is in the same state as others or worse, he cannot be of help to them. If the children come with karma and the sheikh has even more karma, the children will suffer. If the children come filled with illusion and the sheikh is even more steeped in the world of illusion, then the children will suffer even more. If there were no heat in fire, how could a man shivering from the cold be comforted? If the fire were to give off an icy blast, wouldn't it make the man even colder? Like that, if those who are cold should come to one who is like ice, he could cause their death. He could kill them.

My grandchildren, the sheikh must be like a fire that can warm his children and dispel the numbness and chill of their karma. The wisdom of a sheikh must come from the wisdom of God, the words of God, His actions, His truth, and His love. If such wisdom comes from the sheikh, it will give peace and benefit to others.

My grandchildren, you must think about this. From fire you can attain warmth, and from the sheikh, you can attain wisdom and good qualities. You must acquire the qualities of God, but to receive these qualities you must be in the correct state. Know your limits and take the amount of heat appropriate to your state. Then you will attain peace. This is very important for your lives. My love you.

The mountain bears can come out of their caves, but man cannot.

Bears in the Cave

y grandchildren, today we are going up into the mountains. Let us climb onto these high rocks. Do you hear the voices coming from that cave? It sounds like a lot of people are inside speaking in different languages. Listen to all the echoes bouncing back and forth. Come, follow me. Don't be afraid. Let's go and see who's in the cave.

Oh, it's a bear with her children! Listen to them expressing their happiness in their own language. From a distance, they sounded just like people, didn't they? Now they are coming out of the cave, still talking happily. We can't understand what they're saying, but the sound is lovely. Let's watch them for a while. See how the mother tumbles playfully with the children and how they jump and climb all over her? That is how bears play.

My grandchildren, there are many human bears in this world who live in the caves of illusion. When they talk inside those caves, the melody and cadence of their voices makes them sound human, but their words are not words of wisdom, truth, love, God, conscience, or unity, and their actions are not the actions of true human beings. They pounce on each other any way they please. They lack the conduct, values, modesty, sincerity, reserve, and fear of wrongdoing that true human beings have.

These human bears will deliberately seek you out with the intention of harming you. The mountain bears are not like that. They do not analyze before they act. If one of them should chase you, you could escape by simply climbing a tree. But when a human bear decides to come after you, you can never escape from him, no matter where you try to find refuge. He holds onto his vengeance until you are dead.

These human bears who dwell in the caves of illusion are far worse than any bears that live in mountain caves. The mountain bears can come out of their caves, but man cannot. He is trapped in his body of illusion like a caged animal. A mountain bear is strong enough to rip you apart limb by limb, and eat you. But a human bear can do much more harm, for he has the strength of sixty-four people. He contains four hundred trillion, ten thousand kinds of qualities, energies, or *saktis,* and viruses. Each one of these is like a mouth which can tear you to pieces, so you must be very careful. Human bears are extremely dangerous. Do not be taken in by their words or their appearance. Do not get involved with them. And do not let them catch you!

You must try to escape from these bears of arrogance, karma, illusion, ignorance, and the egoism of the I. The worst bear of all is the one which says, "There is no one greater than I!" It will never let go of anyone. You must not get too close to such bears. Do not be fooled into thinking that they are human just because they can talk. Remember that even the bears in the cave sounded human to us from a distance. Do not even waste time listening to their stories. At every moment you have to be careful. Remember, they are bears!

My love you, my grandchildren. Human bears sound exactly like human beings, but you must not think they are. A bear is a bear. You have to consider this with your wisdom and act carefully in your life. This is a very subtle thing. My love you, my grandchildren.

The Four Colors of the Mountain

y love you, my grandchildren. Come, let's walk over to that rocky mountain. Look, one side of the mountain is white, and the other is black. Here in front of us it is earth-colored, almost the hue of marrow, and the far side of the mountain is bluish-green mixed with black. The whole mountain is composed of rocks of four different colors. You can build a beautiful house using the colored stones cut from this mountain.

My grandchildren, come over here and I will show you something. Look what happens when we hit this black stone very hard. Ahh, there is a spark. Where do you think that fire came from? It was within the stone. Now let us strike hard against one of the earth-colored stones. A spark flies out of that one too. Now let's try the white and bluish-green stones. Sparks came from all four stones, didn't they? Even though their colors are different, they all reacted the same way because they all came from the same mother, the earth. Whatever their color, rocks are rocks.

My grandchildren, think about this. People also may be different on the outside, but we are all from the same source. Before we struck the stones, did we know that they would produce sparks? No, we didn't. In the same way, if we strike truth with the wisdom that is within us, sparks will fly. Like a house built with these four colored stones, our bodies are built with the four elements of earth, fire, water, and air. These four also represent the four major religions. When God made Adam ☺, He created him from only one handful of earth, but from that single handful, all these religions have sprung up and become like a huge rock mountain.

Truth and God's power can be found within all four religions. Each religion has a different kind of grace, and it is up to us to dis-

393

Like the four colored stones, people may be different on the outside, but they all come from the same source.

cover it. We have to strike each one with wisdom to release the sparks of the grace of God, His *qudrat,* and His ninety-nine qualities and actions, known as *wilāyats.* The sparks will fly, but to start a fire, we need something for them to ignite, something that will burn, like cotton. Wherever the sparks of grace fall, we must place the cotton of God's qualities and actions, His behavior and good conduct.

If we place that cotton carefully with the faith, certitude, and determination of *īmān,* the sparks of grace will fall upon it, and it will start to smolder. Then we must blow on it with the breath of *"Lā ilāha ill-Allāhu:* There is nothing other than You, only You are Allah," and the fire of God's power will emerge from within His grace. His light will resplend from within His qualities, and His plenitude will radiate from within His light.

My love you, my children, jeweled lights of my eyes. You have to understand the effects of the qualities, actions, and behavior of each of these four major religions, these four colored stones. They may look different on the outside, but they all come from the same source. Truth is one. We must look at the truth within them and see how the fire can be kindled so that it can give warmth to all lives. We have to understand all four, step by step. Then we can help people and live in freedom.

People from the different religions may argue with each other, saying, "This is my God, the true God. Your God is nothing. You are different from me." But they are wrong. It is not like that. If you look at the trees, the rocks, and the bushes, you will see that the same point, the same truth, the same reality exists in everything. You have to extract the point from each thing you experience and then go on. You have to progress and understand the effect of each of your qualities and actions. You must know what is right and what is wrong, what is good and what is evil, what is heaven and what is hell, what is true and what is false, what is permissible and what is forbidden. You have to know the inner mystery and the outer creation, the essence and the manifestation.

You have to discover the meanings within everything. You have to realize the good and the evil in each thing you see or smell. In everything you do, you must push away the evil on the left and accept the good on the right. Only if you gather what needs to be gathered will your life be right.

The four steps of the religions exist so that you can ascend them and go beyond. Strike against each religion with wisdom, and extract God's grace and qualities wherever you find them. Then truth will grow, and you will see the clarity of your soul, the grace of His *rahmat,* and the exalted life of a true human being, an *insān.* Then you will know the meaning of the *qutbiyyat.* You will disappear into the *Nūr,* the Resplendence of Allah, and you will merge with Him. You will exist within Allah and Allah will exist within you. The two will become one.

Once you become perfect, you will see Him as that perfection. Once you become light, He will be the plenitude, the *daulat.* Within that plenitude, His completeness will be seen. He is the Ruler of grace, the Incomparable One. Allah is unfathomable. If you become His slave and do His duty, that will be good. You must do this.

My love you, my grandchildren of one family, one God, and one prayer. When you come to that state you will know peace, tranquility, and love in your own life, and you will have love for all other lives. If each one of you will search for this state with wisdom and understanding, it will be the triumph of your life. That triumph is peace.

My love you, jeweled lights of my eyes, my grandchildren, my sisters and brothers, my sons and daughters. Please think about this a little and try to understand the meaning. My love you.

Beautiful but Deadly Flowers

y love you, my grandchildren. Will you come with me to see a jungle filled with wonders? Within this jungle there are beautiful little glades and many wondrous trees. Can you see their lovely, subtle flowers and leaves? When they open, the leaves display a soft yellow-green color. Some are shaped like ribs but are rounder and more symmetrical, some look like the fingers of a hand, and some look like flowers. But be careful! Do not go too close to them! These plants may smell sweet, but they are carnivorous. They eat the insects and other small creatures that are drawn by the fragrance. Each kind of flower attracts a different kind of insect. Look, a honeybee is approaching that flower over there. It smelled the fragrance from a great distance, flew all the way here, and now it has landed on the flower and is drinking the nectar. Oh, no! The petals are closing! Look how quickly they crush the honeybee and suck out its essence, leaving only an empty shell. Now the flower is opening again.

Look at that plant over there. It is really only a cluster of leaves, but it looks very much like a flower. Here comes a spider. Watch it closely. It climbs down the tree, circles around the plant, and then finally crawls into the center of the leaves. Do you see how the leaves are suddenly curling inward and interlocking like fingers? The plant is as transparent as glass, and you can see the spider struggling inside. In no time at all, the spider is dead. Its essence has been sucked dry, and the tiny hairs inside the plant are pushing out its dried up skin. Look, the plant is opening again. Now here come a few small worms and a large beetle. The same thing will happen to them. How lovely this plant looks, and yet it is so deadly!

Over here is another carnivorous flower whose petals fan out very beautifully. Do you see the little insect sitting there? Attracted by the beauty of the flower, he crept onto its petals, but now he is stuck to

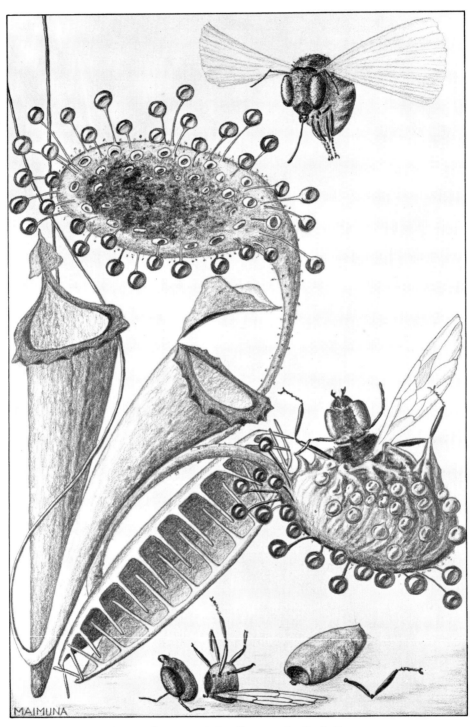

*Attracted by the beauty of the flower, the little bug crept onto
its petals, but now he is stuck to their gum-like surface.*

their gum-like surface. Look how the little bug struggles! Do you think he will escape? Oh, no! The outer petals are beginning to close, crushing his tiny body and sucking out all his blood. Now they are opening once again. All that's left of the bug is an empty shell, which the flower quickly spits out. How can such a lovely thing be so deadly?

My love you, my grandchildren. Think about this. All the insects we saw were drawn to these plants by their beauty and their fragrance. My grandchildren, man's mind catches him in the same way that these deadly plants catch insects. The attraction of this plant of the mind is stronger than any magnet. It seems very beautiful and fragrant, and as you approach it you are very happy. You think, "Ah, there is honey here for me. There is food here for me." But do not be deceived. It only appears to be beautiful. The mind is really filled with arrogance, karma, and illusion.

Children, if you sit on this carnivorous mind for even one second, you will be caught. The moment you touch it, the gum of desire will stick to you. You will be unable to escape if you have even one atom of desire for earth, women, gold, lust, blood ties, titles, the sixty-four sexual games, or the sixty-four arts and sciences. You may approach your mind thinking, "Oh, I'll just sit here for a moment." But as soon as you try to free yourself, you will realize that you are stuck. If you try to use your hands, your legs, your head, or even your chest to pull yourself free, they too will be stuck. Everything that touches the mind gets stuck. You may pull and pull and pull, but the outer petals of illusion will close over you and suck the life out of you. You will never be able to free yourself. Once maya, or illusion, closes in on you, it will crush your life, your soul, and all your goodness. Then it will suck out all your essence, leaving only an empty shell. This is what maya does.

My grandchildren, you must understand these dangers. The finger-like leaves we saw represent the five elements of earth, air, fire, water, and ether. These elements have a fragrance and beauty which attract man. And just as the flowers called out, "Come, come! Spiders, worms, and beetles, all of you, come!" the elements also call out to man. But you saw how quickly the insects who answered this call were captured.

So, beware, my children! A man is caught in exactly the same way. He becomes stuck to mind and desire, to earth, air, fire, water, and ether, to the sixty-four arts, the sixty-four sexual games, and to the desire for earth, women, and gold. He becomes stuck to arrogance, karma, and maya, and to *tārahan, singhan,* and *sūran,* the sons of maya. He becomes stuck to lust, hatred, miserliness, greed, fanaticism, and envy, to intoxicants, obsessions, theft, murder, and falsehood.

This is the world, and it has so many forms, all of which open out like flowers that contain an amazing and alluring beauty. Their fragrance attracts you to them. ''Ahhh, what a lovely smell!'' you say. But you must realize what they will do to you. If the beauty and fragrance of these forms attract you, you will be caught. Did you see the way those insects died? In the same way, the minute you set foot on these tempting things, then your original qualities, the original sound of God, the love of God, His light and peace and tranquility, and the freedom and wisdom of the soul will all be squeezed out of you.

These evil energies will devour all the secrets of God. They will feed upon God's truth and beauty within you. They will suck out every bit of your compassion, equality, unity, and justice. They will suck out all the qualities of God and consume the goodness you were born with. Your bones will become weak, your nerves frayed, and your face wrinkled. Your eyes will sink in, you will lose your vision, your teeth will fall out, your hands and arms will shrivel, and your blood will become thin. Finally, in that state, these evil energies will spit out your empty shell.

My love you, my grandchildren. On the outside you see the creations; on the inside you see your qualities. Everything you see outside is a reflection of what is happening inside. The plants that eat worms and beetles are like the things inside of you which eat you. So you have to be very careful of any magnet that attracts you. Realize that it is dangerous and do not trust it.

My love you, my children, jeweled lights of my eyes. We must leave all these attractions and return to our original state. That original, changeless beauty never kills anyone. That is what we must search for—our Father, our God, and His qualities.

It is very difficult to go to Him. It is easy to find the worldly fragrances, but to find Him we must go beyond this jungle and climb up the mountain. But be careful! Carnivorous flowers grow all along the wayside, very close to our path. They are easy to reach, but you must not get caught by them, or you will perish within them. You will lose your freedom, the freedom of God, and the freedom of compassion and love. This is how life is. All these things will eat you and squeeze you dry. Only God will hold you in a gentle embrace. You have to think about this with wisdom, faith, truth, and good qualities.

My love you, my grandchildren. To find God we must transcend everything, climbing with faith, certitude, and determination. We must try and try. Such an effort will not kill you. It will embrace you and make you live as one with God. *Āmīn. Āmīn.*

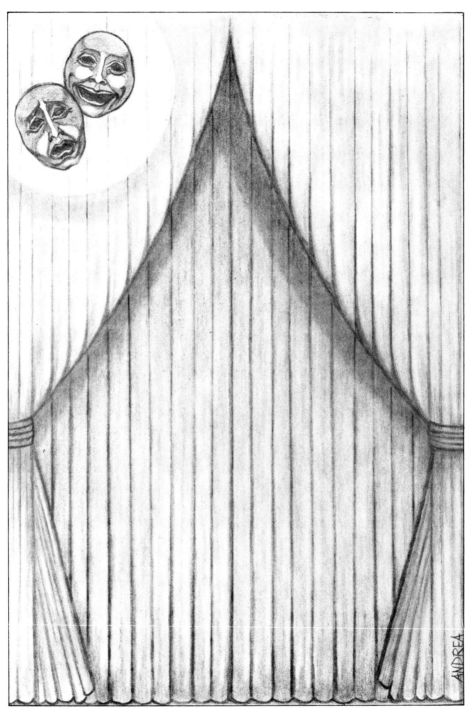

Once you understand the drama of your life, you will realize that all the scenery on the stage is just a backdrop for your life.

The Movie of Life

y love you, my grandchildren, my brothers and sisters, my sons and daughters. Come close and listen carefully, and I will tell you something about life.

You like to watch television and go to the movies, don't you? You enjoy seeing the stories and the actors. You also go to art museums to see the paintings, and to school to read books and study various subjects. You even study about love, don't you? My grandchildren, it is really your own life that you are seeing in all of this. Do not think that these things you are looking at are separate from yourself. Your life is a huge drama, and everything you need to learn can be found within you. Think about this a little.

What do you see on television? Events that happen in real life. You see a drunkard weaving and stumbling. You've also seen that on the street, haven't you? On television you see people taking opium, LSD, and marijuana. You see them go to bars and dance halls and drink beer and whiskey. What wonder is there in this? In the movies you may see a man and woman laugh, wink, and kiss. First they say, "I love you," and they are happy, then later they cry and are sad. Is this anything new? No. You also wink and flirt like that when your parents are not watching. You steal and the actors steal. You shave and wash and they shave and wash in the movies. You run and roll around and lie down, and so do they. You grow a moustache and twirl the ends, or wear a wig, and so do the actors. You even pay money to see these dramas. You rush out to see a fantastic movie about love or an exciting movie about criminals and thieves. When something funny happens, you laugh so hard, and when something sad happens you cry a little, but not very much.

My children, why do you want to see these acts when everything that happens in your own life is a drama? You don't need to go to museums and zoos either. Your life is a museum containing the sixty-four arts and sciences and the sixty-four sexual games, and it is a zoo where you can stare at the animals existing within you. It is not necessary to look at anything outside of yourself, whether it is in the theater, in books, on the road, or anywhere else. What you see in all these, in the cities and towns, at school, or on television is your own secret life. Your own acts and words and speeches are revealed in these outside plays. The secret acts you perform in the darkness are being shown to you on the stage. Everything you do is revealed as an act.

My grandchildren, think about this. Tell yourself, "Everything I see is a part of my own life. What a wonder! All that I look at, all that I do, all that my parents and grandparents and great-grandparents did are all part of my history." From the time you were an embryo, all that was present within your parents formed and grew within you. The way they danced together, their happiness and sadness, and everything that was in their minds later emerged in you. You began to act like them, and someday your children will also copy the things you did.

Is there any wonder at all to be seen on the outside that you will not find within? No, every one of these acts can be seen within your own history. They have all been going on in the world since the beginning of creation. If you think about life you will realize this. Once you understand your own life, you won't experience a sense of awe at any other learning, or at titles and honors, or dramas and singing and dancing, or anything you see on television or in the world. You will see it all as your own act and your own history.

Then once you understand your own act, you will realize that your life is just a drama. Once you understand your drama, you will realize that all the scenery on the stage is just a backdrop for your life. As soon as the lights are turned off and the backdrop is pulled up, the show will disappear and the performance will be over.

Life is like a movie being projected on a screen. The light of desire in the projector of thought and intellect allows you to see your own life on the screen of the mind. As long as the movie is playing, that light of desire allows you to see your own performance and laugh with delight.

But if the house lights in the theater are suddenly turned on during a movie, what happens? The light from the projector merges with the light in the room, and you can no longer see the picture. It disappears. Like that, when the light of God's qualities, truth, and wisdom is turned on, this dark show of life will disappear. Mind, desire, and thought will disappear. Neither the picture nor your acting will be seen. Only the light will be seen. That one power within the soul will draw you into its light. This is the real light: the radiance of God, wisdom, and truth.

My grandchildren, you have to understand the light which exists beyond the screen—the light of God's qualities, truth, and goodness. This light is the form of your soul, the life within your life. There is no wonder in the outside world. Your life itself is the greatest wonder. Nothing else is worth looking at or studying. Your own life is a great school, a great study, and a great drama. But it is very subtle.

What should you look at and try to understand within this drama of life? You have to look deeply at wisdom, goodness, and the subtlety of God's qualities. You have to look deeply at truth, at your inner life, and at your own thoughts. You have to look deeply in order to understand your own acting, and then you must learn how to act correctly in this drama. You must be very clear about what is right and what is wrong, what is true and what is false in your act. Once you understand your own acting, you can understand your birth, your death, the movie of creation, and the movie of life.

Everything is part of your history. It can be found in dramas, movies, dancing, books, science, false wisdom, happiness, sadness, hell, and heaven. These acts are showing you how to cry and how to make love. They mimic what you do and then invite you to watch. If you don't attempt to understand what they are showing you, then watching them will only turn you into a fool. They are really warning you, saying, "Hey, crazy man! Watch this so you won't forget what you do in your own life!" Everything you see in God's creation is only there to help you remember, realize, and understand your own life. Nothing else is of any importance.

My love you, my grandchildren. What is the point of your life? It is to look at each reel, edit out certain scenes, and then splice together the pure speech, pure qualities, pure beauty, and the purity of the soul. You have to put those good scenes into your film and discard the jungle scenes that depict snakes and scorpions, ghosts and demons, elephants, cats, horses, cows, donkeys, ants, and eagles. You must discard them all. They lie between you and the truth. They have no connection to the drama. You have to cut them out and then splice the reels together in the proper way to make the correct connection between you and God.

The most important act in life is truth. If you edit this reel with great care, you and God can then watch it and enjoy the relationship that exists between you. And you can know the flavor that comes from that bliss.

Look at yourself. You came to this world, but what you have to realize is that you came from Him and you must return to Him. The light within you has to merge with that One Light. Then the dark show of life will disappear. My love you, my children. This is the most important thing to understand in life.

This is the act of a good man, the act of a good child of God. This is the most excellent thing in life. Discard all the rest and do what is correct in life. My love you, my grandchildren. May God help you. Āmīn.

Gazing at the Sky Will Never Quench Your Thirst

y love you, my grandchildren. Come, look up at the sky. Do you know where rain comes from? Water from the earth is absorbed by the sky. It collects into clouds and then falls back to the earth in the form of rain. However, this only happens occasionally. You cannot depend upon the rain. For example, you always need drinking water, don't you? But can you count on the rainwater to fall from above? Will gazing up at the sky quench your thirst? No, it is not always raining when you are thirsty. You cannot expect the water to fall out of the sky exactly when you want it. If you stand there waiting for the rain to fall, you will never quench your thirst. You will end up rolling around in your own dirt, and you will die.

Now look at the earth, my grandchildren. There is always water in the earth. If you dig down to the water table and find a spring, then you can drink all you want, whenever you want. Therefore, do not look to the sky. You must make the effort and dig deep down into the earth for your water.

Like this, my grandchildren, you will never quench the thirst of your soul by simply gazing upward for God, saying, "God is there. He will provide." God does exist and He will help at the proper time, but you have to make the effort. You have to try.

Just as moisture from the earth is absorbed by the sky and falls back down as rain, God takes whatever you have and gives it back to you. Whatever qualities you have will come back to you. If you gather the qualities of hell, that is what you will get back. But, my grandchildren, if you gather the qualities of heaven, you will receive heaven. If you gather wisdom and all the good qualities within you and act accordingly, God will make those qualities even more beauti-

If you stand there, waiting for the rain to fall, you will
never quench your thirst.

ful with His light. He will transform them into the freedom of the soul and have them rain down upon you. God will take what you have and turn it into something far greater, something far more valuable. He will make it complete and return it to you.

There is a God. He is everywhere, but you must dig deep within yourself and find Him there. All of His actions must come into you. Then you will have the wealth of grace. Therefore, children, do not keep thinking, "God will do it. God will provide." It is ignorance to gaze up at the sky and think, "I don't have to do anything. It will come all by itself." There is no benefit in that.

My love you, my grandchildren. Think about this. Think about the work you must do. Do not look up at the sky, look within yourselves. All things are within you, just as the water is deep within the earth. My love you, my grandchildren. You must understand this.

The Subtle Ship on the Ocean of 'Ilm

y love you, my grandchildren, my sisters and brothers, my sons and daughters. The history of God, to whom all praise is due, and the history of man, who is His most exalted creation, are both very subtle. If we want to understand the subtlety of these two histories, we must first acquire wisdom and the divine knowledge known as 'ilm.

Listen carefully, my children, and I will tell you about the purpose of man's life. There is a mind within the mind of man, and within that mind is the innermost heart, the *qalb*. Within that *qalb* is the light *qalb* of God, and within that light *qalb* is the soul, which is God's treasure. Within that soul is a resplendence, and within that resplendence is the power of His kingdom. Within that power is our Father. He is present as a power in all beings, performing His duty, both within and without. In this way He protects and sustains all His creations everywhere. The purpose of man's life is to understand this.

But, my grandchildren, it is very difficult for man to reach this understanding, because he is in a constant state of torpor. His mind is like tissue paper that crackles every time he touches it. It is always making noise. How many different sounds and melodies and rhythms the mind produces! It evokes the music of the sixty-four arts and the sixty-four sexual games and puts man into a state of torpor. The intellect interprets these noises to the mind and only increases its torpor. Neither his feeling, his awareness, nor his intellect know anything beyond those sounds.

Like a monkey, the mind can only mimic and grin. It lacks the wisdom to understand what it has not seen. It cannot think. It does not have the capacity to go beyond. Desire, which arises from the mind, is also limited in this way. So are thoughts and dreams, which are the essence of the mind. The mind shows man all these desires and thoughts and dreams and keeps him in a state of torpor. Thus he remains limited and cannot go beyond, to where God exists.

My grandchildren, you have seen the shore, where the ocean meets the land. But when you are far out in mid-ocean, you cannot see any shore at all. The ocean of the mind and illusion is also like that. You cannot see its end. It covers everything, everywhere. And in that vast ocean of illusion there are as many different beings as there are creatures in the sea. Those beings produce endless sounds and melodies. We have to understand the noises that we hear coming from the ocean of illusion and put them behind us, for there is something that lies far beyond them, something truly limitless.

Beyond that ocean of illusion lies the ocean of wisdom, and beyond that lies the ocean of grace-awakened wisdom, of *gnānam*. And within that you will find God and His kingdom, His beauty and His resplendence, His bliss and His perfection. Within that perfection you can discover how God rules His kingdom.

But, my grandchildren, to understand and know all this is very difficult. It is easy to research into the ocean of illusion, just as it is easy to learn about the oceans of the world. You can look at them and analyze them. But the ocean of *'ilm*, of divine knowledge, is secret. If you want to explore this ocean, your soul must climb into the ship of wisdom. It is a very subtle ship, and it can travel to places that you cannot reach by any other means. However, to board this ship, you have to discard your self and all that you have. This too is difficult. You have to leave behind on the shore all the things that belong to the ocean of illusion and to the world. You must discard the sixty-four sexual games and the sixty-four sexual arts. You must discard fanaticism, arrogance, the pleasures of the monkey, and the desires of the dog. As long as you fail to discard these, you will remain attached to illusion, mind, and desire. However, if you do leave these behind and go beyond, you can swim in the fathomless depths of the heart. You can swim in divine knowledge.

My grandchildren, come. Before you reach that ocean of *'ilm*, you must still pass through much in the ocean of illusion. Along the way you will see many different creations. Can you see the crabs, the sharks, and all the other kinds of fish that live here?

But you must cross over this ocean and go still farther. In this

411

To survive in these waters, we must wear a special mask and inhale the oxygen of Lā ilāha ill-Allāh. A huge secret exists in this.

place the water is very heavy and filled with many gases. No living creature can exist here. None of those creatures of illusion, nothing with a form, not even a germ can survive here. Some things appear to have forms, but when you touch them you will find that they are merely gas. We are the only beings here. It is also like this in the *qalb,* the innermost heart. None of the creatures of illusion can exist there.

Look children, on the surface the gases are bubbling with great force, and below they are churning up and down. The heaviness of the water pulls us down, then lifts us up. It is in constant turmoil.

Like that, when we try to go toward God's kingdom, the heavy weight of the world of mind and desire pushes us down on one side, while the force of the five elements lifts us up and pushes us away on the other side. For us to travel through these waters we must wear a special mask and inhale the oxygen of *Lā ilāha:* there is none other than You, *ill-Allāh:* only You are Allah. This is the only way we can survive. A huge secret exists in this. No being can survive here without knowing this secret.

⸙

My grandchildren, now we have come to God's kingdom. Here you will never see any forms. Nor will you find creatures that eat one another, or beings that tell lies or have pride, jealousy, envy, deceit, revenge, anger, ego, or the differences between the I and the you. You will not find separations between religions, races, or languages. You will not find mantras, *tantras,* or tricks. These things are only needed by mind and desire.

What will you find here, beyond all these? You will find God's truth, His love, grace, compassion, equality, tolerance, justice, conscience, unity, light, His three thousand gracious qualities, and His ninety-nine duties and actions, His *wilāyats.*

Do you want to enter this kingdom of souls and see what is there? Do you want to understand the fullness and power of God's kingdom, His grace, and His love? If you do, my children, then you must discard all the illusion and move forward, continuing to say, "*Lā ilāha:* there is none other than You, *ill-Allāh:* only You are Allah." You need this oxygen for survival. It must be contained within the tank of *īmān,*

413

of faith, certitude, and determination. And it must flow through the valve of the *Kalimah*.

You must make all these preparations to travel through the ocean of grace, the ocean of love, and the ocean of awakened wisdom, or *gnānam*. All kinds of difficulties will come to attack you on this journey and you will have to pass by each one of them. So strap on this oxygen tank of faith, and then you can enter His kingdom and see His treasure and His qualities.

My grandchildren, peace, equality, justice, and the quality of considering the lives and hunger of others as one's own all exist in His kingdom. To go there we must have those same qualities. We cannot enter any other way. This is the path of peace for the soul.

If you follow this path, you can enter God's kingdom of grace and see Him. You will see His treasure and His qualities. Then you will be able to see yourself and the essence of all beings. You will see the lights and the effulgence of those lights. You will be able to understand the explanations of God and find true happiness.

My grandchildren, it is not easy to make this journey. It is very difficult. To open this path and proceed, you must learn from a wise man. He must be one who performs his duty without selfishness. Only such a one can teach you how to accomplish this. But even if the wise man tries to guide you, it will not be easy for you to accept his teachings and to learn from him. Some of you will look for an easy way out or even oppose what he teaches you. You may kick and bite and try to run away. For many people this path will have a very bitter taste. Only a very few in this world will find it sweet.

May all praise and praising be offered to Allah alone, the One who is limitless grace and incomparable love. May He grant us His qualities, His actions, His conduct, His wisdom and knowledge, His compassion and patience. May He give us His wisdom and grace and the treasure which will bring us peace. *Āmīn*.

Twelve Years with the Sheikh

y love you, my grandchildren, my sons and daughters, my brothers and sisters. *Bismillāhir-Rahmānir-Rahīm.* All praise and glory belong only to Allah. We need His protection in the world of the souls, in this world, and in the hereafter. We need His help every second of our lives. We must search for Him with every breath and never let go of Him. He is always ready to help. If you look for Him, He will look for you. If you think of Him, He will think of you. If you intend Him, He will intend you. If you call Him, He will come. He is expecting you to call upon Him, and He is ready at all times.

My love you, my grandchildren. Please think about this. I am telling the truth. No one but God can help us. No other god has that power, for that grace and that point are in His hands alone. If you search for God's qualities, His wisdom, and His truth, you will understand what I have said. If you trust in Him without a single doubt or suspicion, your intentions will be fulfilled, and you will attain freedom both in this life and in the kingdom of the soul.

To do this, you need to find a true human being, a man who has God's qualities, a man of wisdom. Once you find such a man, you must carefully observe his qualities and his wisdom. You have to see that ideal beauty. If you can exist in such a state, if you can acquire qualities and wisdom like his, then you will be able to understand everything. But you must not harbor a single doubt or suspicion, you must have absolute certitude. That will bring you peace, tranquility, and serenity in your life and in all three worlds.

This man of wisdom will be a map for your life. All you need to do is follow the map with understanding. He has not come here to show you any miracles or rub his hands together and magically produce something for you. He will not teach you to recite mantras or do tricks. Does the truth of God's grace need magic or miracles? No, truth performs no miracles. Does the wisdom of truth need makeup? No, good qualities, truth, and wisdom need no embellishment. If you are beautiful, you don't need any artificial decoration. Your light and your beauty will be seen in you, as a free, open, and natural beauty. You will know it and others will see it and enjoy it. What is natural never changes, but when you cover it with makeup, its beauty is diminished. Don't hide that original beauty. If you can return to your original state of good qualities and wisdom, that state itself will become the map which will show you the way from this world to God. At that point, everything will occur automatically, and as each thing happens, you will understand it.

Children, only a true human being can show you how to achieve that state. You have to follow him, step by step. Watch what he does, and then do it. Look at the way he acts, and then act in the same way. He will show you each step and tell you what it means. He will teach you about your birth and about those who have been born with you. He will explain all of creation to you, and you, in turn, must look at each creation as he speaks of it. Listen and reflect with your experience and understanding. See what path he takes, and then follow him. To walk with him in this way is the learning. After a while your understanding will be the map and you can go forward, knowing your path.

Children, until you can proceed on your own, you must be with your sheikh. Hold on to the truth he teaches you with your faith and with your innermost heart. Focus on his words and his actions. Watch very carefully. Do not drift away for even a second, or you will miss the point. He will have left that place, talked about something else, and gone on. If you look to one side or the other, or fall even one step behind, it will not be good. Focus only upon him. Follow exactly in his footsteps, and then he will take you on the path he travels. He can take you from the very creation of your soul to your merging with the resplendent state of your Father. Until you reach that state, you have to travel with him.

My love you, my children. Books cannot take you where you want to go. It is quick and easy to study and memorize the scriptures, the Bible, the Qur'an, and the Purānas, but it is long and difficult to learn about the soul, the freedom of life, and the secrets of the kingdom of

God. It's true that there is a time for you to wander around with books. And at that time they will have a meaning for you. But once you come on this path, you cannot gain any more from books. What you really have to understand now is your life, who you are, who your Father is, what the soul is, and what wisdom is. You must understand the actions, the goodness, and the qualities of God, your Father.

You can learn all these by following an *insān,* a man of wisdom. That will give you the understanding you need. People say that to learn this properly you must surrender to the sheikh and stay with him for twelve years. But they say these things without understanding. What do those twelve years really mean? And what does surrender mean? What do you have to surrender to?

You have seen how a flashlight works. The bulb is connected to a battery by a small piece of metal, and when you push the switch, the current flows to the bulb and the light goes on. Each thing has to touch the next connection in exactly the right way, or it will not work. The same process holds true for your body. Your food has to taste good, be the proper temperature, be suitable for your blood, and provide you with the necessary vitamins, or you will be ill. Even the water you drink must agree with you. Your body has certain needs, doesn't it? Everything has to be just right for it to function well.

In the same way, my grandchildren, your thoughts, your intentions, and your gaze have to be just right to connect with those of the sheikh. They have to follow him just as the shadow of a man follows him wherever he walks. Where does this shadow come from? It comes from the man, doesn't it? Everything has a shadow, even a tree. You have to be connected to the sheikh like a shadow, following his innermost heart and turning wherever he turns. This is the way it is at first.

You must remember that during this time the sheikh will be the one who is doing everything, and you will be merely his shadow. You will be separate from him, yet following him. And just as a shadow comes closer and closer as the sun rises higher and higher, your qualities, your body, your soul, and your possessions must draw closer and closer to the sheikh. Finally they will be hidden within him. At noon, when the sun reaches its zenith, no shadow can be seen. The shadow has merged with the man. Like this, when you are fully

Do you know what it means to be with the sheikh for twelve years? It means we must stay with him until we understand the twelve worlds within us.

mature you can disappear into the sheikh. You will walk as one and go on the journey as one. Until then, you have to follow him and cling to him, drawing closer and closer. This is what surrendering to the sheikh means. Once you attain a mature state, you will merge with him and will no longer be in the world. You must think about this.

My love you, my grandchildren, my sons and my daughters. Until you fully understand, you will become tired and depressed when you see sorrow and suffering. Religion, race, color, and the languages of the world will keep you separate from your sheikh. These things might even cause you to look back and turn away.

My grandchildren, the world that we see on the outside does not belong to us. We have only the worlds inside, the worlds of heaven and hell. We have the happiness and sadness of heaven as well as the happiness and sadness of hell. We have the vast worlds of ignorance and lack of wisdom within us. There are eighteen thousand universes within us.

Do you know what it means to be with the sheikh for twelve years? It means that we have to stay with the sheikh until we understand the twelve worlds within us. What are these twelve worlds? In the lower part of your body there are two worlds, two openings: the place from which you were born and the place of fecal arrogance. Then there are seven worlds in your head: the mouth which is the opening of hunger and hellfire from which you drank and shouted and howled, the two nostrils that carry the two breaths in and out, the eyes that you see with, and the ears that you hear with. The tenth opening, the navel, was cut and sealed at birth. The navel is the opening through which the jealousy and pride and vanity of satan entered.

The other nine openings are called the nine planets, which keep whirling us about and tormenting us. These nine worlds are also represented in the zodiac by the forms of crabs, scorpions, and other animals. We must use our *imān* to cut away these animal qualities. We need to understand all ten openings. We must learn about the cause of fecal arrogance and the source of our birth, as well as the source of our speech and hunger and taste, of our breath, and of our vision and hearing.

To understand those ten openings, or worlds, and to overcome and control them, you need ten years. In the tenth year you must learn who you are. You must understand your self and close that self off, just as the navel is closed. Then, in the eleventh year, you look at the world with the eye in the center of the forehead, the *kursī*. As you are looking at others, trying to help them and to satisfy their needs, the *kursī* is opened. In the twelfth year, after you have understood your self and controlled the worlds within you, and after you have understood everything in the world, you then give yourself up to God. You merge with your Father and both of you live together in the *'arsh*.

You do need a sheikh, and you need to be with him for twelve years to understand these twelve worlds. Whether you are far away or in his presence you must keep him in front of you, within you, behind you—everywhere. You must look at each of these worlds, one by one. Do not turn to mantras, saying, "Om, ahm, eem," hoping those sounds will produce miracles. They will not help you. Instead, try to know and understand what must be thrown away and then throw it away. If you can do that, it will be enough of a miracle.

This is why you have to find a true human being, an *insān*. You have to follow his qualities and his wisdom like a shadow in order to overcome these twelve worlds and merge with God. Only if you proceed in this state can you reach the kingdom of your Father. Otherwise, you will experience nothing but the world. You will live in the world, die in the world, and be reborn in the world. You will have nothing else. Your pleasure and sorrow, your laughter and tears, your happiness and sadness will come from the world. All that you praise or blame and all the miracles that you perform will be of the world. Even the path you take to hell will be the path of the world. Hell is all you will find on the path.

My grandchildren, search for a man who has the qualities of God and follow him. What you need to learn is very difficult, and therefore you need a true man of wisdom. It is easy to read religious scriptures. Many people have done that. Once you have memorized them you are finished, but you can never finish studying God and His qualities and the truth. The more you progress, the deeper it will be, until finally you merge with your Father. But even when you attain that state, there is still more to be learned. You have to stay within God and learn for so many ages.

My love you, my grandchildren. As long as you are not in this

420

realized state, you will have difficulty understanding what you need to know. This is why you must stay with the sheikh for twelve years. You must understand. You have to become like him and learn with him, so that one day you can reach the kingdom of your Father. Don't talk about your horoscope. Don't turn to the zodiac for your understanding. Avoid those things.

My love you, my grandchildren. Understand yourselves and correct yourselves. This is the point. This is what you have to know in your life. You have to understand the real qualities of God. They are your map. As you grow in your understanding, the truth and wisdom that come to you will bring you so much beauty. And the resplendent light within you will become brighter and brighter.

My grandchildren, the right path is truth, the wisdom of truth. This is not something that we can just talk about, we must bring it into our actions. Talking about something is one thing, but doing it is another. You have to act upon the truth. Nothing will happen just from talking, whether the words come from you or from a man of wisdom. In the same way that the ink from your pen sticks to a piece of paper, your actions must stick to your words. It is easy to talk about wisdom, but you have to hold on and stick to it. Learn only that which can never be erased. Do not bother to learn anything that can be erased. That kind of learning is like writing on water. You write, but a second later, it disappears, and there is no way of knowing what was written. You will never be able to benefit from that kind of learning, and neither will anyone else. Think about this. What you learn must be firmly established and printed in a way that will stick. Only if you stay with the sheikh will you be able to do this.

Allah is sufficient unto all of us. May He give us the wisdom of truth. May He make us go on the straight path and take us to that point. *Āmīn*. May Allah protect us and keep us from making mistakes. May He give us His grace. *Āmīn*. *Āmīn*.

The Seven Levels of Wisdom

y love you, my grandchildren, my sisters and brothers, my sons and daughters. Last night I attended a meeting. About nine hundred or a thousand children were gathered there. The older ones were sitting in the back, and the smaller ones up front were asking questions.

"How can we know God? In what way should we lead our lives so that we can understand God? Is there proof of God's existence? Why do they say that man is the most exalted of all creations? Some creations are stronger than man, some are more subtle, and some are more beautiful. So why do they say that man is the most exalted?"

These are very good questions. They have been asked the world over, but people usually ask without having any understanding of their true selves. However, last night these children were asking so that they could understand both God and themselves.

My love you, my grandchildren. Do you want to know God? Listen carefully and I will tell you how. What do you do if you want to meet a king? First you have to travel to the city where he lives, and then you must find his palace. But still it is not easy to meet a king, for he is always protected by many people, and you have to get past all of them before you can see him.

First you have to go through the crowd in front of the gates and then past the guards. Once inside, you have to talk with the officers in charge, and after that with several levels of ministers. As you approach each official, you have to insist over and over again, "I want to meet the king. Where is the king?" To succeed in going beyond all these people you need to be aware of each one's qualities and actions. And you must be careful to ask the right questions at the right time and place. Otherwise, you will be stopped over and over again.

Even if you manage to get this far, you still have to pass through every room in the palace, until you reach the one in which the king resides. Only then will you finally be able to speak to him.

My grandchildren, finding God is also difficult. First you must have the faith and certitude to accept that there is a God. Then you must have the absolute determination to see that Treasure and to establish a connection with Him. This yearning must be very strong in you.

Now, what kind of being is God? What is His state? Where did all the countless creations come from? They did not come into being all by themselves. They must have been created by someone, so there must be a Creator. For every effect there is a cause. That Creator is God, the Father who sustains all of His created beings. To know the identity and value of such a Treasure, you must know all about the creations which have come from Him bringing His message. You must understand all the birds, animals, reptiles, insects, worms, viruses, and atoms; the sun, moon, and stars; the sky, sea, and land; the earth, fire, water, air, and ether. You must understand the good and the bad in everything: the pure and impure spirits in man, the good thoughts and bad thoughts, the good qualities and bad qualities, the wisdom and ignorance. There are countless matters you must know and understand, one by one, before you can know God.

Therefore, my children, if you want to reach that perfectly pure kingdom of heaven, you must first pass through all His other kingdoms. You must know the kingdom of heaven and the kingdom of hell. One is a kingdom of equality and love where peace exists, and the other is a kingdom of destruction, where one being seeks to ruin another and there is no peace. We have to understand both of these kingdoms.

If you want to know what kind of being God is, if you want to understand His ways and receive His treasure, you must discover His qualities by studying everything that you encounter before reaching Him. You must study each of His creations and understand their qualities, their actions, and their levels of wisdom. But always remember, my children, that beyond all of these is a wisdom much greater and qualities that are beyond and beyond and beyond. God's qualities and His plenitude are so much more valuable than anything you will see along the way. He is far, far beyond everything. But if you observe His creations, you can discover how, through them, He has shown His state, what He is capable of, and what kind of power He has.

My grandchildren, if you want to learn about God, first look at yourselves. You have feeling, awareness, and intellect. These three levels of consciousness are also found in every creation. But beyond these, man has four higher levels: judgment, subtle wisdom, analytic wisdom, and divine luminous wisdom. You have to climb up each of these levels one by one, learning and understanding, step by step. You must start with feeling, then move on to awareness, and then to intellect. Only after you have progressed to a certain extent will wisdom come. If you want to understand His kingdom, you must have faith and start this climb correctly.

Feeling

The very first step is feeling. You must learn from each created being about its feelings. To conduct your research, you have to put your own feeling into the feeling of each other being and mingle with it. What is the state of its body? What are its qualities? What has God given to each creation? If you can change your own feeling into the feeling of each created thing, then you will be able to understand the state that God has given to it. You will realize what is within that being. You will know its body, its blood, its awareness and intellect, how it functions, what it is capable of, and how it will behave in certain situations. Only then will you understand the point of that life and see God's work within it.

Have you understood the worm? Do you know what life is like for four-legged animals? Or what the life of a fish is like? To know this, you must go into the feeling of each being and find out how it behaves under different circumstances. What will a cow do when it has an itch? It will lick itself or scratch itself with its hooves. What will a fish do when it feels an itch? It will flap its fins and then jump up and down in the water. What will worms do? They will wiggle this way and that in the earth. Birds, snakes, crocodiles, scorpions, and all created beings have this feeling of itching, but each has a different way of dealing with it.

My grandchildren, only if you place your own feeling within the different creations will you know how they would act in each particular situation. And once you have understood that, you should think, "What would I do? What is the state of these created beings and what can it show me about my own state? What was their state in the womb as an embryo, and what was I like then?" Once you have completed this step of understanding the feelings of other beings, and of understanding your own feelings, you must go on to the second step.

Awareness

In this step you must learn what each creation is aware of. Send your own awareness in to mingle with the awareness of all the countless beings. Find out what they are aware of and what you are aware of. Know good and bad with your own awareness, then observe their awareness of good and bad. Put what you learn back into yourself, and then look deeply into your own awareness and see what effect it has on you. "Their awareness works in this way. What is my awareness like? What is the difference between the two?" Do this research within yourself. Understand the qualities and actions of the animals, birds, worms, insects, and fish, and see what kind of peace they have. See the differences between you and them and decide for yourself which is the more exalted. Once you have understood their awareness and your own, then go on to the third step.

Intellect

You must research into the intellect of each created being. Place your intellect within the intellect of another being and observe it. Each life has a specific function. A magnet has the power to draw any metal that touches it, an electric current has its own manner of functioning, and fire has another way of behaving. Look carefully at each life. Mingle your intellect with that life until you see and understand the full extent of its intellect. What is the state of this life? How much does it know? What is its function? What work does it do? What pain does it experience? What kind of illness does it have? What is good for it and what is bad? What part of it will perish and what part is permanent? What dangers come to it and how does it escape from them? How does it avoid accidents? Then understand how this life is similar to your own and how it differs from yours. For example, does

As your intellect analyzes both the dangerous and the peaceful animals, you must say to yourself, "Their forms and limbs are different from mine; but they have qualities similar to mine."

it take food for its hunger in the same way that you do? In this way, thoroughly research into the actions and intellect of each being.

All lives, the sun, the moon, the reptiles, the sky, and the earth have this section of intellect, but it is limited. The intellect can only imitate what it sees. Like a monkey, if you laugh it will laugh, if you cry it will cry, and if you throw something it will throw something. The monkey only mimics what it sees. In the same way, the intellect can only explain the things it has seen. It can identify something and tell you how it works, but it cannot differentiate between right and wrong.

My children, after you have researched into the intellect of all other beings, then with your own intellect analyze yourself. Compare their intentions with your intentions and their qualities with your qualities. Inquire into your own state and theirs and ask yourself, "What is the difference between us? What is the limit of their intellect, and what is the limit of my intellect, the human intellect? They have feeling, I have feeling; they have awareness, I have awareness; they have intellect, I have intellect. This being has two eyes and a nose, and I have two eyes and a nose. Birds have four limbs, two wings and two legs. I also have four limbs, two arms and two legs. A worm has no outer legs, but it has segments which push it forward by expanding and contracting when it breathes in and out. Fish use their two fins to swim. I use my hands and feet to swim, but in a different way."

With your intellect you must analyze the dangerous animals as well as the peaceful ones. Lions and tigers are dangerous, deer are peaceful. An elephant makes trumpeting sounds, but only when it senses danger will it trample people or grab them and throw them about with its trunk. Man also makes a big noise, shouting, "I, I, I!" But unlike the elephant, he beats and tramples down others and tosses them about with his trunk and legs of arrogance, even when there is no danger. The elephant hurts others with its body, but man hurts them in a subtle way with his arrogance. There is also not much difference between the actions of a bear and those of man. There is a saying that an attacking bear has five mouths. It strikes with its two paws, kicks with its two hind feet, and bites with its mouth. Man also bites, pinches and kicks others. A snake will lie curled up and then all of a sudden hiss and strike. Man may also lie still and look peaceful, but if he is attacked, he will strike back with force and sometimes even commit murder.

As your intellect investigates all these animals, you may say to yourself, "Their forms and limbs are different from mine, but they have qualities similar to mine. It seems that all the beings existing in the outer world also exist in a huge world within me. Each animal has its own particular quality, but I have all of those qualities within me!"

My precious grandchildren, you must look within yourself and identify the animals there. "This quality is like that of the snake and this is the quality of the elephant. This is the quality of the scorpion, the wasp, and the honeybee. This is the quality of the crocodile, the lion, and the tiger. This is the quality of the bird, the parrot, and the mynah. This is the quality of a demon, a ghost, and satan. This is hell and this is heaven."

Everything in that outside world is also within you: heaven and hell, the sea, the earth, the sun, the moon, the netherworlds, the spirits, the five elements, the five senses, good and bad, wisdom and lack of wisdom. Your intellect must find and know the state of each one of these. Once you have identified all these outer things, understood how they work, mingled with them, and discovered how they can be controlled, you must then apply that learning inside. And once you can control them within you, you will also be able to control them on the outside. You have to start controlling and cutting them with the intellect, telling them one by one, "You do this work. You do that work."

This is what intellect can do. But it cannot go beyond that level. Intellect and philosophy can only understand what can be seen by the eye, that which has a created form. Beyond this is the step of understanding what cannot be seen: the difference between right and wrong, good and bad, and heaven and hell. Questioning and judgment go beyond the level of intellect. And God, His resplendence, His light, and His kingdom are beyond even that level of understanding.

Judgment
My grandchildren, all creations function with three levels of

consciousness: feeling, awareness, and intellect. After you have understood the outside world, after you have finished learning about the animals and other beings in that world, you must then control all the beings in the world inside of you. Do this with your feeling, awareness, and intellect. Then you can climb up to the next step, estimate, or judgment. This is the level of researching into the human being. Now you can begin the study of your own nature, the study of the connection between yourself, God, and creation. At this point you must estimate and judge your own limits as well as the limits of everything else.

You must ask yourself, "Where did man come from? Did he come from the sea of illusion or from God? How did this fetus come into being? Is there a particular point from which it was formed? From what was it created? On what is it built? On what does it survive? Did the embryo come from the five elements? Or did it come from a ray, or from His grace, or His gaze, or His thoughts?"

With your judgment you must research into the five kinds of life: earth life, fire life, air life, water life, and ether life. What are these lives made of? What are their qualities? What will they do? How do they function? What is their world like? Where do they come from? What were they created from? When will these lives be destroyed and perish? What is their time limit? How many energies do they have? What can they do? The whole world functions with these five elements. In Tamil they are known as *Shīva-sakti* (earth), *Varuna baghavan* (water), *Vāyu baghavan* (air), *Agni baghavan* (fire), and *Parāsakti* (ether or illusion). Through your research you will see that the energies of these five can turn land into water and water into land. They can turn fire into water and cold into heat. They do all this work of confusion. They go on twisting and turning like this, and when something goes wrong, even the slightest mistake, there is destruction.

You must understand the connections these five kinds of lives have. Earth life has a connection to earth, fire life to fire, water life to water, air life to air, and ether life to ether. Each of these five elements is controlled by an angel. The Angel Mikā'īl ☺ controls water, the Angel Isrāfīl ☺ controls air, Izrā'īl ☺ controls fire, and Rukial ☺ controls the ether. And all of them can be found within the element of earth, or Adam ☺. Each of these lives has a connection to its respective element, but all of them are connected to the earth, even the lives in the sky. Torpor, selfishness, jealousy, mind and desire, the differences of I, you, mine, yours, race, color, and religion—all have that connection to the earth. Using the energies of these five, man can only be a leader of evil. He can perform magic and mesmerism and do everything evil, but he cannot do anything true or good.

My grandchildren, beyond these five elements is found the sixth life, the light life. That is the perfectly pure soul, the ray from God. Its connection is to God and it will reunite with Him. The food for the soul comes from God; it takes its qualities and actions from Him alone. The other five lives draw their food from the energy of the five elements. After you assess the limits of the five lives, then you can begin to investigate the limits of the sixth.

First you studied the birds, animals, dogs, foxes, and horses. Then you asked, "Am I a donkey or a horse or any of these? What am I?" And you found out, "I am a man." Next you researched into the five kinds of lives, their qualities, and what their energies are capable of. Now you can begin your research into the sixth life, the soul of man, and see what it does. The five kinds of life were created from the impurity of the elements and were formed in torpor, but the soul, man's life, came from the light of God and is pure. That sixth life is the pure spirit, God's ray, the soul life. And where is the kingdom of the soul to be found? What is the soul life connected to? You must enter that kingdom and research into it.

My grandchildren, it is with this fourth level of consciousness called judgment that you must learn all about these six kinds of lives within you. After you have understood the state of the five kinds of lives and their destruction and end, and once you have begun your investigation into the sixth life, then you must climb up to the fifth step, the step of subtle wisdom.

Subtle Wisdom
My grandchildren, with your subtle wisdom you have to analyze again each of the five lives you have already studied, and then extend that wisdom to analyze the light life, the soul of man. You must study the qualities and actions of God and start taking His qualities

into yourself. What would God do in a particular situation? Analyze what His qualities would do and what the power of the soul's wisdom would do, as opposed to what the qualities and energies of the five elements would do. Understand this clearly within yourself.

Next you must spend time with God. With your subtle wisdom, start to look for Him within you. That power of our Primal Father can be found in the kingdom of heaven, but so many are guarding His palace. The angels, the *olis* or lights of God, the *ambiyā'* or prophets, the *auliyā'* or friends of God, the *qutbs,* and the houris are all there guarding God's palace. Before you can enter and reach Him, you must pass and analyze and understand each one of them.

You have to start by inquiring into the angels. What is their state? What are their actions like? What duties do they have? You have to change yourself into their state. Place your subtle wisdom into that of the angels and analyze it. Your wisdom should fall into their wisdom and compare the work they do within you with the work they do outside. Once you have completed that, my grandchildren, you must climb up to the sixth step.

Divine Analytic Wisdom

Here you must strive to reach the light of the pure wisdom of *Qutb Muhaiyaddeen* ☺. This is the level of divine analytic wisdom, or the *qutbiyyat,* and with this level of wisdom you must once again analyze all that you have understood so far. You have to analyze the three worlds of *awwal, dunyā,* and *ākhir,* the world of the soul, this world, and the hereafter, and know the state of each one. You must separate all that you have learned and discard what has to be discarded. "This belongs to this. That belongs to that." Divide your kingdom and give each part whatever belongs to it. Then, with the analytic wisdom of light, control each one. Give the section of earth to earth, but keep it under your control. Give the section of fire to fire and water to the water, but keep them under your control. Give the section of air to air, but control it. And give the section of ether, or illusion, to illusion but keep it under your control. Then separate out the section of wisdom and give that to the kingdom of the soul.

At this point you will be controlling all these angels. You will have the wisdom of the *qutbiyyat* to separate what is right from what is

431

wrong. This is the step of analyzing the kingdom of the soul, analyzing the prophets, the lights of God, the *qutbs,* and the friends of God.

Divine Luminous Wisdom

Next you must analyze the kingdom of heaven. You have come now to the seventh level of consciousness, the level of divine luminous wisdom. This is the wisdom of the *Nūr,* the resplendence of God. Now you are with the prophets. What is their work? To act with Allah's qualities, follow His commandments, and carry out His word and His justice. Without His word, they will not act. And when you reach that state, you are connected to the power of Allah. You take your words from Him and act according to that. You take His qualities and act with those qualities. You take the plenitude and completeness from Him, and with that you can do His work, His duty. You take the grace and light from the kingdom of the soul, and then you share that grace and light with others.

When you come to this state, you will control all other lives. They will be your life, and you will be in charge of their lives. You will be the one in control of the ocean, the land, and the netherworlds. When you understand all this and control these energies, that will be your kingdom of heaven and you will be its ruler. You will understand yourself and discover your power. You will know yourself and find completeness. You will see the Father of your soul, the Perfectly Pure One. You will hear His voice and see His state and His kingdom. This is the seventh step, the level of divine luminous wisdom.

My love you, my grandchildren. You must come to know your Father. Until you reach this seventh level of wisdom you will not understand yourself. As long as you do not understand all the other lives, you will not understand your own life. As long as you do not understand your life, you will not know the secret of your Father or understand His pure wisdom of light, the soul. And if you do not know pure wisdom, you will not understand the connection between yourself and your Father. You will not know anything about His kingdom.

Only when you understand yourself, only when you have wisdom, will you consider all lives as your own and know that state. Then all duties will be yours, and you will be helping all lives. As long as you do not have this wisdom, no matter how much learning and education you may have or how many philosophies and scriptures you have read about bliss, no matter what other kinds of wisdom you have learned or meditations you have done, or explanations you have understood or status and titles you have received—all that will only be like writing on water.

✳

My love you, precious jeweled lights of my eyes. This is the way you have to learn. Until you realize this state of wisdom within, you cannot understand yourself. To do this work you need faith, certitude, and determination. You need *imān*. From those first two levels, feeling and awareness, you must climb up step by step. You have to climb up and go beyond to understand your Father. Only if you understand all of this can you see Him.

Once you know all other creations and compare them with yourself, you will finally realize why man is the most exalted being. Man is the one who can see the state of all others as well as his own state. Only man has a life beyond the five lives. He has the sixth kind of life in him, the light life. Because this sixth life is beyond what all other creations have, man is exalted. Because he knows right from wrong, he is exalted. And because he has that wisdom which understands with more than just the intellect, he is exalted.

My love you, my grandchildren. You have to go past all these guards one by one and finally go to Him.

My love you. May God protect you. *Āmīn.*

433

The loveliness of Allah's garden is indescribable. Beautiful swings hang from the trees, and the flowers and fruits sparkle like gems.

The Magnificent Garden of Allah

y love you, my grandchildren. Come, let us go to the Peradeniya Royal Botanical Gardens in Kandy. You will have to buy a ticket to go in. It used to cost ten cents, but gradually the price has increased and now you must pay almost two dollars.

Children, these gardens are very old. They have existed here in Sri Lanka for over two hundred years, since long before the British arrived. But the British expanded the gardens and made them even more beautiful. Many tourists visit here, as well as local people and students from the nearby Peradeniya University. They wander about enjoying the fresh air and the lovely trees and flowers, hoping to find some peace and relaxation.

My grandchildren, shall we take a look around? Let us walk down the road that wanders along the banks of the two rivers that flow on either side of the gardens. Many of the trees and plants along these banks have been growing here for a very long time. Each variety is labeled with its botanical name and the part of the world it came from.

Look at all the people gathered here. Some are sitting together in twos and threes, some are talking and laughing, and a few couples are walking hand in hand, smiling at each other. People come here with certain ideas about the kind of peace they seek. Those who want to sit, sit. Those who want to talk, talk. Those who enjoy smiling, smile. Those who like to rest under the trees, rest. And yet, these people do not attain the peace and freedom they came for. That is not to be found here. No matter how many times they come to these gardens, they cannot find the lasting peace they are seeking.

Now, my children, we also have come to these gardens. Have you found peace here? Has it given you any comfort? To truly find peace and comfort we must look for a different kind of garden.

Allah has placed in our lives a river of milk, a river of honey, a river of wisdom, a river of His knowledge, and a river of His divine power. Amidst those flowing rivers we can find the botanical garden of Allah's kingdom.

Even if you were to see all the wonders of all the universes in this world and the next, you still could not describe the beauty or measure the vastness of His botanical garden. Each fruit has seventy thousand tastes, each leaf has seventy thousand fragrances, and each flower has seventy thousand varying colors and hues. The loveliness of this garden is indescribable. Beautiful swings hang from the trees, and the flowers and fruits sparkle like gems. Look at that fruit! It shines like a ruby, and that flower is like a cinnamon stone. And this flower has seeds which glisten like sapphires. It seems as if a path of diamonds has been outspread on the earth before us. Children, if you should want milk, water, honey, sherbet, or fruit, you need only to think of them and they will appear. You cannot stop gazing in wonder at all the beauty. This flower garden is so blissful, cooling, tranquil, and serene. Here you can find so much peace and fulfillment from everything you see.

God, His celestial messengers, the houris, angels, and heavenly beings who work in this flower garden, all exist within the grace and divine power of God. All who are His followers, all those who have received the treasure of His wealth, His *daulat,* live here in His kingdom: the prophets, the *qutbs,* the *olis,* or the lights of God, and the *auliyā',* who are the friends of God. All who have the absolute faith, certitude, and determination of *īmān,* all who know wisdom and the divine knowledge of *'ilm,* all the loving ones who understand Him, and all who have understood themselves dwell in this garden. It has been made for those who have justice and compassion and who live with God's qualities and love.

One who understands that grace will never regard anything in the world as large or important. One whose wisdom understands the clarity of *īmān* will know that the world is not worthwhile. To such a one the world is tinier than a mustard seed, tinier than the point of a needle. And my children, when you too acquire Allah's qualities and actions, then nothing in this world will be a wonder. Wisdom and truth cannot be impressed by the trees and bushes of the world. Do not look for peace in this shrubbery. You will never find it there.

My grandchildren, the flower garden of Allah's kingdom in the world of the souls is incomparable. Nowhere else is there such splendor and majesty. Nothing is more beautiful than Allah. Nothing is more beautiful than His wealth, His qualities, His actions, His behavior, and His love. And nothing is as perfect as the justice of the One who has no comparison anywhere.

This is what you must search for. If you reach the kingdom of God, then everything you need will come to you and bring you peace. Your soul and your heart will be at peace, your wisdom and *imān* will be at peace, and each of your qualities will be at peace.

In this heavenly flower garden you will find a wondrous palace filled with angels, celestial beings, and houris who will serve you. The fragrances from the perfumed breezes of rose, sandalwood, and jasmine will come to you and give you wondrous peace, a peace such as you will never find anywhere else in your life. Please understand this and realize that no beauty can equal His. This flower garden has been made with the incomparable beauty of God's *qudrat,* His power, and these palaces have been made with the qualities of God.

My love you, jeweled lights of my eyes, my children and grandchildren. Try to see Him. Try to know the bliss. Try to attain that peace and live in His garden. With the wisdom I have, I cannot begin to fully describe its splendor to you. No one can describe it. You have to see it for yourself. You have to see His palace, His kingdom, His gardens, and all the paths of His justice. There is no comparison, no equal to that anywhere. You can know it only if you go there.

My grandchildren, there is much more to learn about the garden of Allah. I only told you a small part. You must try to go to Allah's garden yourself and see it with your own wisdom. Then one day, when you go there, perhaps I will be there too, and we will meet again. *Āmīn.* May Allah help us.

OTHER BOOKS BY
HIS HOLINESS M. R. BAWA MUHAIYADDEEN

Truth & Light: brief explanations

Songs of God's Grace

The Divine Luminous Wisdom
That Dispels the Darkness

The Guidebook to the True Secret of the Heart
(Volume One and Volume Two)

God, His Prophets and His Children

Four Steps to Pure Īmān

Asmā'ul-Husnā:
The 99 Beautiful Names of Allah

The Truth and Unity of Man
Letters in Response to a Crisis

The Wisdom of Man

A Book of God's Love

My Love You, My Children:
101 Stories For Children of All Ages

The Golden Words of a Sufi Sheikh

Sheikh and Disciple

Maya Veeram or The Forces of Illusion

The central branch of the Bawa Muhaiyaddeen Fellowship is located in Philadelphia and serves as the residence of His Holiness Bawa Muhaiyaddeen, while he is in the United States. The Fellowship also serves as a meeting house and as a reservoir of people and materials for all who are interested in the teachings of Bawa Muhaiyaddeen. For information, write or call:

The Bawa Muhaiyaddeen Fellowship
5820 Overbrook Avenue
Philadelphia, Pennsylvania 19131

Telephone: (215) 879-8631